A History of Cambodia

Also of Interest

Profiles of Contemporary Asia

* Available in hardcover and paperback.

About the Book and Author

A History of Cambodia
David P. Chandler

Prominent though Cambodia has been in world affairs in the last two decades, remarkably little is available in the way of historical studies of that ancient country. Recent events have been documented and there are histories of the medieval kingdom known as Angkor, but this book is the first to chronicle Cambodian history from its beginnings to the twentieth century. It also is the first scholarly history of Cambodia to appear in English, the first in any Western language since Adhémard Leclère's *Histoire du Cambodge* appeared in 1914, and the first to draw on nineteenth- and twentieth-century Khmer archives and documents.

Within the framework of a narrative of historical events, Dr. Chandler examines the roots of today's Cambodia (Kampuchea), exploring how patterns of Cambodian thinking and the style of Cambodian politics have been derived from the past. His work is based on research conducted in Cambodia, Thailand, France, and the United States, supplemented by more than twenty years' study of documents relating to Cambodia.

Dr. Chandler is associate professor of history and research director for the Centre of Southeast Asian Studies at Monash University in Australia. He is author of *Cambodia Before the French: Politics in a Tributary Kingdom, 1794–1847* and *The Land and People of Cambodia,* coauthor of *In Search of Southeast Asia: A Modern History,* and coeditor of *Revolution and Its Aftermath in Kampuchea: Eight Essays.*

THAILAND

LAOS

CAMBODIA

•Samrong

•Siem Reap

Angkor

Battambang•

TONLE

SAP

•Kompong Thom

Pursat•

Kompong Chhnang•

CARDAMOM CHAIN

MEKONG

•Stung Treng

•Lomphat

•Kratie

Senmonorom•

Kompong Cham•

Udong•

•Krong Koh Kong

PHNOM PENH

Kompong Speu•

MEKONG

TONLE BASSAC

Prey Veng•

VIETNAM

Koh Kong

Takeo•

Svay Rieng•

Koh Rong

•Kompong Som   •Kampot

Gulf of Thailand

N

0   25   50   75   100

Kilometres

David P. Chandler

A History of Cambodia

Westview Press • Boulder, Colorado

Copyright © 1983 by Westview Press, Inc.

Published in 1983 in the United States of America by
  Westview Press, Inc.
  5500 Central Avenue
  Boulder, Colorado 80301
  Frederick A. Praeger, President and Publisher

Library of Congress Cataloging in Publication Data
Chandler, David P.
  A history of Cambodia.
  Bibliography: p.
  Includes index.
  1. Cambodia—History. I. Title.
DS554.5.C46 1983   959.6   83-1391
ISBN 0-86531-578-7

Printed and bound in the United States of America

For Elizabeth, Margaret, and Tom

Every nation in the world has its own history and its own strengths and weaknesses. Since earliest times excellent things and rotten things have mingled together and accumulated over long periods. To sort them out and distinguish the essence from the dregs is a very difficult task, but we must not reject history because of this difficulty. It is no good cutting ourselves off from history and abandoning our heritage. The common people would not approve.

—Mao Zedong
Talk to music workers
24 August 1956

Contents

Illustrations

Preface

I have studied Cambodia since 1959, when I enrolled as a student of Khmer at the Foreign Service Institute in Washington, D.C. Since then, in the Foreign Service, graduate school, and my years of teaching, I have contracted a multitude of intellectual debts, which it's a pleasure to acknowledge here. Since I began my research for this book in 1977–1978, many people have helped me to maneuver the manuscript into print. I am grateful to them all.

The last four chapters of this book are based for the most part on research with primary sources. Chapters 6 and 7 are drawn in large part from my doctoral dissertation, *Cambodia Before the French: Politics in a Tributary Kingdom, 1794–1847* (Ann Arbor, 1974). Chapters 8 and 9, which deal with the colonial era, reflect archival work I carried out in Paris and in Aix-en-Provence in 1977. The chapters also benefit from valuable work on this period by Milton Osborne, V. Reddi, and Alain Forest. Much of the material in Chapter 10 can be traced to work in the archives of Aix-en-Provence and Phnom Penh by Benedict Kiernan, and other parts are drawn from private papers entrusted to me by Maj. Gen. Chana Samudavanija in Bangkok in 1981.

The earlier chapters, on the other hand, rely largely on secondary sources. My debt to the writings of George Coedes and L. P. Briggs should be evident from the footnotes to Chapters 2, 3, and 4. I'm also grateful to my colleague Ian Mabbett for his comments on these chapters, which contain several references to his work. The material presented in Chapter 5, which traverses a *terra incognita* of Cambodian history between the abandonment of Angkor and the end of the eighteenth century, owes much to the work of Michael Vickery, a fellow sojourner in Cambodia in the early 1960s and since then a colleague in graduate school and most recently in Australia. For all of these chapters, I've benefited from discussions and correspondence with friends like these and with such faraway colleagues as Hiram W. Woodward, Jr., Saveros

Pou, Evéline Porée-Maspero, O. W. Wolters, Khin Sok, and Sumedh Chhim.

A major intellectual influence that might, I hope, be perceptible at many points in the book is that of the late Paul Mus, whose insights into Southeast Asian society and culture illuminated my first two years of graduate study. Other teachers, students, and friends have also made important contributions along the way. These include the late Harry Benda, J. D. Legge, David J. Steinberg, David Wyatt, David Marr, Alexander Woodside, and Robert E. Elson. Ben Kiernan, when still a student, taught me a great deal about the history of Cambodian radicalism, as readers of Chapter 10 will notice. While the book was in its final stages, I was encouraged by discussions of Cambodian history with Serge Thion, William Shawcross, Laura Summers, Anthony Barnett, and Chanthou Boua.

I'm grateful for access to the facilities of Harvard University, where I began my research for the book in 1977, and to those of Cornell University, which I visited in 1977, 1978, and 1979. Staff members of the French colonial archives in Aix-en-Provence were extremely helpful when I worked there in 1977, and so was the staff of the National Library in the People's Republic of Kampuchea, which I visited briefly in 1981. Closer to home, I have been assisted ably and often by the interlibrary loan personnel of the Monash University Library.

In other publications, I have recorded my gratitude to Cambodian friends in 1960–1962, 1970, and 1971. I doubt if many of them have survived the holocaust of the 1970s. None of them has written to me to say so. All the same, it seems appropriate to record my gratitude to them all once again, singling out especially Long Anar, Chhea Ton, the villagers of Krol Ko hamlet, Kompong Speu, and the late Dik Keam, formerly librarian of the Institut Bouddhique, who was murdered near Kratie as a "class enemy" in 1977.

In closing, three people have urged me, over the years, to write this book: J. D. Legge, a long-time colleague; my wife, Susan; and editor Mervyn Adams Seldon, who finished her punctilious work on the manuscript in a period of great personal distress. Susan McRory, my copy editor at Westview Press, was vigorous with an editorial brush and comb and provided many helpful substantive suggestions.

My colleagues at Monash, Ben Kiernan and Ian Mabbett, read the book in draft and suggested several improvements. Nguyen van Hung provided the translations from the Vietnamese that appear in Chapters 6 and 7. Translations from French, Thai, and Khmer, unless otherwise noted, are my own. Two of the photographs were kindly supplied by my colleague

Walter Veit, three by Jacques Nepote, and one by Roger M. Smith. The remaining photographs are my own.

Pam Sayers has typed my work for many years, impeccably and without much harm, it seems, to her sense of humor. In the final stages of writing, the manuscript benefited from Bess Brudenell's expert help. The index was prepared by Edythe Porpa, and the maps were drawn by Susan Tomlins and Vicki Tipping.

Any mistakes that have slipped past so many skilled and helpful people are obviously mine.

A NOTE ON THE NAMES "CAMBODIA" AND "KAMPUCHEA"

Throughout the book, except where I refer to the regimes that have governed Cambodia since 1975, I have refrained from using the name "Kampuchea." I have preferred to use "Cambodia" because it is still more widely used in English than "Kampuchea" and also because I do not accept the right of a regime to say how its name is to be pronounced *in a foreign language.* I feel this especially in the Cambodian case, because Democratic Kampuchea's documents, written in Khmer, show so little respect for local pronunciation of other countries' names and in fact often preserve the *French* pronunciation, transliterated into Khmer! In other words, I respect the fact that "Danmark," "Italia," and "Republica Dominicana" are, inside those countries, preferred pronunciations to the anglicized "Denmark," "Italy," and "Dominican Republic." But should the man on the street in one of these countries, talking about America, be required to say "United States"?

Moreover, it is not as if we had been asked, after 1975, to give the Cambodian people back the name of an ancient empire or of an ethnic grouping battered by colonialism. *That* task was attempted by the ill-fated Khmer Republic. "Kampuchea" derives from the Sanscrit "Kambuja," the name of a tribe in northern India associated (as we see in Chapter 2) with a myth of Cambodian origin. The name is as "Cambodian" in origin as New York is "American."

In recent times, among foreigners especially, the use of the word "Kampuchea" has been a way of expressing, usually from afar, one's sympathy with the Cambodian revolution. For this reason, one scholar of the region has recently argued that "Cambodia" is "the imperfect imperial rendering of Kambuja or Kampuchea."[1] Why is a hard "C" less perfect, or more imperial, than a "K"? How, in any case, is "Kambuja" to be pronounced? Or is one transliteration system to be seen as more patriotic than another?[2]

David P. Chandler
Monash University

NOTES

1. Laura Summers, "In Matters of War and Socialism Anthony Barnett Would Shame and Honor Kampuchea Too Much," *Bulletin of Concerned Asian Scholars,* Vol. II, No. 4 (October-December 1979):18, note 2.

2. See Serge Thion, "The Ingratitude of Crocodiles: The 1978 Cambodian Black Paper," *Bulletin of Concerned Asian Scholars,* Vol. 12, No. 4 (October-December 1980):40, for an eloquent defense by an apologist for much of the revolution of the use of "Cambodia" in preference to "Kampuchea."

CHAPTER 1

Introduction

This book will examine roughly two thousand years of Cambodian history. Chapters 2 through 5 carry the story up to the end of the eighteenth century; the remaining chapters deal with the period between 1800 and 1953, when Cambodia regained its independence. In Chapter 10, I have made an attempt to analyze the country's history in terms of the traumatic shocks that it suffered in the 1970s. The narrative begins with the onset of Indianization, at the beginning of the Christian era. It pauses when Cambodia became independent; the 1950s and 1960s, which have been ably treated by many authors, are not discussed in detail. At the same time, events in the 1970s have had such a profound effect on Cambodia's people and institutions that it was felt they should be sketched in at the end of the book so as to cast their pall over the preceding chapters.

One reason for writing the book has been to close a gap in the historiography of Southeast Asia. No lengthy history of Cambodia has appeared since the publication of Adhémard Leclère's *Histoire du Cambodge* in 1914.[1] Subsequent surveys, in French and English, have limited themselves to the study of particular eras or have relied primarily on secondary sources.[2] Over the last fifty years or so, moreover, many of Leclère's hypotheses and much of his periodization—to say nothing of his style of approach—have been revised by other scholars, weakened by new documents, or altered by archaeological findings. The colonial era has ended and needs examination in terms of preceding history; moreover, the so-called dark ages, discussed in Chapters 5 through 7, have often been ignored even though they form a bridge between Angkor and the present. The time has come, in other words, to reexamine the primary sources, to synthesize other people's scholarly work, and to place my own research, concerned mainly with the nineteenth and twentieth centuries, into the framework of a general history, with a nonspecialist audience, as well as undergraduates, in mind.

I have not covered the years since 1953 in detail because I am satisfied with the form of the book I set out to write. This is a circular argument, and my decision needs to be defended. The best reason for not dealing with the Sihanouk years, I think, is that so much excellent narrative and analytical work in political history has already appeared.[3] It is impossible to approach the period from other perspectives because of the destruction of the 1970s. We cannot discover, for example, what effects the introduction of widespread primary education had on the generation of Cambodians who reached maturity in time for revolution. Moreover, to close the book with the anti-Sihanouk coup of March 1970 would place more emphasis on this event than it deserves. A far more profound set of developments was set in motion five years later, when the Communists gained control. But 1975 is also a poor year for ending a general history, partly because almost insurmountable methodological problems confront a historian of the Lon Nol period.[4] As for the years of Communist regimes, from 1975 until the present, I feel that a great deal of basic research, much of it now under way, remains to be done. In ten years or so, it may be feasible to extend this book to cover another thirty years of Cambodian history. For the time being, it is perhaps enough to say that looking back at Cambodia in 1953 means looking through a billowing cloud of smoke.[5]

As it stands, the book examines several themes. One of these has to do with the effects on Cambodian politics and society of the country's location between Thailand and Vietnam. This theme, which is discussed in Chapters 6 and 7, has been crucial only since the second half of the eighteenth century. For nearly two hundred years, the presence of these two powerful, antagonistic neighbors has forced the Cambodian elite to prefer one or the other or to attempt to neutralize them by appealing to an outside power. Cambodian kings tried both alternatives in the nineteenth century. Sihanouk, Lon Nol, and Pol Pot all attempted only one—the second; the current regime in the People's Republic of Kampuchea (PRK) has committed itself to the patronage of Vietnam.

Another theme, really a twentieth-century one, has to do with the relationship of present-day Cambodians to the past. The history of Angkor, after all, was deciphered, restored, and bequeathed to them by their colonial masters. Why had so many forgotten it? What did it mean to have the memories and the grandeur brought back to life, in times of terror and dependence? And in what ways are the dark ages and the colonial era connected to these earlier times?

A third theme arises from the pervasiveness of patronage and hierarchical terminology in Cambodian thinking, politics, and social relations. For most of Cambodian history, it seems, people in power were thought (by themselves and nearly everyone else) to be more meritorious than other people. Despite some alterations, this belief remained essentially unchanged between Cambodia's Indianized phase and the onset of Theravada Buddhism.[6] The widespread acceptance of the status quo meant that in Marxist terms Cambodians went through centuries of mystification. If this is so, and one's identity was so frequently related to subordination, what did "independence" mean?

A final theme, related to the third, springs from the inertia that seems to be characteristic of rural society. Until very recently, alternatives to subsistence agriculture and incremental social improvements of any kind were rarely available to most Cambodians and were in any case rarely sought, as the outcome could be punishment or starvation. In the meantime, crops had to be harvested and families raised as they had been harvested and raised before. The way things had always been done, in the village and the palace, was also seen as the way things should be done. Clearly this suited elite interests and kept the rest of society "in line"; but perhaps because mystification was so widespread, the process may well have been less cynical than we might wish to think. Throughout Cambodian history, in any case, government (or *rajakar,* literally "royal work") was the privilege enjoyed by people freed in some way from the obligation of growing their own food. The governed grew food for them in exchange for their protection.

This conservative cast of mind, perceptible at so many stages of Cambodian history, has led some writers to suggest that Cambodia and its people were "unchanging" and "asleep." This myth of changelessness, on occasion, suited the French administration, as it implied docility; for later observers, there has been something "un-Cambodian" about revolutionary efforts, however misguided and inept, to break into a new kind of life.

The notion of changelessness is a myth or at least an oversimplification of events, but it has persisted for too long among students of Cambodian history and among some Cambodians who make a virtue of a conservative point of view. It must be used with caution, especially in this book, for each of the chapters that follow records a major transformation in Cambodian life. The first perceptible one came with the mobilization of population and resources to form an Indianized polity at the start of the Christian era, discussed in Chapter 2. Another followed the concentration of power at Angkor in the ninth and tenth centuries, which is described in Chapter 3. A state emerged that some scholars would see as a classic example of Wittfogel's notion of oriental despotism or of Marx's concept of an Asiatic mode of production.[7] Still another transformation, discussed in Chapter 4, overtook the Khmer when their capital was destroyed by Cham invaders in 1177 and was rebuilt into a Buddhist city by Jayavarman VII, who was a Mahayana Buddhist. Soon after his death, around 1220, still another transformation occurred: the conversion of most Cambodians from a loose-fitting form of Shaivistic Hinduism, with perhaps some Mahayana overtones, to Theravada Buddhism. The implications of these changes are treated in Chapter 5. The abandonment of Angkor two centuries later and the southward drift of Cambodia's demographic center of gravity probably had even more profound effects.

Because the sources are so thin and unreliable, what I have called Cambodia's dark ages are difficult to study, but it is clear that they were very different in many ways from the Angkorean era. For one thing, the spread of Theravada Buddhism (and its corollary, Thai cultural influence) diminished the importance of brahmanical advisers to the king and broke down the influence of brahmanical families who had crowded around the throne looking for preferment. In Angkorean times, these families had controlled much of the land and manpower around Angkor through their connections with royally sponsored religious foundations. As these foundations were replaced by *wats* (Buddhist temples), the forms of social mobilization that had been in effect at Angkor diminished in importance; so did extensive irrigation. The two or three annual harvests of rice that had been reported at Angkor came to a halt. The elite undoubtedly grew less numerous as a result; at the same time, foreign influences, particularly from the Islamicized regions of Southeast Asia, became apparent at the Cambodian court.

Unfortunately for us, these transformations occurred in a poorly documented era. Through documents, we can examine Cambodian society before and after them, but not while they were taking place. We have no clear idea, for example, why so many people changed religions when they did. Similarly, although there were clearly some economic incentives involved, it is hard to say why (and when) a landholding priestly elite transformed itself into, or was replaced by, an elite more interested in patronage and trade.

In the seventeenth and eighteenth centuries, Cambodia became a victim of its location. Its capital region (Phnom Penh/Udong/Lovek) lay at the eastern edge of the Theravada cultural zone that included Burma and Siam, and very close to the expanding frontier of Sinicized Vietnam. The region, in other words, lay along a cultural fault line. This affected the thinking and behavior of Cambodia's leaders, drawn into games of realpolitik that they could never expect to win. By the end of the eighteenth century, Cambodia had been devastated by civil wars and invasions from both sides; it was even without a monarch for fifteen years. The early 1800s, discussed in Chapters 6 and 7, formed perhaps the darkest portion of the dark ages. After a brief taste of independence in the 1850s under King Duang (r. 1848–1860), the kingdom succumbed to French protection. Its rulers may have preferred this state of affairs to Thai hegemony, but

French rule soon came to resemble the "civilizing mission" imposed upon them earlier in the century by the Vietnamese.

The economic, social, and cultural changes of the colonial period in Cambodia resembled those that occurred elsewhere in Southeast Asia, but they were less intense than those that affected Java, Burma, and the Philippines over somewhat longer periods of systematic colonial rule. As in these other colonies, however, the changes that swept Cambodia helped to put together the framework for the Cambodian nation-state that emerged very briefly in 1945 and again, perhaps for good, in 1953.[8]

The three most obvious transformations in this period, discussed in Chapters 8 and 9, were in foreign trade, communications, and demography. Rice and corn, grown for the first time in large quantities for export, and rubber, grown for the first time altogether, now linked Cambodia with a world outside Southeast Asia. Its economy, never especially strong, became dependent. Nothing altered, in fact, with political independence; most of Cambodia's foreign exchange throughout the 1950s and 1960s came from earnings on the export of rice, rubber, and corn.

Perhaps the most visible difference between colonial and precolonial Cambodia, however, had to do with communications. By the 1920s, one could travel across Cambodia by car in a couple of days—a journey that had taken months in the nineteenth century. Cambodians began moving around the country by road and rail and found markets for their products opening up. The social changes that accompanied this new freedom of movement were obviously important, although they are hard to document precisely.

Finally, for every Cambodian who had greeted the French (if the image is appropriate) in 1863, there were four to say goodbye. Cambodia's population, estimated at slightly less than a million when the protectorate was declared, had risen to more than 4 million by 1950. By keeping the kingdom at peace and by introducing some improvements in hygiene the French presided over a demographic revolution that, when it intensified in the 1960s, soon put serious pressures on Cambodian resources.[9]

It is difficult to say how decisive the Japanese occupation of Cambodia was, particularly as the French remained in nominal control until early 1945. With hindsight, however, it is clear that the summer of 1945, when Cambodia was granted independence, had a profound effect on many Cambodian nationalists, both conservative and radical. In the late 1940s, a new political ideology based on resistance rather than cooperation and independence rather than subordination also took hold among many rural Cambodians, as well as in sectors of the Buddhist clergy and among the educated elite. Some of these people opted very early for a revolutionary alternative to the status quo, occasionally with disastrous effects. These developments in the 1940s and early 1950s, discussed in Chapter 10, have continued as an undertone to Cambodian political ideology ever since.

The book says very little about Cambodia's resources or its economy, except in passing. These have been remarkably consistent over the two millennia to be examined. In early times, discussed in Chapter 2, the cultivation of grain, probably wet rice, supported the people of the Mekong Delta, in the region known to the Chinese as Funan. Chinese accounts tell us that farmers stored water in small, man-made ponds, which they used for bathing and perhaps for irrigation, much as they were to do until the upheavals of the 1970s, when Cambodia's rural economy expanded rapidly and to a large extent broke down. The hydraulic works at Angkor, discussed in Chapter 3, amplified this earlier technology. The relationships between the seasons, water, rice, and subsistence agriculture have remained the same throughout Cambodian history. Supplements to the diet, however, may have changed somewhat. The amount of wild game has undoubtedly decreased, and in the colonial and postcolonial eras, imported and processed items became available. The mainstay supplements, however—fish, roots, locally grown spices—appear to have changed very little from one century to the next.

Until very recently, the same could be said for much of Cambodia's rural technology. Pots, sickles, ox-carts and cotton cloth—to name only four—appear to have changed little between the twelfth century, when they appeared on bas-reliefs at Angkor, and the 1980s.

A third consistency in the Cambodian economy lies in the field of exports. Until the colonial era, when plantation crops that were grown for export (primarily rubber, pepper, and rice) transformed Cambodia's national economy, the goods Cambodia exported for the most part were ones that grew wild in the woods. These included such things as rhinoceros horns, hides, ivory, cardamom, lacquer, and perfumed wood. Because these exports paid for the luxuries imported by the Cambodian elite, it is important to note the symbiosis that existed between woodland populations responsible for gathering these products and the people settled in the agricultural plains. This relationship is examined in a nineteenth-century context in Chapter 6.

Another theme of the Cambodian economy is the country's victimization by monsoons. Like many other countries of Southeast Asia, Cambodia has two distinct seasons rather than four. The rainy season, dominated by the southeasterly monsoon, lasts from May to November. The rest of the year is dry. Over the years, rice farmers and administrators have calibrated their activities to the ebb and flow of these conditions. In the wet season, much of Cambodia is under water. Because of this, in precolonial times at least, military campaigns almost never began in wet weather. At the same time, because there was little to do in the fields once the rains had started, these months came to be favored by young men who wanted to spend short periods in monasteries as Buddhist monks.

Unlike the other countries of mainland Southeast Asia, Cambodia has no mountain ranges running north to south, providing barriers for east-west penetration. Low ranges of hills mark off its northern frontier and parts of its frontier with Vietnam, but these have never posed serious problems for invaders. Cambodia's vulnerability to attack, especially after the decline of Angkor in the fifteenth century, is a recurrent feature of its history and a theme of its foreign relations. Conversely, in its periods of greatness, Cambodia expanded easily into the plains of southeastern and central Thailand.

On the other hand, because Cambodia had no deep-water port of its own until the 1950s, overseas commerce reached the Cambodian capital by coming upriver from the China Sea. For this reason, foreign influences, like foreign armies, tended to come overland. The conversion of the kingdom to Theravada Buddhism in the thirteenth and fourteenth centuries, discussed in Chapter 4, is an example of this process of infiltration and osmosis.

The transformations and continuities I have listed came under systematic and variegated attack in the 1970s, particularly after 1975, when Cambodia's entire historical experience was attacked vociferously by the regime of Democratic Kampuchea, which worked hard to dissolve continuities, real or imagined, between revolutionary Cambodia and anything that had happened there before.[10] We also have little idea how severe the damage was to rural Cambodian society during the U.S. bombing of 1973, when for six months U.S. planes dropped nearly twice as many tons of bombs on Cambodia as they had dropped on Japan in World War II. To put it mildly, the destruction of the countryside and the repudiation of history and institutions have had important effects on the status quo. For this reason, among others, it is too early to say much that would be accurate or helpful about Cambodian society in the 1980s. As I suggest at the end of the book, this is primarily because Cambodia is still a *postwar* society, and the directions it will take after such tremendous damage (in addition to the effects of the U.S. bombing, perhaps a million people died of hunger, disease, or executions between 1975 and 1979) are difficult to predict. For similar reasons, it may be too soon and it is certainly very difficult to decide what happened to Cambodian society in the 1970s, or indeed since independence. But the time that came before this, covering what spokesmen for Democratic Kampuchea were accustomed to call "two thousand years of history," deserves discussion.

CHAPTER 2

The Beginnings of Cambodian History

No one knows for certain how long people have lived in what is now Cambodia, where they came from, or what languages they spoke before writing was introduced, using an Indian-style alphabet, around the third century A.D. Carbon-14 dates from a cave at Laang Spean in northwestern Cambodia, however, suggest that people who knew how to make pots lived in the cave as early as 4200 B.C. Another cave, near the ocean, was inhabited about a thousand years later. Presumably the first Cambodians arrived long before either of these dates; evidence of a more primitive, pebble-working culture has been found in the eastern parts of the country. Skulls and human bones found at Samrong Sen, inhabited since around 1500 B.C., suggest that these prehistoric Cambodians resembled Cambodians today, after account is made for recent infusions of Chinese and Vietnamese blood.[1]

Whether the early people came originally from China, India, or island Southeast Asia is still debated by scholars, and so are theories about waves of different peoples moving through the region in prehistoric times. But recent finds suggest that mainland Southeast Asia had a comparatively sophisticated culture in the prehistoric era; some scholars even attribute the first cultivation of rice and the first bronze-casting to the region. In any case, it is likely that by the beginning of the Christian era the inhabitants of Cambodia spoke languages related to present-day Cambodian, or Khmer. Languages belonging to the Mon-Khmer family are found widely scattered over mainland Southeast Asia, as well as in some of the islands and in parts of India. Modern Vietnamese, although heavily influenced by Chinese, is a distant cousin. It is impossible to say when these languages split off from one another; some linguists believe that the split took place several thousand years ago. Unlike the other national languages of Southeast Asia, then—aside from Vietnamese—Khmer is not a newcomer to the area. This continuity is one of many that strike students of Cambodia's past. What is interesting about the cave at Laang Spean is not merely that it was inhabited, on and off, for so long—the most recent carbon-14 date from the cave is from the ninth century A.D.—but that the methods used to make pottery found at the earliest level, and the patterns incised on them, have remained unchanged for perhaps six thousand years.

The "changelessness" of Cambodian history was often singled out by the French, who in the nineteenth and twentieth centuries saw themselves as introducing change and civilization to the region. Ironically, this theme was picked up by Pol Pot's revolutionary regime, which claimed that Cambodians were asleep or enslaved for two thousand years. Both points of view ignore a great deal of evidence; arguably, the revolution of the 1970s was the fifth Cambodia has undergone since prehistoric times. But prerevolutionary Cambodians were less contemptuous of tradition. "Don't choose a straight path," a Cambodian proverb tells us. "And don't reject a winding one. Choose the path your ancestors have trod." Part of this conservatism, perhaps, is characteristic of a subsistence-oriented society, in which experimentation can lead to famine and in which techniques of getting enough to eat are passed from one generation to the next.

We know very little about the daily lives of Cambodians in prehistoric times; we do know that their diet, like the diet of Cambodians today, included a good deal of fish. It seems likely that their houses, from an early date, were raised above the ground and made accessible by means of ladders. Clothing was not especially important; early Chinese accounts refer to the Cambodians as "naked." After about 1000 B.C., perhaps, they lived in fortified villages, often circular in form, similar to those inhabited nowadays by some tribal peoples in Cambodia, Laos, and Vietnam. The Cambodians, like other early inhabitants of the region, had domesticated pigs and water buffalo fairly early, and they grew varieties of rice and root-crops by the so-called slash-and-burn method, common throughout the tropics, as well as in medieval Europe. These early people probably passed on many of their customs and beliefs to later inhabitants of the region, although we cannot be sure of this, for there are dangers of reading back into prehistoric and early Cambodia what we can see among so-called primitive tribes or twentieth-century peasants. We cannot be sure that these modern customs have not changed over time. Hairstyles, for example, changed dramatically in Cambodia as recently as the early eighteenth century, and in the 1970s they were changed again by the revolutionary regime.

All the same, it is unlikely that certain elements of Cambodian life and thinking, especially in the countryside, have changed a great deal since Angkorean times (ninth to mid-fifteenth centuries) or even over the last few thousand years. These elements might include the village games played at the lunar new year; the association of ancestor spirits (*nak ta*) with stones, the calendar, and the soil; the belief in water-spirits, or dragons; the idea that tattoos protect the wearer; and the custom of chewing betel, to name only a few.

INDIANIZATION

The notion of changelessness dissolves, however, when we discuss the first set of revolutionary changes that swept Cambodia at the beginning of the Christian era. This was the phenomenon known as Indianization, whereby elements of Indian culture were absorbed or chosen by the Cambodian people in a process that lasted more than a thousand years.[2] No one knows precisely when the process began or how it worked at different times. All-inclusive theories about it advanced by French and Dutch scholars usually put too little emphasis on the element of local choice; a few writers, on the other hand, have tended to exaggerate it. Generally, as George Coedes has remarked, scholars with training in Indian culture emphasize India's "civilizing mission"; those trained in the social sciences stress the indigenous response.[3]

Historians must deal with both sides of the exchange. The process by which a culture changes is complex. When and why did Indian cultural elements come to be preferred to local ones? Which ones were absorbed, revised, or rejected? In discussing Indianization, we encounter the categories that some anthropologists have called "Great" and "Little" traditions, the first connected with India, Sanskrit, the courts, and Hinduism, and the other with "Cambodia," Khmer, villages, and folk-religion. In the Cambodian case, these categories are not especially useful. We cannot play down the Great Tradition in Cambodian village life; where does monastic Buddhism fit in, for example, or Little Tradition activities, like ancestor worship and folk stories, at the court? Village wisdom always penetrated the court, and princely values, enshrined in Hindu epics and Buddhist legends,or *jataka* tales, penetrated village life. The two aspects of society were complementary and antagonistic at different times.

Nevertheless, the process of Indianization made Cambodia an Indian-seeming place. In the nineteenth century, for example, Cambodian peasants still wore recognizably Indian costumes and in many ways they behaved more like Indians than they did like their closest neighbors, the Vietnamese. Cambodians ate with spoons and fingers, for example, and carried goods on their heads; they wore turbans rather than straw hats, and skirts rather than trousers. Musical instruments, jewelry, and manuscripts—to name only three items—were also Indian in style. It is possible also that cattle-raising in Cambodia had been introduced by Indians at a relatively early date; it is unknown, to a great extent, in the rest of mainland Southeast Asia.

Trade between prehistoric India and Cambodia probably began long before India itself was Sanskritized. In fact, as Paul Mus has suggested, Cambodia and southern India, as well as what is now Bengal, probably shared the culture of "monsoon Asia," which emphasized, among other things, the role played by ancestral, tutelary deities in the agricultural cycle.[4] These were often located for ritual purposes in stones that naturally resembled phalluses or were carved to look like them. Sacrifices to the stones, it was thought, ensured the fertility of the soil. Cults like this, of course, were not confined to Asia, but it is useful to see, as Mus did, that an Indian traveler coming across them in Cambodia would "recognize" them as Indian cults honoring the god Siva or one of his consorts. Similarly, a Cambodian visiting India, or hearing about it, would see some of his own cults in those that honored the Indian god.

During the first five hundred years or so of the Christian era, India provided Cambodia with a writing system, a pantheon, meters for poetry, a language (Sanskrit) to write it in, a vocabulary of social hierarchies (not quite the same thing as a caste system), Buddhism, the idea of universal kingship, and new ways of looking at politics, sociology, architecture, iconography, astronomy, and aesthetics. Without India, Angkor would never have been built; yet Angkor was never an Indian city, any more than medieval Paris was a Roman one.

Indian influence in Cambodia, unlike Chinese influence in neighboring Vietnam, was not imposed by colonization or by force. As far as we know, Indian troops never invaded Cambodia, and if individual Indians enjoyed high status, as they often did, it was partly by convincing local people that they deserved it. When Indian colonists came, at first as adventurers perhaps, they were absorbed into the local population. Until very recently, therefore, Indianization failed to produce the identity crisis among Cambodians that Chinese influence produced among the Vietnamese. Cambodia never resisted India, which was not, in any case, a unified state; moreover, unlike Vietnam vis-à-vis China, Cambodia never looked to India—after the fourteenth century or so—for new ideas, approval, or advice. Indianization gave a format and a language to elite Cambodian life, but it was not narrowly political. Moreover, the hierarchical arrangements that came to characterize the language and behavior of the Cambodian elite, although owing much to Indian models, never sprang from a recognizable caste system affecting Cambodian society as a whole. At the village level, caste considerations never took root; what resembled a caste "system" at the medieval Cambodian court, moreover, probably was little more than a set of ritual procedures that showed respect for

Indian traditions.[5] Another by-product of Indianization in Cambodia is that Cambodian nationalism, unlike its Vietnamese counterpart, has not generally pictured itself as the product of a struggle against foreign invaders and advice. Instead, national identity, until recent times, was seen as the sum of social arrangements in effect inside Cambodia. Indianization and elements of life that are traceable to India were merely components of the sum. The fact that they came from India (just as our polysyllables so often come from Greece and Rome) was not considered a reason for alarm.

Like many Southeast Asian countries, Cambodia has a legend that traces its origin back to the marriage of a foreigner and a dragon-princess, or *nagi,* whose father was the king of a waterlogged country. According to one version of the myth, a brahman named Kaundinya, armed with a magical bow, appeared one day off the shore of Cambodia; a dragon-princess paddled out to meet him. Kaundinya shot an arrow into her boat; this action frightened the princess into marrying him. Before the marriage, Kaundinya gave her clothes to wear and her father the dragon-king in exchange "enlarged the possessions of his son-in-law by drinking up the water that covered the country. He later built them a capital, and changed the name of the country to 'Kambuja.'"[6]

This myth is of Indian origin, as is the name "Kambuja," and perhaps it describes some obscure confrontation that had occurred in the Aryanization of southern India, rather than an event in Southeast Asia. But if it is useless as a "fact," it is interesting in several ways as a starting point for Cambodian history. In the myth, Cambodians see themselves as the offspring of a marriage between "culture" and "nature." Kaundinya's acceptance by his father-in-law, who drains the kingdom for him, is crucial to his success. This idea would have been familiar to Cambodians, for a prospective bridegroom often had to gain his in-laws' approval by living with them before his marriage. In the myth, the local people (i.e., the dragons) respect the brahman and in his honor give the kingdom an Indian name (which first appears in a Cambodian inscription in the ninth century A.D.).[7] Later on, monarchs would trace their ancestry to this mythical pair, who represented, among other things, a "marriage" between the sun and the moon. To be a legitimate king, it seems, one had to be a Cambodian and an Indian at the same time.

FUNAN

This myth of origin was first recorded by Chinese officials, and indeed, for the first few centuries of the Christian era, written sources for Cambodian history are almost entirely Chinese. These are supplemented, luckily, by archaeological findings, especially from the remains of an ancient trading city located near the modern Vietnamese village of Oc-Eo in the Mekong Delta, excavated during World War II by an archaeological team supervised by Louis Malleret.

Roman coins found at the site date from the second and third centuries A.D., and some Indian artifacts, including seals and jewelry, can be dated to the same period. Malleret believed that the port declined in importance in the fourth century. No contemporary records about it have survived, however, and we do not know what it was called by its inhabitants.[8] Because of its location, and some of the artifacts found at the site, Malleret concluded that the port was used by pilgrims and traders moving between India and China in the first centuries of the Christian era. Its extent suggests that it played an important part in this trade, and its location was ideal for ships hugging the coast and "turning the corner" from or into the South China Sea.[9] The city probably provided warehousing for goods in transit between India and China and was an outlet for products collected from the forested interior of Cambodia and Vietnam.

Until the twentieth century, indeed, forest products made up the bulk of Cambodia's export trade. These included elephants, ivory, rhinoceros horn, feathers, wild spices like cardamom, and other products such as lacquer, hides, and aromatic wood. Plantation exports like rubber and pepper were developed in the colonial era; rice exports also, which made up the bulk of twentieth-century Cambodian foreign trade, were of little use in early times, when nearly everyone in the region produced enough themselves. The point to make about these high-value, low-bulk goods is that they were cultivated or caught by forest people rather than by inhabitants of cities. Many of them probably traveled considerable distances before they reached Oc-Eo, and so did the goods or coins traders used to pay for them. Oc-Eo, then, may well have been the principal gateway through which Indianization extended into the heartland of Cambodia. There were other gateways, such as the Indianized kingdom of Champa, which developed in the early Christian era along the south-central coast of Vietnam.

Until very recently, many scholars believed that Oc-Eo was the seaport for an important kingdom, identified by Chinese sources as "Funan," and located by George Coedes (using linguistic evidence rather than archaeological findings) near the small hillock known as Ba Phnom, in southeastern Cambodia, east of the Mekong. According to Coedes, "Funan" derives from the old Khmer word for mountain (*bnam*), and he located the ritual center of the kingdom at Ba Phnom. A cult to Siva as a mountain deity existed in Cambodia as early as the fifth century A.D. and may well have been enacted on Ba Phnom. An Indian traveler to China reported: "It is the custom of the country to worship the celestial god Mahesvara [Siva].

This deity regularly descends on Mt. Mo-Tam so that the climate is constantly mild and herbs and trees do not wither.''[10]

Paul Wheatley has recently suggested that the cult originated in southern India and that the mountain was not Ba Phnom, but another hillock not far away, in what is now Vietnam.[11] The evidence that either mountain was a cult site is stronger than the evidence that Funan was a major, unified kingdom.[12] What made the place important to the Chinese was that a principality of this name (or more likely, one dubbed Funan by the Chinese) offered tribute to the Chinese emperor, on an irregular basis, between A.D. 253 and 519. Toward the end of this period, stone inscriptions in Sanskrit and Khmer are available for study, but these do not provide evidence for a major kingdom. It is possible, nonetheless, that small chiefdoms in Cambodia occasionally banded together and called themselves a kingdom for the purposes of sending tributary goods to China (an ideal occasion for encouraging trade) or of seeking Chinese help against their neighbors. It is possible that Funan was thought to be a major kingdom because the Chinese wanted it to be one and later because French scholars were eager to find a predecessor for the highly centralized kingdom of Angkor, which developed in the ninth century A.D.

Despite their usefulness in many ways, Chinese sources present peculiar problems to the historian, as many of them repeat uncritically data from previous compilations as if they were still true. Nonetheless, Chinese descriptions are often as vivid as this one about Funan:

> The King's dwelling has a double terrace on it. Palisades take the place of walls in fortified places. The houses are covered with leaves of a plant which grows on the edge of the sea. These leaves are six to seven feet long, and take the form of a fish. The king rides mounted on an elephant. His subjects are ugly and black; their hair is frizzy; they wear neither clothing nor shoes. For living, they cultivate the soil; they sow one year, and reap for three. . . . These barbarians are not without their own history books; they even have archives for their texts.[13]

There is evidence that the major step during the Funan period toward the integration of the small, dry-rice-growing and root-cultivating principalities, whose people worshipped Siva, with hunting and gathering societies inland from Oc-Eo was the introduction, perhaps as late as A.D. 500, of systematic irrigation; drainage probably came earlier. We have seen in the Kaundinya myth that drainage was attributed to the good offices of a dragon king; one of the few inscriptions from Funan mentions a king "rescuing" his territory from the mud. But the most important passage related to this innovation, and to Indianization, is a Chinese one, which appears at first to be a garbled version of the original myth:

Then the kingdom was ruled by a brahman named Kaundinya. A spirit announced to him that he would be called upon to govern Funan, so he travelled there . . . and the people of Funan came out to meet him, and proclaimed him king. He changed the institutions to follow Indian models. He wanted his subjects to stop digging wells, and to dig reservoirs in the future; several dozen families could then unite and use one of these in common.[14]

Now seventh- and eighth-century inscriptions speak of rice fields adjacent to Hindu temples, suggestive of irrigated rice, and aerial photographs of the Mekong Delta show silted-over canals, which may have been used for drainage as well as transport.[15] If irrigation was widely used before the ninth century A.D., it was not on an especially large scale and, with the exception of the seventh-century agglomeration of Isanapura (now known as Sambor Prei Kuk, near Kompong Thom), the village was the most characteristic unit of pre-Angkorean Cambodia. Indeed, Isanapura may well have consisted of villages grouped around a common ritual center, whose stone buildings have survived. Even after the introduction of wet-rice technology, perhaps in the fourth or fifth century A.D., the area under irrigation, which is to say, under control of supravillage organizations, was never very great. Moreover, it seems likely that most villages in the hinterland continued to grow dry rice and to cultivate roots, supplementing their diet by hunting and gathering, long after irrigation and wet-rice cultivation had taken hold in Hinduized communities.

People, rather than land per se, are needed to cultivate wet rice. With this in mind, as well as the low density of the population in the entire area (always excepting Java, Bali, and the Red River Delta in Vietnam), it is easy to see why throughout Southeast Asian history overlordship and power were so often thought of and pursued in terms of controlling people rather than land. There were periods of Cambodian history, under Jayavarman VII in the twelfth century, for example, when far-flung territorial control was an important part of a king's prestige. Nonetheless, territory per se (mere forest in most cases) was never as important as people.

Indeed, the notion of alienable ownership of land, as distinct from land use, does not seem to have developed in traditional Cambodia. Land left fallow for three years reverted to state control. The king, theoretically at least, was the lord of all the land in the kingdom. This meant that he could reward people with the right to use it. Many of the Cambodian-language inscriptions from the Angkorean period, as we shall see, dealt with complicated quarrels about access to land resources. Many of these might never have arisen had there been a system of titles, survey maps, and ownership.

The record of inscriptions and, by inference, of architectural remains from the first eight centuries A.D. fails to provide evidence of large-scale

SOUTHERN CAMBODIA: PRE-ANGKOREAN SITES
[after B.P. Groslier and E. Lunet De Lajonquiere]

unified kingdoms on Cambodian soil and very little evidence of the development of urban centers. There seems to have been some continuity among members of the elite, traceable in part to their tendency to marry among themselves. At the same time, it seems likely that Cambodia, like much of the rest of early Southeast Asia, contained a collection of small states, each equipped with a court and an elite, and that these segments had entourages, or "strengths" of people growing food for them who could also be called upon to fight. Presumably, these states traded among themselves and raided each other, particularly for slaves, but these suppositions are not directly supported by the evidence. It seems likely also that each "king," when undisturbed (or when disturbing others), thought of himself as a universal monarch, benefiting from Indian teachers, as well as a local chieftain, performing identifiable Cambodian tasks.

Leadership was measured by prowess, which was measured by success in battle, by the ability to attract a large following, and by the perceived capacity to provide protection. As J.D.M. Derrett has pointed out, protection, along with rainfall, is the sine qua non of peasant society: protection from enemies, from rival overlords, from the forces of nature.[16] In recognition of this necessity, overlords in the time of Funan and throughout Cambodian history often included in their reign-names the suffix *varman* (originally "armor"; hence "protection").

The overlords themselves thought that they could not live without supernatural protection, and most of them sought this, in part, through their devotion to Siva. Here they were assisted, for a time at least, by a group of renegade Indian brahmans, the so-called *pasuputa,* who enjoyed a vogue in India and elsewhere in Southeast Asia around the fifth and sixth centuries A.D.[17] These wandering ascetics preached that personal devotions to Siva were more rewarding than meticulous attention to brahmanical rituals or to the law of destiny, or *karma.* Technically, an overlord's devotion did not require the intercession of the *pasuputa,* and some of them presumably did without it. In any case, these self-made Hindus were perceived, and saw themselves, as superior men, vehicles of Siva, the god who "ceaselessly descended" onto the holy mountain. The transmission of Siva's potency via the overlord and his ritual acts to the people and the soil was an important source of cohesiveness in Cambodian society.[18] It has also been a source of continuity. As late as 1877, human sacrifices to a consort of Siva were conducted at Ba Phnom at the beginning of the agricultural year. Like those described in fifth-century Chinese sources, these had the objective of transmitting fertility to the region; and like the Chinese rituals, they were sponsored by local officials.[19]

In the Funan era, Buddhism also flourished in Cambodia, and the Buddhist concept of merit, which until very recently suffused Cambodian thinking about society, resembles, in some ways, the notions of prowess and salvation just discussed. In both schemes of thought, power and ability were seen—especially by those who did not have them—as rewards for virtuous behavior in previous lives. The loss, diminution, or absence of power, moreover, revealed to people that a previous existence had been in some way flawed. A person's status in society, therefore, was programed by performance in the past, while one's behavior here and now determined where one would stand when one returned to life. To improve personal status, then, one must accumulate merit by performing virtuous acts, like subsidizing a temple, or being generous to monks, donating a gilded image of a god, or financing religious festivals. Acts like these were thought to redeem the person sponsoring them. As we shall see, the great temples at Angkor were also thought of as redemptive gestures of this kind, a bargain struck by kings with their immediate ancestors and, through them, with the gods. No one here and now could see if the bargains were a success, but the thought of neglecting to make them, especially when the afterlife meant a return to earth, occurred seldom, if at all.

The notions of "patron," "client," and "entourage" become important at later stages of Cambodian history—they are probably the key to nineteenth-century Cambodian life—but it would be dangerous to assume that precisely similar arrangements were in effect in Cambodia in the sixth and seventh centuries A.D. We do not know how overlords came to power, for example, or how they recruited followers. We do not know what made followers linger in their service, and we lack a clear idea of what the services entailed. The evidence suggests that we can describe pre-Angkorean society in Cambodia as an aggregation of leaders and followers, occupying spaces of territory and spaces in society that were thought about in terms of centers and peripheries. With such a multiplicity of centers, Cambodia was decentralized; segments of what we would call "society" (i.e., the total of the aggregations) acted independently of each other or were related in sporadic ways.

Things were not quite as simple as this, of course. Localized religious cults, like the ones Evéline Porée-Maspero and others examined in Cambodia in the 1940s and 1950s,[20] generally stressed the welfare of the community rather than that of the individual, for without communities to perform the work, irrigated rice cannot be grown. Rural life requires alliances. The human sacrifices at Ba Phnom were one example of this communal orientation. Others included the complex of rituals ushering in the agricultural year (the sacred furrow, the towers of sand, and so forth); the royal cults that in effect negotiate with the dead for the welfare of the kingdom; and the boat-races that take place in flooded rivers at the end of planting. Although these cults at first appear to be antagonistic to each other (the Great and Little Traditions once again), in fact they were complementary.

Because genealogies were not maintained in Cambodia, except among the elite, the *nak ta,* or ancestor people, had no family names. They thus became the symbolic ancestors of people in a particular place, or by dying in a place they came to patronize its soil. *Nak ta* in inhabited sites could be spoken to and tamed; those in the forest or in abandoned places were thought to be more powerful and more malignant. As a place was inhabited, over the years ancestral traditions gathered around it, although seldom to the same extent as in China or Vietnam.[21] The pre-Angkorean record is almost silent about *nak ta,* but we can assert, by reading back from modern data, that a confrontation between Hindu and local beliefs was rarer than a blending of the two.

The tendency to syncretize, in fact, was noted by early Chinese visitors. The passage that refers to Siva's continuous descent onto Mt. Mo-tan, for example, also mentions a *bodhisattva,* or Buddha-to-be, that was held in reverence at the time. Frequently two Indian gods blended with each other, as Siva did with Vishnu to form Harihara, a composite deity much favored by Angkorean kings.

The process of blending different religions meant that here and there local spirits received the names of Indian gods, just as localized Greek and Roman deities were renamed in the early years of Christianity. Hindu temples also were often built near sites favored by pre-Indian celebrations; there are Neolithic remains underneath the palace at Angkor.[22] What was being stressed at times like this was the continuity of habitation and a continuity of sacredness—ideas in themselves with deeper roots in Cambodia than in most of India. If ancestors became Indian gods in times of centralization and prosperity, the gods became ancestors again when the rationale for Hinduism and its priestly supporters disappeared. Thus at Angkor, and in Cham sites in Vietnam studied in the 1930s by Paul Mus, Indian images and temples were worshipped in quite recent times merely as mysterious products of the *nak ta*.[23] This is partly because the literature of the Cham and Cambodian elites, which was used to explain and justify the images and temples, had disappeared or could no longer be deciphered, while the language village people used in their religious lives remained to a large extent unchanged from the pre-Indian era to colonial times.

The most enduring cult, as Mus has shown, was the cult of the lingam, or stone phallus. This widely diffused motif, and the cults associated with it, exemplified links between ancestor spirits, the soil where they and the lingam "grew," and the fertility of nearby soil for agricultural use. Because of the territorial aspect of the cult (a lingam could be moved from place to place, ceremoniously, but was only potent in one place at a time) and the notion that the lingam was a patron of a community, it was closely supervised by local overlords and, in the Angkorean era, by the king. As early as the fifth century A.D., a cult honoring a mountain god at the hill of Lingaparvata in southern Laos—nowadays known as Wat Ph'u—involved human sacrifices; the site was notable because it contained an enormous natural lingam, some 18 meters (59 feet) high.[24] Lingaparvata, like Ba Phnom, was patronized as an "ancestral" site by several Angkorean kings.

The period of Funan, then, which lasted until the sixth century A.D., was one in which Cambodia's political center of gravity was located south and east of present-day Phnom Penh. During this period, trade between India and China was intense, and one of the principal components of this trade was Buddhist religious objects. Local religious practices emphasized devotion to Siva, Vishnu, and the Buddha, as well as to minor Hindu deities. Politics centered on villages and groups of villages, rather than on a tightly organized kingdom; irrigated rice allowed for surpluses and for some social differentiation, but not as much as developed later on. The main point to stress about the period, from the historian's point of view, is that we know about it from Chinese sources, which tell about local customs, centralization, and commodities for trade. We hear no Cambodian voices, as we do from the seventh century onward in the form of stone inscriptions. After the waning of "Funan," in fact, our sources become richer and harder to use.

GOVERNMENT AND SOCIETY IN EARLY CAMBODIA

The first dated Khmer-language inscription from Cambodia was incised in A.D. 611, with the earliest Sanskrit inscription being carved two years later.[25] There are some datable inscriptions, in both languages, from the seventh century, and these give us a picture of the way Cambodian society was put together. The picture is different from the one we get from Chinese sources because the inscriptions are religious rather than secular in orientation. According to the inscriptions, Cambodian society was divided, informally at least, into those who understood Sanskrit and those who understood only Khmer. For several hundred years, Sanskrit was used in inscriptions that spoke directly to the gods. Khmer, on the other hand, has always been the language of Cambodian men and women, those who were protected by the gods and descended, as gods did not, from the *nak ta.* Sanskrit inscriptions, in verse, praise the meritorious actions of kings and the elite, such as building temples, financing monasteries, and offering gifts to brahmans. Some of the speakers trace or doctor their genealogies, as if to cash in on or invent ancestral merit; many praise brahmans at the expense of other segments of the society; and all are fulsome in praise of those in power. Much of the verse, according to Indianists, is highly polished, subtly worded, and well composed, comparing favorably with Sanskrit poetry composed in India at the time.

Khmer inscriptions, on the other hand, are all in prose. They record the founding of temples and the details of temple administration, such as the numbers and names of slaves attached to a particular place. They also give inventories of temple treasures and list the dimensions of rice fields, orchards, and ponds in a temple's jurisdiction. Many of them outline the duties of slaves and set the amount of taxes—payable in labor or in kind—levied to support the temple priests. Usually they close with a curse threatening people who neglect, rob, or disrupt the temple in question with punishment over many generations.

A little too neatly, perhaps, the line between Sanskrit and Khmer separates the so-called Great and Little Traditions. On the one hand, there are wealth, poetry, intricacy, word-play, priests, direct access to the gods—i.e., a language that protects. On the other, there are poverty, prose, straightforward catalogs, slaves, and the world of ordinary people— i.e., a language about what receives protection. Both sets of inscriptions used the same sort of alphabet derived from India and, as a rule, were carved by the same masons. Presumably poets and priests, if they wanted to do so, could read them both. But were they intended to be read? In general, they are accessible enough, carved on temple door posts or on independent steles; probably the texts were also kept on perishable material in archives somewhere else. The reason they were carved at all may be that writing on stone, the medium of the gods, served a special purpose. Stone was not used in secular sites; these, including palaces and ordinary dwellings, were built of wood, bamboo, and other perishable materials. Sanskrit, moreover, was the language of the gods; stone was associated with permanence, which is to say the dead. In incising the stones, Cambodians were speaking, collectively, to their ancestors; the inscriptions themselves, if in Sanskrit, spoke directly to the gods. A curse, or an oath of allegiance, inscribed on stone was thought to be stronger as a result.

Moreover, the juridical aspect of the inscriptions should not be over-looked. By recording land grants on stone, for example, it was thought that beneficiaries would be recognized and protected; similarly, curses (in Khmer) might serve as burglar alarms and preserve the sites from depredations.

The division between Sanskrit and Khmer was also the division between those who grew rice and those who did not. It was everyone's ambition to be "rescued from the mud," but very few succeeded; most of those who did were placed, in Angkorean times, into various *varna,* or caste groupings, which made up perhaps a tenth of the society as a whole. These people included clerks, artisans, concubines, artists, high officials and priests, as well as royal servants, relatives, and soldiers. Because they seldom served as slaves, and only a few of them were important enough to patronize a temple, they appear rarely in Cambodian inscriptions. This gap means, among other things, that we never know the names of the people who designed and carved the magnificent statuary and temples of Angkor. By the seventh century, in fact, the city of Isanapura was already the most extensive complex of stone buildings in all Southeast Asia, built a century ahead of similar constructions in Java. All the same, the presence of these free people somewhere between the summit of society, symbolized by the king's palace and his sacrificial mountain, and the rice fields that surrounded them should not encourage us to call them a "bourgeoisie" or even a "middle class," because our information about them is too sparse.

The connotations of Western-oriented social terms like these bedevil us when we look to other Cambodian social groups. We have already noted that the term "king," or *raja,* probably meant less in Funan than it did in medieval Europe. Another important term, *knjom*—which can be translated as "slave"—seems to have meant something more ambiguous to the Khmer than our word "slave." For one thing, as Judith Jacob has shown, *knjom* was only one of some fourteen categories of slaves in pre-Angkorean Cambodia.[26] They had many levels of social status, different origins, and many kinds of duties. Those toiling in the fields, on the one hand, resembled black slaves in the antebellum American South. Others, especially those attached to temples, may have seen themselves as enjoying clerical status. And yet, as all of these groups of people apparently could be bought, sold, and given away and had no freedom to escape, they were not servants either. Many of them were probably bondsmen, working off debts contracted by themselves or by their parents. Were they serfs? The question should make us wary of the interchangeability of terms, and recent Communist statements that early Cambodia was "feudal" are inaccurate even when it is granted, as the inscriptions enable us to do, that the society was certainly exploitative and divided sharply between haves and have-nots. The evidence that connects slaves to *places* is incomplete, although some of them appear to have been attached to certain places for several generations. This suggests hereditary servitude, or a liability to be called on, attached to a place rather than to a particular lord. Some villagers were free to grow their own rice but were not free to move; others appear to have been owned by temples; still others by members of the elite. Practice and theory seem to have varied from time to time and from place to place; generalizations about Cambodian society in this period are difficult to make.

Evidence from inscriptions suggests that slaves of various kinds made up the majority of the Cambodian population at any given time. Free peasants were liable to calls on their time and energy to perform public works, favors for an overlord, or service to a temple or to serve in wars. Many of them, in fact, were prisoners of war or their descendants.

The slaves themselves pass in and out of Cambodian history as mere names. These are a mélange of Sanskrit and Khmer words. From one inscription to another, they range from respectful references (some *knjom* are referred to by the equivalent of "Mr." or "Ms.," for example) to derogatory ones, in which slaves have names like "dog," "imperfect," "red in the face," and "bad-smelling." By and large, slaves with recognizably Sanskrit names (such as "loves justice," "slaves of Siva," or merely "Dharma") tend to have slightly higher status than the others, and many of them may have served as musicians and dancers. Many of their names would be recognizable in Cambodia today; the names of flowers, for instance, are still widely used for girls.

Another difference between pre-Angkorean slaves and those of the ante-bellum United States is that the villages they lived in, the food they ate, and the beliefs they shared were not very different from those found in times of "freedom" (whatever the term meant to a rice farmer at this

A ninth-century statue, buried in the forest near Kompong Cham. Author's photo.

time) or from those of the masters whom they served. If the *knjom* had been uprooted, they usually came from fairly similar cultures; the gap between the city and the countryside, which was to be so exploited in the Cambodian revolution of the 1970s, for example, was not yet meaningful or wide. As servants of temples, moreover, many *knjom* participated in rituals that punctuated the year, such as the times when gilded images were washed, clothed, and paraded round a temple, or later on when the eyes of a Buddha-image were ceremonially "opened." They crowded around royal processions and made decorations for palanquins as these passed through. The *knjom* lived in the vicinity of grandeur. Among themselves, they explained grandeur, in turn, in terms of merit, and merit in terms of protection. They saw themselves as engaged, like others in the society, in plotting their own redemption; what better way to do this than to serve the priests who served the temple gods?

We can come to these tentative conclusions by reading back from recent Cambodian life, or by studying bas-reliefs, statues, artifacts, and inscriptions. But as almost always in Cambodian history, we write the peasants' words, as it were, without having access to their voices. What would they have said? It is difficult to imagine without asking a second question: To whom would they be talking? Among themselves, of course, Cambodian peasants are frank and egalitarian, but they take few risks in the presence of outsiders. The peasants' apparent acceptance of superiors has led some scholars to argue for an essential harmoniousness in traditional Cambodian society. But Cambodian history is filled with rebellions and civil wars. The absence of peasant voices makes it almost as hard, all the same, to make a case for persistent tumult as for harmony. Most of the time, there was plenty of cause for both.

Yet pre-Angkorean Cambodia was not an integrated despotic state. Instead, it was a collection and a sequence of principalities sharing a despotic language of politics and control. Because the principalities saw themselves as absolute, they were rivals of each other and thus independent. And yet throughout the eighth century (a period about which Chinese sources are silent, for no tribute arrived in China) Cambodia was gradually becoming more politically coherent. What brought this about is still being argued by scholars; it is likely that integration involved increased population, increased wet-rice technology, and apparently random inputs, like victories in war or protracted periods of peace. The area of Aninditapura, in the vicinity of present-day Angkor, grew in importance in relation to the principalities along the upper Mekong, at Sambor and elsewhere. The distribution of pre-Angkorean inscriptions indicates that the more populated sections of Cambodia—as in the twentieth century, but not in the Angkorean era—were along the banks of the Mekong and lower Tonle Sap, particularly to the south of present-day Phnom Penh, with other settlements along the upper Mekong near present-day Kratie.

Until quite recently, scholars sought to consolidate this assortment of small kingdoms under the name "Chenla," given to one of them by the Chinese and preserved in nineteenth-century Vietnamese as a name for Cambodia. The Chinese, in fact, distinguished between two "Chenlas," one associated with the Mekong Delta (and known as "water Chenla"), the other ("land Chenla") apparently located somewhere on the upper reaches of the Mekong, perhaps near present-day Wat Ph'u in southern Laos. The Chinese were not averse to exaggerating the importance of the "barbarian" states from which they received tribute. European scholars in the nineteenth and twentieth centuries, perhaps forgetting the multiplicity of kingdoms that had characterized medieval Europe or precolonial Africa— to name only two examples—also chose to see Chenla as a centralized successor state to Funan, thus making a neat progression from the earliest of these "mighty" kingdoms to the one concentrated at Angkor.[27]

In a brief and persuasive essay, however, Claude Jacques has crippled the usefulness of this interpretation, although one contributor to the collection in which Jacques's essay appears still referred to Chenla as the predecessor of Angkor. In Jacques's words,

> Inscriptions give evidence in the Khmer country of a multitude of little realms and princedoms; those which the Chinese called Funan and Zhenla, on grounds unknown so far, were among them and may have been the most important. It seems that some princes managed, sometimes, to take the leadership of a more or less large group of realms; but this situation was to all appearances only temporary.[28]

It is clear nonetheless that, by the seventh and eighth centuries A.D., coastal trading states in Cambodia like Funan (and others like it elsewhere in Southeast Asia) had faded or changed into polities further inland, known in the Cambodian case by the collective term "Chenla." The wealth of these new kingdoms derived primarily from wet-rice agriculture and from the mobilization of manpower rather than from subsistence agriculture and trade. Ideologies from India, which survive today in architecture, sculpture, and inscriptions, seem to have played a prominent role in molding and directing these societies, perhaps because ideas of this hierarchical kind were useful in legitimizing the extraction of surpluses more or less by force. Rituals may have become associated with wealth as time went on, and wealth may have become tied to supernatural skills, in a process of state formation discussed by Jonathan Friedman.[29] It is impossible, however, to recapture the process from the documents that have survived. What is important in terms of the sweep of Cambodian history, as we shall see in Chapter 5, is that the geographical and economic shifts of the seventh and eighth centuries reversed themselves in the fourteenth and fifteenth centuries, and just as the first set of changes can be associated with the formation of Angkor in the ninth and tenth centuries, the second set can be associated with its decline.

CHAPTER 3

Kingship and Society at Angkor

Scholars usually place the Angkorean period of Cambodian history between A.D. 802 and 1431. In fact, these years mark neither a beginning nor an end. The northwestern part of Cambodia, where the state we know as Angkor (the name derives from the Sanskrit word *nagara*, meaning "city") sprang up in the ninth century, had been inhabited by Khmer-speaking peoples for several hundred years. Moreover, although the city was abandoned in the fifteenth century, it was restored as a royal city briefly in the 1570s. More important, one of its major temples, Angkor Wat (i. e., the "City that has become a Buddhist temple"), was probably never abandoned by the Khmer, for it contains Buddhist statuary from every century between the fifteenth and the nineteenth and inscriptions on its walls from as late as 1747.[1] When the Angkor complex was "discovered" by French missionaries and explorers in the 1850s, Angkor Wat contained a prosperous Buddhist monastery inside its walls, tended by more than a thousand hereditary slaves.

The two dates are useful all the same, for they mark off Cambodia's period of greatness. At various times in these six hundred years, and only then, Cambodia—known in its own inscriptions as Kambuja-desa— was the mightiest kingdom in Southeast Asia, drawing visitors and tribute from as far away as present-day Burma and Malaysia as well as from what were later to be Thai kingdoms to the west.

SOURCES FOR ANGKOREAN HISTORY

At the same time, these periods of systematic domination were infrequent and relatively short. We know too little about social conditions at this time, moreover, to classify all Cambodian kings as "oriental despots." Some of them, as far as we can tell, accomplished little or nothing; others left scores of inscriptions, temples, statues, and public works.

Some kings ruled over a centralized, many-layered administration; others seem to have controlled only a few hundred followers. One fact that emerges from studying the kings in order—as L. P. Briggs and G. Coedes have done—is the variety of people and regions they were able to command.[2] Seen from the top, where written records emerge, the Angkorean period is easy to generalize about but hard to penetrate. Seen in terms of artistic styles, media, and motifs—including the facility of Cambodian poets in Sanskrit—it is possible to talk about "progress," "development," and "decline" without being able to say why some periods were "progressive" and others "decadent." Seen from the bottom, it is easy to generalize again about continuity between the era and recent times, but we are handicapped by the poverty of our sources.

Sources, indeed, pose major problems. Those connected with Sanskrit inscriptions on the one hand and Khmer-language ones on the other have been discussed in Chapter 2, but it is important to see how the biases of these documents produce a skewed picture of Cambodian society at Angkor. The Sanskrit poems proclaim the grandeur of kings; the Khmer inscriptions exhibit the precision with which jurisdictional squabbles were prosecuted and slaves registered. Here and there, we can use inscriptions to cross-reference official careers; here and there—especially when they provide inventories of temple treasures and personnel—they give us a glimpse of material culture. But it is as if U.S. history had to be reconstructed from obituary notices, wills, deeds, and Fourth of July orations and little else.

These kind of documents, of course, are meticulously dated. This means that, with some exceptions, the chronological framework of Angkor—particularly for the monarchs who reigned there—has been reconstructed after having been forgotten by the Cambodians themselves. The job of chronological reconstruction was never easy; it occupied much of the career of perhaps the greatest scholar associated with early Southeast Asian history, the French savant George Coedes (1886–1968). Coedes was unwilling to speculate about matters not dealt with by inscriptions and left his successors with a variety of tasks concerning the corpus of Cambodian inscriptions he established.[3]

The inscriptions themselves, being dated, are rooted in time; being parts of permanent buildings, they are rooted in the landscape too. In spite of this, with rare exceptions, the inscriptions are not the place to look for details of life among Cambodia's rural poor, or for clear statements of the political process as it operated at Angkor. Instead, they usually refer to extraordinary events—contracts entered into by people and gods— observed from "above" in poetry or from "below" in prose. The *history* they give us is comparable, in a way, to the lighting and extinction of hundreds of torches, here and there, now and then, over the landscape

NORTHERN CAMBODIA: ANGKOREAN SITES
[after B.P. Groslier and E. Lunet De Lanjonquiere]

of eastern mainland Southeast Asia. As each is lighted, we can look around and discern a few details of historical fact: Temple X was dedicated to such and such an Indian god, by so and so, on such and such a date. It had a particular number of slaves attached to it, identified by name and sex, and with children identified in terms of whether they could walk or not. The temple lands stretched east to a stream, south to a small hill, west and north to other landmarks . . . and then the light goes out. We know little about the way this temple fitted into the context of its time, whether its patrons enjoyed official status, or whether the temple remained in use for months or for centuries. In some inscriptions, descendants return to the site to restore it in honor of their ancestors; other temples seem to have lasted only as long as individual patrons did.

The other sources we have for the study of Cambodian history are the temples themselves, and the statues and bas-reliefs they contain, as well as artifacts dating from Angkorean times that have been unearthed throughout Cambodia. These tell us a good deal about the sequence and priorities of Cambodian elite religion, about the popularity of certain Indian myths, and about ways in which they reflect the preoccupations of the elite. They also tell us about fashions in hemlines, hairstyles, and jewelry; these have been used to arrange a chronology of artistic styles. The bas-reliefs are informative about weapons, armor, and battle tactics, and those from the thirteenth-century temple-mountain, the Bayon, are a rich source for details about everyday Cambodian life.[4]

So in addition to deeds, obituary notices, and orations, we can work with tableaux showing the people of Angkor, for the most part, disguised as mythical figures and with bas-reliefs showing them going about their daily business. What is missing from our sources are documents that stand above the others, giving an overall view of the society, or those that in a sense come from "underneath" it, providing details about such things as taxes, land ownership, social structure, and folk belief.

JAYAVARMAN II AND THE FOUNDING OF ANGKOR

What happened in 802? From the Sdok Kak Thom inscription, incised in A.D. 1050 in northwestern Cambodia—a major source for Cambodian chronology and religious history—we learn that in this year the monarch we call Jayavarman II, residing in the Kulen hills to the north of what was to become the Angkor complex, participated in a ritual whereby he became a "universal monarch."[5] The ceremonies also celebrated a cult with which the inscription is particularly concerned, that of the *devaraja,* a Sanskrit term that translates as "god king" or "king of the gods," unquestionably a cult linking the monarch with Siva. The ceremony was apparently preceded some years earlier by an "auspicious magic rite" celebrated at the cult site of Ba Phnom in the southeast.[6]

Jayavarman II and his son, Jayavarman III, left no inscriptions of their own, and this has encouraged scholars, until recently, to suggest that the importance granted to these kings as "founders of Angkor" has been exaggerated. The Sdok Kak Thom inscription is primarily concerned with the sacerdotal family that, for more than two hundred years, officiated at the *devaraja* celebrations. And yet the biographical details that the inscription provides are very useful. Jayavarman II apparently resided in five parts of Cambodia at different times in his career. He appears to have moved from the southeast, near Ba Phnom, to the upper Mekong Basin, near Sambor, before moving west to occupy Aninditapura, to the north and east of the Tonle Sap, or Great Lake.

What was Jayavarman doing in these places? With all the facts we know about him—more extensive than for many later kings—there is still something mysterious about him. Who was he? Where did he come from? In a persuasive essay, Claude Jacques has argued that he arrived (or returned) from a place called "Java" (perhaps the island of that name, perhaps a kingdom in Sumatra) around A.D. 770, when he was about twenty years old.[7] One of his first actions, according to a tenth-century inscription found in the area of Ba Phnom, was to perform a special ceremony that "made it impossible for Java to control holy Cambodia." We do not know what the ceremony involved or why Jayavarman II was impelled to declare his independence at this time and in this way. Coedes has pointed out that although the ceremony clearly preceded the one performed on Mt. Kulen, it could easily have been one of several, in many parts of the kingdom, as Jayavarman moved through them over the next thirty years.

The references are tantalizing and incomplete. Was the ceremony performed at Ba Phnom imported from Java? Or was it one that linked Jayavarman II with ancestral spirits at Funan? The ceremony was important enough to be noted in an inscription concerned primarily with other things, two centuries later. Given Ba Phnom's enduring importance as a cult site, as recently as the 1940s, the second explanation is tempting, but evidence is lacking to support it.

The rest of Jayavarman's early career has been traced by Jacques and Oliver Wolters.[8] Primarily, it involved a series of military campaigns and the formation of alliances, through marriages and grants of land, with locally powerful people willing to transfer some of their allegiance to a newcomer claiming to be a universal monarch. An undated inscription gives the borders of Jayavarman II's kingdom as being "China, Champa, and the land of cardamoms and mangoes"—perhaps located to the west.[9] Reading "Vietnam" for "China," it seems as if more or less the current land area of Cambodia—with the addition of southern Laos—was involved.

The assimilation of the Angkorean region into "Kambuja-desa" occupied more than twenty years. No inscriptions have survived from this period, and temples appear to have been small or made of perishable materials. These undocumented years are crucial all the same, for at this time the related notions of nationhood and kingship, remolded to fit the Cambodian scene, appear to have been gathering force. Both terms should be used with caution. "Nationhood" may have meant little more than having a name (Kambuja-desa) with which to contrast one's fellows with outsiders. Cambodians were insiders, owing their allegiance to a particular "universal" king, whose relation to them resembled Siva's relationship with the other gods. Perhaps both these ideas came in from Java, but they were probably already known from the Indian literature of statecraft, familiar to brahmans known to have been in Cambodia at this time.

The evidence for these suggestions springs from inscriptions carved long after Jayavarman's death. But Wolters and Jacques argued convincingly that in his progress through Cambodia, the future king had welded together an assortment of disparate regions into some sort of self-aware community. Whether or not, in the long run, Jayavarman II succeeded in this task (or even if the task was what he had in mind) is open to question because of the obscurity that surrounds his reign. But it is clear that the kings who came after him honored him as the founder of a dynasty and as the instigator of a particular way of looking at Cambodia that was different from what their own, more provincial ancestors had been able to achieve. Jayavarman II also served a more practical purpose. Cambodian folk thinking has always placed great emphasis on the veneration of ancestors, or *nak ta,* associated with particular places. Once the royal capital of Cambodia came to be at Hariharalaya (present-day Roluos), where Jayavarman II finally settled, subsequent kings came to honor him as a kind of ancestral "founder-spirit" of the sort that every Cambodian village, until recently, possessed.

Although it is no longer tenable to say that the cult of the *devaraja* was in some way a ritual process by which a king *became* a god, or a "god-king," the evidence of ritual and ideological connections between Cambodian kings and the god Siva is extensive (up to the twelfth century at least), even if the *devaraja* cult as such may not have played as large a part in the sacralization of Cambodian kingship as the authors of the Sdok Kak Thom inscription would like us to believe. The cult, in other words, was *a* royal cult, rather than *the* definitive one; Hermann Kulke has argued persuasively that the cult involved a statue of Siva, himself *devaraja,* or king of the gods, that was paraded through the streets of Angkor—and other royal capitals at festivals—in remembrance, perhaps, of the role the cult had played at the beginning of the Angkorean period, when Jayavarman II freed Cambodia from Java.[10]

YASOVARMAN AND HIS SUCCESSORS

His son, Jayavarman III, came to the throne young, was an elephant hunter, and died after ruling "wisely," in A.D. 877.[11] The elephant hunting may be an impenetrable metaphor, and "wisely" may disguise inaction. The writer who provided this information had a special interest in continuity, after all, with regard to the *devaraja* cult, for the Sdok Kak Thom inscription presumes, perhaps mistakenly, that the ruler who patronized the *devaraja* cult was the legitimate and unique ruler of Cambodia. This may have become the case, especially after the middle of the tenth century, but it is interesting that Jayavarman III's successor, the first to embark on a systematic program of temples and inscriptions at Hariharalaya, made only one muted reference to this predecessor, tracing his own legitimacy to relatives of a wife of Jayavarman II (not Jayavarman III's mother) and to a pair of "kings" about whom nothing else has come to light. Presumably, this was a way of casting his genealogy back beyond Jayavarman's usurpation, thus connecting himself with the pre-Angkorean rulers to enhance his own legitimacy.

In fact this very king, Indravarman (r. A.D. 877–889) was himself a usurper, which may account for his muddled genealogy. His reign is important because it was the first of many to be marked by a triadic pattern of royal behavior described in the 1930s by the art historian Philippe Stern.[12]

The first phase was to sponsor irrigation works in honor of his subjects and the watery divinities of the soil. In Indravarman's reign, a large reservoir was constructed at Hariharalaya to trap rain water. It was known as the Indratataka and covered 300 hectares (650 acres). An inscription tells us that as soon as Indravarman became king, he made this promise: "In five days, I will begin to dig."[13] Another purpose of such reservoirs was to indicate the extent of a king's power, and of his alliances with the gods, by recreating on earth geographical features associated in people's minds with the mythical home of the gods, Mt. Meru, where lakes surround the central mountain. This north Indian fantasy, translated to waterlogged Cambodia, is not devoid of irony; but neither are Gothic towers in U.S. college towns.

The second phase was for a monarch to honor his parents and his other ancestors by installing statues of these people, usually in the guise of gods. Indravarman sponsored statues of his parents (as well as of others, including his mother's parents, and Jayavarman II and his wife, depicted as embodiments of Siva and his consort) in the stuccoed brick temple complex known today as Preah Ko (sacred cow).

This charming temple, completed in 879, inaugurated what is now called the Roluos style of Cambodian architecture.[14] In this style, several features that were to become important later—including the custom of enclosing temples in a series of concentric moats and walls—appeared for the first time. The sophistication of carving and the predominance of floral motifs suggest that these skills had been developed earlier by carving wood. Although of modest size in comparison with later temples, Indravarman's monuments of Preah Ko and Bakong—his "temple-mountain"—were far more grandiose, in conception and appearance, than anything that had preceded them and hint at developments in religious ideology and social mobilization for which other evidence is lacking.

An inscription from Preah Ko indicates that Indravarman had become a universal monarch by subduing unspecified contenders: "In battle, which is like a difficult ocean to cross, he raised a pathway, made up of the heads of his arrogant enemies; his own troops passed over on it." The inscription also tells us: "It seems that the creator [Indra] tired of making so many kings, had fashioned this king named Indravarman [literally 'protected by Indra'] to form the joy of the three worlds, uniquely."[15]

Inscriptions far from Roluos suggest that Indravarman commanded, at least briefly, loyalties in northeastern Thailand and the Mekong Delta that confirm his seemingly inflated rhetoric. One of these, carved in honor of one of his teachers (himself a cousin of Jayavarman II) goes even further:

> Ruler of the entire world which he had conquered, established on the slopes of Mt. Meru, he was even steadier than the sun, which occasionally was distant.
> Atop the lordly heads of the kings of China, Champa and Yavadvipa [Java?] his reign was like a flawless crown, made from a garland of jasmine flowers.[16]

Statements like this about kings, which may strike us as flowery, were circumscribed by the traditional characteristics of the gods the kings were being made to resemble. The poet's skill was thought to consist of piling up these characteristics and half-concealing some of them behind metaphors, similes, and puns. Just as the verses enumerated the ways in which a king was like the god, the temples were catalogs and pictures of the world of the gods—a sort of mirror image. In this sense, the temples can be seen as puns, or plays on words, and mirror images of another world.

The final phase of Indravarman's program, as detected by Philippe Stern, was to erect a temple-mountain. This is now known as the Bakong and took the form of a stepped pyramid. Unlike the reservoir, or the Preah Ko, the Bakong was dedicated to the king himself and was to serve, after his death, as his sarcophagus. Coedes estimated that thirteen Angkorean kings, beginning with Jayavarman II, built such temple-mountains.[17] Not all of them have survived. Those that have can be read in different ways. First, they were planned as duplicates of the mythical mountain, Mt. Meru, which stood north of the Himalayas at the center of the universe. Like Mt. Meru, they were homes for the gods and for deceased worthies—not only kings—who had been assimilated into heaven. They were also tombs, housing the ashes of the king. In some cases— particularly Angkor Wat—they were astronomical observatories as well.[18] In sum, the temples were cities of the dead.

Bakong was the first Cambodian temple to be built primarily of stone rather than brick; it was also the first to assume a precisely pyramidical shape. The temple was reconstructed by French archaeologists in the 1930s. By then, nearly all of its bas-reliefs had disappeared.

Indravarman's son, Yasovarman, who reigned from 889 to about 910, was an important king. His inscriptions and his buildings suggest that he wanted to do more than his father and to focus Cambodia around a royal *city*. Yasodharapura, the "city" of Angkor, bore his name until the fourteenth century.

Yasovarman's first official action appears to have been to endow "a hundred" religious hermitages, equipping each with a royal rest-house and a set of regulations.[19] Twelve nearly identical inscriptions related to these hermitages have been discovered. Two are near Roluos; six of the others are from southeastern Cambodia, where Yasovarman, through his mother, claimed family connections from pre-Angkorean times. The spread of the inscriptions suggests that "Kambuja-desa" was becoming a recognized and accepted concept as well as an ideal.

Soon after this, Yasovarman honored his parents by building the four brick temples, now known as Lolei, on an island he built in the middle of his father's reservoir. At the northeast corner of the reservoir—often an honored direction in Cambodian religious thinking[20]—he built a raised highway running northwestward toward the area 16 kilometers (10 miles) away where he planned to establish his capital city. This area now houses the Angkor complex.

Yasovarman's choice of Angkor was probably influenced by his plan to build his own temple-mountain there on the summit of a natural hill. His choices included a hill (Phnom Krom) that was too close to the Tonle Sap and another (Phnom Bok) that was too far away.[21] He constructed small temples on these two hills, however, and built his main temple on the hill known today as Phnom Bakheng (literally "Mount Mighty Ancestor") and then as *phnom kandal* (the central mountain), which still lies close to the center of the Angkor complex.

The Sdok Kak Thom inscription tells us that Yasovarman "established the royal city of Sri Yasodharapura and brought the *devaraja* from Hariharalaya to this city. Then he erected a central mountain (*phnom kandal*)."[22] Yasovarman's mountain was not identified as Phnom Bakheng until the 1930s. In conception and execution, it is far more grandiose than any of his father's monuments. Its symbolism has been studied in detail by Jean Filliozat, who has shown that the number of levels, statues, towers, and stairways, when "read" separately and together, correspond to various numbers—particularly 33 and 108—endowed by Indian religion with metaphysical significance; in some cases, pilgrims approaching the monument would be able to catch this allusion by counting the number of towers they could see.[23]

To the east of Phnom Bakheng, Yasovarman built a reservoir, the Yasodharatataka, roughly 6.5 kilometers (4 miles) long and 3 kilometers (2 miles) wide. Along its southern shore he had monasteries built for sects that honored Siva, Vishnu, and the Buddha. Elsewhere throughout his kingdom, he ordered temples built on natural hills, the most notable being Preah Vihear, on the edge of the precipice that nowadays forms part of the frontier between Cambodia and Thailand.[24]

These activities suggest that Yasovarman was able to command a far larger pool of manpower than his predecessors had done. It is likely that many of these were unwilling workers, captured in raids or battles or forced to immigrate from elsewhere in the kingdom. Yasovarman's inscriptions show him to have been a cosmopolitan monarch, aware of the grandeur of Indian civilization and tolerant of different religious beliefs. As usual, however, the sources reveal very little about his political activities, his alliances, or his idiosyncratic ideology. We have tantalizing glimpses of administrative reforms, including evidence that in Yasovarman's legal code fines were levied in relation to one's ability to pay and a suggestion that taxes were efficiently collected, in kind, throughout the kingdom. But for the most part we must settle for proclamations of his greatness: "He was a lion-man; he tore the enemy with the claws of his grandeur; his teeth were his policies; his eyes were the Veda. His glory was like a roar in all directions; his virtues made up his name."[25] Here as so often in Sanskrit versification, many of the words are deliberate double entendres; the phrase "his eyes were the Veda," for example, plays on the similarity between the verb "to see" and the noun "sacred teachings." These double meanings, as we have seen, appear at many points in Angkorean verse, as well as in the architecture of the temples.

Yasovarman died around 910. He was succeeded by two of his sons in turn. Little is known about them, and by 921 a brother of one of Yasovarman's wives had set up a rival city at Koh Ker, in what is now an inhospitable area about 85 kilometers (60 miles) north of Angkor. The rival began at once to perform kingly actions, such as building a reservoir and beginning work on a temple-mountain. In 928, when the reigning king died at Yasodharapura, the usurper proclaimed himself king with the title Jayavarman IV. Work continued on his temple-mountain, known today as Prasat Thom, until about 930. The temple itself, housing a lingam estimated to have been 18 meters (59 feet) high and about 5 meters (16 feet) in diameter (and probably made of metal, or encased in metal, for it has disappeared), was in fact the highest of the temples erected in Cambodia, with the exception of Angkor Wat.[26] Jayavarman IV's inscriptions boasted that the construction surpassed those of previous kings.

We do not know the roots of his colossal self-esteem, the basis of his following, or what prompted him to shift the capital so far from Yasod-harapura. Kulke has argued that Jayavarman's declaring himself king while the *devaraja* image was still at Yasodharapura weakened the legitimacy of the cult.[27] Jayavarman, in fact, extended it by proclaiming himself and his kingship to be a *portion of the god* housed in his temple-mountain. In this way, he claimed to draw his legitimacy directly from Siva, a notion adopted by several later kings after the capital had returned to Yasodharapura.

Although Jayavarman's claims may seem hollow or pompous to us, it is clear that by force or persuasion he was able to rule at Koh Ker over large numbers of people, and in considerable splendor, for twenty years. After his death in 942, one of his sons reigned briefly, and in 944 one of his nephews (on his mother's side, a nephew of Yasovarman as well) returned to Yasodharapura as King Rajendravarman II. In the words of a later inscription, this king "restored the holy city of Yasodharapura, long deserted, and rendered it superb and charming by erecting houses there that were ornamented with shining gold, palaces glittering with precious stones, like the palace of (Indra) on earth."[28]

Although little is known about Rajendravarman's reign, his imitation of procedures enacted by Yasovarman, such as building a temple honoring his ancestors in the middle of a lake, indicates that he wished to restore Angkorean kingship, rather than to start a dynasty of his own or to connect himself with Jayavarman's dynasty at Koh Ker. Under Rajendravarman, two temple-mountains were built—the Mebon and Pre Rup—as well as numerous other temples, especially in the north. His reign appears to have been peaceful, except for a successful campaign against Champa; and it ushered in a period of prosperity at Angkor that lasted for almost a hundred years. One aspect of this prosperity is the literary polish of Rajendravarman's Sanskrit inscriptions. One of these, the Pre Rup stele, runs to almost three hundred stanzas, glorifying Rajendravarman's genealogy, his learning, and his performance as king.[29] Another aspect of his reign was the commercial expansion of the Khmer kingdom westward into what is now northeastern Thailand; and a third was his public tolerance for Buddhism. Rajendravarman appears to have studied Buddhism himself, and the minister in charge of public works throughout his reign was a prominent Buddhist.

Rajendravarman died in 968 and was succeeded by his son Jayavarman V, who was still a boy and appears to have spent several years under the close supervision of relatives and high officials. These men and their families figure largely in the highly polished inscriptions from his reign. Perhaps the loveliest of the temples at Angkor, now known as Banteai Srei (Fortress of Women), was dedicated at the beginning of the reign by an official who was later Jayavarman's guru, or tutor.[30] There is evidence that this delicate, small-scale temple, carved of pinkish sandstone, once served an important urban area. Today it lies half-concealed in light

A heavenly angel (*thevoda*) from the eleventh-century temple of Thommanon. Author's photo.

forest about 16 kilometers (10 miles) north of the main Angkor complex; it was discovered by a French surveying party only in 1916.

Although Shaivite like his father and many of the brahmans at the court, Jayavarman V was tolerant of Buddhism, and Buddhist scholarship flourished during his reign. An elegantly written inscription from Wat Sithor in Kompong Cham dating from this period shows how syncretic

Buddhist thinking inside Cambodia had already become, fusing elements of Buddhism and Shaivism in a way that led the nineteenth-century Sanskritist Emile Senart to note: "Everywhere one senses a manifest preoccupation to disturb people's habits as little as possible, and to submerge deep differences inside surface similarities."[31] Inscriptions play down Jayavarman V's role as a builder of temple-mountains. His own, the Takeo temple, appears to be unfinished. Instead, they emphasize architecture on a more personal scale, such as his royal palace. He died in 1001.

His death ushered in a turbulent and destructive period, but by 1003, another king, whose origins are unknown, was reigning at Angkor. The rest of the kingdom was not under his control. In the north, a prince calling himself Suryavarman—later to be king as Suryavarman I—was mentioned in several inscriptions.[32]

Some scholars have argued that neither of these kings was Cambodian by blood. As Michael Vickery has recently shown, however, Suryavarman was almost certainly a Cambodian member of an elite family with links to the northeastern part of the kingdom as well as to a Buddhist kingdom in the south of present-day Thailand.[33] It is intriguing that the blueprint used by Suryavarman to take power in the first decade of the eleventh century so closely resembles the one chosen two centuries before by Jayavarman II. The process involved sporadic warfare as well as the formation of coalitions—by force, marriage, and cajolery—which enabled the pretender to reduce or buy off the power of local chiefs. Vickery suggested that Suryavarman had powerful allies among the priestly families that dominated the government at Angkor, and inscriptions of the time show him moving slowly westward, toward a partly depopulated capital, over a period of years—an indication in itself about the intricacy with which the alliances he needed had to be put together.

Suryavarman won his final battle, an inscription tells us, "from a king surrounded by other kings." One new element in his rise to power is his patronage of Buddhism. There is evidence from hostile inscriptions that as he rose to power he destroyed *vrah,* or religious images.[34] The meaning of this charge is unclear. Had Suryavarman been a Buddhist, perhaps the destruction would represent iconoclasm pure and simple. It is more likely that it was connected with the delegitimation of certain religious foundations whose patrons had been slow or unwilling to cooperate with him. Another inscription, in fact, suggests that during his reign the king deliberately impoverished members of the elite who had amassed great fortunes and thus represented distinct political threats.

One of Suryavarman's first actions in reaching Yasodharapura was to arrange that an oath of loyalty be sworn to him, publicly, by as many as four thousand officials, known as *tamvrac,* at the newly constructed royal palace. The oath has survived in an inscription, the only one of its kind. It states that the officials will be loyal to the king, and adds:

> If all of us who are here in person do not keep this oath with regard to His Majesty, may he still reign long, we ask that he inflict on us royal punishment of all sorts. If we hide ourselves in order not to keep this oath . . . may we be reborn in the thirty-second hell as long as the sun and moon shall last.[35]

The oath closes by asking that those who keep it be awarded religious foundations to administer as well as food for their families—as "recompense due to people who are devoted to their master." Loyalty, in other words, was to be rewarded by the right to extract surpluses from regions under some sort of control by *tamvracs,* who were linked by allegiance to the king. The oath as a whole marks an intensification of royal power and also the imposition of a newly constituted, or reconstituted, elite connected to the control of land.

Suryavarman's reign, in fact, was characterized by the intensification of several aspects of kingship, coming at a time, as Vickery has shown, when bureaucratic power rivaled or even surpassed the power of the king. Suryavarman expanded the territory under Angkorean control, colonizing the western end of the Tonle Sap with new religious foundations. Further away, in the same direction, he annexed the Theravada Buddhist kingdom of Louvo, centered on present-day Lopburi in central Thailand.

He also expanded the irrigation works at Angkor, in a move that suggests that his other policies had increased the population of the city. Because this hydraulic program was linked to increased bureaucratic centralization, it is possible to refer fruitfully to Suryavarman's reign as one that employed the "Asiatic mode of production" referred to by Marx and others.

Under Suryavarman, priestly and bureaucratic functions, seldom separate in practice, were institutionalized. Government-sponsored religious foundations became conduits for government revenue and largesse in ways that remain obscure but that probably were connected with the power of priestly-bureaucratic families around the king.

His administration was an urbanizing one. A French scholar, Mestrier du Bourg, has shown that whereas for the preceding three reigns roughly twenty toponyms contained in inscriptions end with the suffix *"pura,"* or city (cf. Singapore, the "lion city"), under Suryavarman the number jumped to forty-seven, further evidence that his rise to power involved herding people into conglomerations from less tightly administered rural areas. Perhaps some of these *pura* were cities in name only, to enhance the prestige of locally based elites, but the evidence for urbanization coincides with other things we know about Suryavarman's reign.[36]

There is also evidence that merchants engaged in local and overseas trade became more active while Suryavarman was king. Throughout Cambodian history, the majority of such people appear to have been, in ethnic terms, outsiders—Chams, Chinese, or Vietnamese—but references to merchants as a group became more frequent in inscriptions dating from Suryavarman's reign. As usual, foreign trade involved the exchange of "wild" goods from forested areas for "civilized" ones, such as cloth or porcelain; but as Kenneth Hall has shown, commodities such as land, rice, buffalo, and slaves were also traded by Cambodians at this time for manufactured or exotic goods from other countries.[37]

The extent to which Suryavarman's reign mobilized bureaucratic and coercive talents to concentrate people at Yasodharapura marked a noticeable departure from the past. The success of these tactics showed subsequent kings that the kingdom could be organized and expanded by forcing its cultivators to work throughout the year. The food needed to support the coercive apparatus (priests, kings, bureaucrats, and armies) could not be supplied by the single annual harvests that previously had sufficed for ordinary people to survive.

In extending his power in this way, Suryavarman enjoyed the advantages of the usurper. He was free to choose and reward his trusted followers, rather than finding himself hemmed in at the beginning of his reign by hangers-on from other courts. At first, governing the country with new officials probably meant that more attention was paid to local issues, for the new officials would still have debts to their clients in the countryside that their successors could ignore.

Suryavarman's successor, Utyadityavarman II (r. 1050–1068) was a devotee of Siva. Guided by a powerful guru, he revived interest in the *devaraja* cult and also revived the custom of building a massive temple-mountain—in his case, the Baphuon—to house the lingam associated with his reign. As an inscription carved under his successor tells us:

Seeing that in the middle of Jambudvipa, the home of the gods, there rose up a golden mountain, he made a golden mountain in the center of his city, out of emulation. On the summit of this mountain, in a golden temple, shining with celestial brilliance, he set up a Sivalinga made of gold.[38]

ANGKOREAN KINGSHIP

There are three ways of looking at Cambodian kingship in its heyday at Angkor. One is to study the king's relationship with Siva. Paul Mus,

44

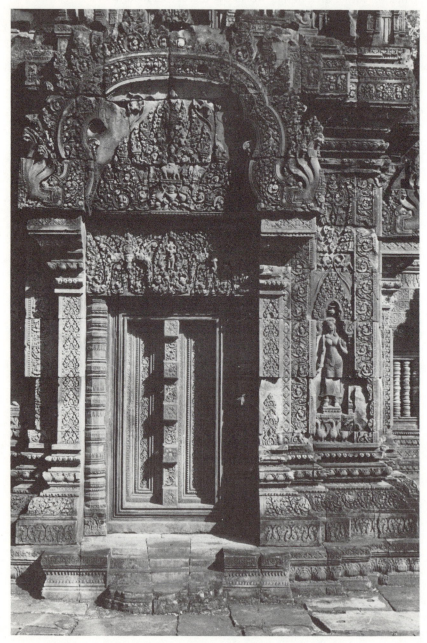

Doorway and lintel, Banteai Srei (late tenth century). Author's photo.

in a brilliant essay written in 1933, has shown that Siva's popularity in classical Southeast Asia may be traced in large part to his role as an earth and an ancestral spirit, emerging from the earth (and thus from the ancestors) at first "accidentally" in the form of an outcrop of stone, later purposefully, carved into the shape of a lingam representing the ancestors and, later still, one representing the rulers *and* ancestors of a particular place. Siva in this sense was a literary form of an ancestor spirit, held responsible for fertilizing the soil by inducing rain to fall on the region under his jurisdiction. This aspect of Cambodian kingship (found elsewhere in Southeast Asia, particularly in Vietnam) endured into the 1960s in the countryside. Siva and his consort, Uma, were gods to whom sacrifices—buffalos or human beings—were addressed because they were thought of as divinizations of what lay under the earth. Intriguingly, when looked at in this way, the Cambodian king, as a patron of agriculture, resembles a Chinese emperor far more than a *raja* of traditional India.

Now the role of a Cambodian king, of course—or of the emperor for that matter—was not merely to bring rain or to keep everyone's ancestors contentedly at bay. A second way of looking at Cambodian kingship, through the eyes of the people, is to see it in terms of the king's repeated and ritual enactment of lordliness and superiority in battle, sexuality, poetry, possessions, ceremony, and so forth. Seen in this way, the king was not an earth spirit or a priest, but the hero of an Indian epic. This is the view taken, in fact, by most of the Sanskrit-language inscriptions of Cambodia that praised kings as embodiments of virtue, actors *above* society, associated in many cases with the sky, the sun, Indra, Vishnu, and Rama rather than with earthly or ancestral forces. As living superlatives (for each king was seen as "the greatest" rather than one of many), kings provided the poets with a point of comparison, a kind of polestar, from which society, flowing outward and downward, metaphorically organized itself, first through the *varnas* near the king and then on to free people, villagers, and slaves. The king was superhuman without being helpful in any practical sense. He was a hero, occupying the top of society because of his merit and his power.

To members of the Angkorean elite, this reenactment of lordliness had at least two purposes. The first was to present godlike behavior (e.g., building a temple-mountain in imitation of Mt. Meru; or defeating "hordes" of enemies) in order to obtain blessings for the king and the kingdom. The correct performance of rituals—especially exacting with regard to the timing of particular rites—was crucial to their efficacy. In this context, the word "symbol," in a twentieth-century sense, is rather empty. The king believed in the rituals. So did his advisers. Ceremonies were the vehicles through which his lordliness—in which he also believed—was acted out.

A third way of looking at kingship is in terms of everyday Cambodian life. Sanskrit inscriptions are far less useful here than the Cambodian ones. Although society at Angkor, at first glance, appears to have been almost mechanically organized into strata, the inscriptions point to webs of relationships, responsibilities, and expectations within which everyone appears to have been contentedly, or at least perpetually, entangled. Seen in this way, the king, as a polygamist, a patron, and a giver of names was perhaps the most entangled of them all. Ian Mabbett's thoughtful study of Angkorean kingship shows the range of things a king was expected to do, approve, and know about.[39] These included bestowing titles and emblems on his high officials; granting land and slaves to numerous religious foundations; constructing and maintaining irrigation works; constructing, decorating, and staffing temples; and conducting foreign relations, particularly, in this era, with Champa to the east of the capital and with various tributary states to the north and west. The king was also the court of last appeal, and the inscriptions tell us how obscure squabbles involving landholdings often floated up through the judicial system to reach him—a feature of kingship that endured into the twentieth century, as we shall see in Chapter 8.

At the same time, although the inscriptions tell us little about it, to survive a king had to be a political operator. As Mabbett pointed out, many Sanskrit inscriptions praise the political acumen of kings in terms of their resemblances to Rama or their knowledge of Indian political texts. As political manuals, these learned writings certainly gave Cambodian kings plenty of room for maneuver, but it is in just this area—the day-to-day preferments, quarrels, and decisions—that the inscriptions are of so little help. The *flavor* of life at court is inaccessible.

The inscriptions are of more assistance in telling us about the other levels of Cambodian society—freepeople and slaves—but again only at the moments described, recalled, or honored by an inscription. Mabbett's study of slavery at Angkor, which builds on earlier ones by Yves Bongert and A. Chakravarti, shows the bewildering complexity of categories in use for what we would call "slaves" and the bewildering number of tasks that were assigned to them.[40] As suggested in Chapter 2, it is still impossible to sort the terms out either diachronically or across the corpus of inscriptions. There are cases, for example, of "slaves" who owned slaves; "slaves" who married members of the royal family; and "free" people who were disposed of by others, just like slaves. Working back from later periods, one gets the impression that most of the people at Angkor were subjects (*reas*) rather than objects, or free people. They were at the disposition of patrons, who had the right to sell them to other people. In many cases, they disposed of "lower" people themselves. In the inscriptions slaves are listed as commodities.

These people, about whom we know so little, were certainly the "giants" who were once thought to have built Angkor. What can be gleaned about their everyday lives, especially from bas-reliefs, shows us that their technology, clothing, and houses changed little between Angkorean times and the period of the French protectorate. The bas-reliefs also depict their domestic animals, games, and marketing, and clowns, shamans, ascetics, and peddlers. We are on less firm ground, however, when we seek to reconstitute their beliefs or the stories they told each other. No popular literature can be traced back to Angkor. Post-Angkorean Cambodia, discussed in Chapter 5, was radically altered by its close association with Thai society and Thai ideas. This absence of written sources makes it difficult to bring the ordinary people of Angkor to life, except through the things they made—reservoirs, temples, statues of stone and bronze, unglazed pottery, and so on. What did a slave at Angkor think about his master? Was a master to be imitated, hated, or revered? How far "down" into the society—or into a person's mind—did recognizably Indian ideas, gods, and vocabulary penetrate? There is evidence that the population was more literate in Khmer than it was in Sanskrit, but nothing is known about the way literacy was taught. The picture that emerges is one of familiarity with Indian culture (and perhaps knowledge of occasional Indian visitors as well) among the elite, thinning out in the rest of the society, until in the villages, as in the nineteenth century, we find ancestral spirits given Hindu names and Hindu statues treated as ancestral gods.

As we have seen, Cambodia's imitation of India stopped short, even among the elite, of importing the Indian caste system, although, as Mabbett has shown in yet another penetrating essay, a set of ritual orders using *varna* nomenclature formed part of the king's repertoire of patronage, for caste standing was occasionally bestowed by the monarch on his own clients or on the clients of his associates. Except at the beginning of a dynasty, a Cambodian king, like most Chinese emperors, could rule only by extending networks of patronage and mutual obligations outward from his palace, at first through close associates and family members but becoming diffuse—and more dependent on local power-holders—at the edges of the kingdom. Villagers far from Angkor would probably seldom have known the king's name any more than they did in the early twentieth century, when the following passage was recorded by French ethnographers working among the Cambodian population of southern Vietnam:

> In former times . . . there were no canals, and no paths; there were only forests, with tigers, elephants, and wild buffaloes; no people dared to leave their villages.
>
> For this reason, hardly anyone ever went to the royal city. If anyone ever reached it, by poling his canoe, the others would ask him about it:

"What is the king's appearance like? Is he like an ordinary man?" And the traveler, seeing all these ignorant people asking questions, would reply: "The king has an elegant, beautiful appearance, unstained by dust or sweat; he has no scars . . . " but of course often he had never seen the king at all.[41]

ANGKOR WAT

The last years of the eleventh century, although notable for several interesting developments in Cambodian architectural motifs, foreshadowing the twelfth-century monument of Angkor Wat, were years of turmoil and fragmentation. At different times, two or even three "monarchs" contended for the title of absolute ruler. At the end of the century, however, a new dynasty, which was to last for more than a hundred years, began to rule at Angkor. Little is known about the first two of its kings, Jayavarman VI and his brother, Dharanindravarman I, but their great-nephew, Suryavarman II, under whom Angkor Wat was built, was, like Yasovarman II and Suryavarman I, another unifying monarch. If his inscriptions are to be believed, he gained power while still young, after winning a crucial battle against a rival prince: "Leaving the ocean of his army on the field of combat . . . he bounded to the head of the elephant of the enemy king, and killed [him] as a *garuda* on the slope of a mountain might kill a snake."[42]

Suryavarman II indeed was the first king to rule over a unified Cambodian kingdom since Utyadityavarman II's death in the 1060s. The parallels with Suryavarman I, who was probably no relation, are numerous and instructive. Both kings came to power following periods of fragmentation and disorder. They responded to this, once Yasodharapura was in their hands, with vigorous administrative policies, with a recognizably pragmatic style of kingship, and by expanding the territory and manpower under their control. Suryavarman II campaigned in the east, against Vietnam and Champa, using mercenaries drawn primarily from tributary areas to the west. He established diplomatic relations with China—the first Angkorean king to do so. Like Suryavarman I, he also sought to separate himself in religious terms from his immediate predecessors. Suryavarman I had done this by his patronage to Buddhism, whereas his namesake chose to exhibit a devotion—unusual for a Cambodian king—to Vishnu. In both cases, innovative or personal policies went along with a legitimizing cluster of actions, which linked the kings with pre-Angkorean pilgrimage sites like Wat Ph'u, with Hindu gurus associated with previous kings, and with artistic styles extending back into the reigns of the people they had managed to overthrow.

Suryavarman II's devotion to Vishnu led him to commission the largest, perhaps the most beautiful, and one of the most mysterious of all the monuments at Angkor—the temple, tomb, and observatory now known as Angkor Wat.[43] The temple was begun at the start of his reign, and it was not completed until after his death, about 1150. There is striking evidence, recently uncovered, that its central statue of Vishnu, long since vanished, was dedicated in July 1131, which was probably Suryavarman's thirty-third birthday—a number, as we have seen, with important cosmic significance in Indian religion.

What is so mysterious about the temple? First, it opens to the west, the only major building at Yasodharapura to do so. In addition, its bas-reliefs—more than a mile of them around the outer galleries of the temple—are to be followed by moving in a counterclockwise direction, starting from the northwest quarter. Now the customary way of reading a bas-relief or of walking around a temple was to keep it all on one's right by moving in a clockwise direction, known by the Sanskrit term *pradaksina.* The reverse direction was usually associated with the dead; so was the west, for obvious meteorological reasons. Some French scholars argued, therefore, that Angkor Wat, unlike the other temples at Angkor, was primarily a tomb.[44]

The arguments raged in learned journals until 1940, when Coedes proposed that Angkor Wat, like fifteen other royally sponsored Cambodian monuments, be thought of as a temple *and* a tomb. He cited stone receptacles, perhaps sarcophagi, that held part of the "treasure" of these other temples. As for the unusual orientation of Angkor Wat, Coedes suggested that this may have been in honor of Vishnu, Suryavarman's patron-deity, often associated with the west; Angkor Wat is the only temple at Angkor that we know to have been dedicated to him. The twelfth century, in fact, saw a vigorous revival of Vaisnavism, associated with popular religion, on the Indian subcontinent; this revival, it seems, like earlier ones in Indian religion, had repercussions at Angkor.

Between 1940 and the 1970s, little scholarly work was done on Angkor Wat. Scholars and tourists were content to marvel at the artistry of its bas-reliefs (many of them concerned with the prowess of Rama), the delicate and yet overwhelming proportions of the temple, and its continued hold on the imagination of ordinary Cambodians. In the mid-1970s, however, Eleanor Moron began studying the dimensions of the temple in detail, convinced that these might contain the key to the way the temple had been encoded by the savants who designed it.[45] After determining that the Cambodian measurement used at Angkor, the *hat,* was equivalent to approximately 0.4 meters, (1.3 feet), Moron went on to ask how many *hat* were involved in significant dimensions of the temple, such as the distance between the western entrance (the only one equipped with its

Giant guarding the gates of Angkor Thom (twelfth century). Photo by Walter Veit.

own causeway) and the central tower. The distance came to 1,728 *hat.* Three other components of this axis measured, respectively, 1,296, 867, and 439 *hat.* Moron then argued that these figures correlated to the four "ages," or *yuga* of Indian thought. The first of these, the Krita Yuga, was a supposedly golden age, lasting 1,728 years. The next three ages lasted for 1,296,000, 864,000 and 432,000 years respectively. The earliest age, therefore, was four times longer than the latest, the second earliest, three times longer, and the third earliest, twice as long. The last age is the Kali Yuga, in which we are living today. At the end of this era, it is believed, the universe will be destroyed, to be rebuilt by Brahma along similar lines, beginning with another golden age.

The fact that the length of these four eras correlates exactly with particular distances along the east-west axis of Angkor Wat suggests that the "code" for the temple is in fact a kind of pun that can be read in terms of time and space. The distances that a person entering the temple would traverse coincide with the eras that the visitor is metaphorically living through en route to the statue of Vishnu in the central tower. Walking forward and away from the west, which is the direction of death, the visitor moves backward into time, approaching the moment when the Indians proposed that time began.

In her research, Moron also discovered astronomical correlations for ten of the most frequently recurring distances at Angkor Wat. Astronomers working with her found that the sighting of the temple was related to the fact that its western gate aligned at sunrise with a small hill to the northeast, Phnom Bok. Moreover, at the summer solstice "an observer . . . standing just in front of the western entrance can see the sunrise directly over the central tower of Angkor Wat."[46] This day, June 21, marked the beginning of the solar year to Indian astronomers and was sacred to a king whose name, Suryavarman, means "protected by the sun" and who was a devotee of Vishnu.

The close fit of these spatial relationships to notions of cosmic time, and the extraordinary accuracy and symmetry of all the measurements at Angkor, combine to confirm the notion that the temple was in fact a coded religious text that could be read by experts moving along its walkways from one dimension to the next. The learned *pandits* who determined the dimensions of Angkor Wat would have been aware of and would have reveled in its multiplicity of meanings. To those lower down in the society, perhaps, fewer and fewer meanings would be clear. We can assume, however, that even the poorest slaves were astounded to see this enormous temple, probably with gilded towers and probably painted white, reflected in the water of its moat, with towers rising 60 meters (200 feet) above the ground and above the thatched huts of the people who had built it.

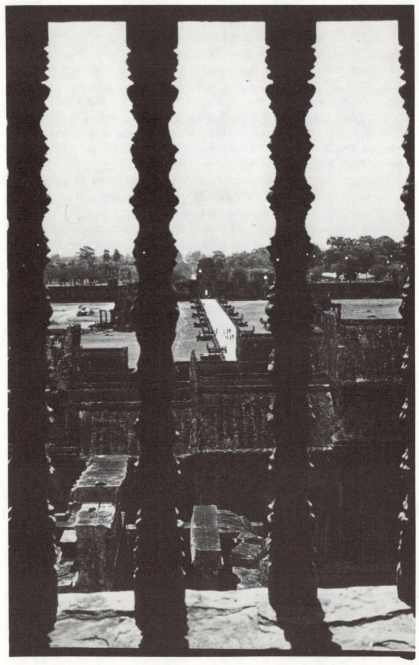

Angkor Wat (twelfth century), view from the upper gallery. Photo by Walter Veit.

Two implications of Moron's research are, first, that other temples at Angkor might well be studied and decoded and, second, that this decoding can provide insights into religious and astronomical texts that have disappeared but on which the architecture of temples was based.

Although Suryavarman II probably led a campaign against Vietnam as late as 1150, the date of his death is unknown. In fact, the period 1145–1180 produced almost no inscriptions and its history must be recreated from later sources. Suryavarman's successor, perhaps a cousin, reached the throne under mysterious circumstances, probably in a coup d'état. This new king, Dharanindravarman II, appears to have been a fervent Buddhist, although there is a possibility that he never reigned as king at Yasodharapura. Around 1160, he was succeeded by Yasovarman II, whose reign is recalled in one of Jayavarman VII's inscriptions. There Yasovarman is given credit for putting down a mysterious revolt in the northwest. The people who led this revolt, according to the inscription, were neither foreigners nor members of the elite; in bas-reliefs at the temple of Banteai Chhmar, they are depicted as people with animal heads.[47] Perhaps the revolt, like the Communist rebellion in the 1970s, was a supposedly unthinkable one, organized by the downtrodden segments of the society and by "forest people," against an allegedly unassailable elite.[48]

Instability continued in the 1160s; Yasovarman was assassinated by one of his subordinates, who then declared himself to be king. At this time also, the tributary state of Louvo sent tributary missions to China, suggesting at least partial independence from Angkor. The absence of inscriptions and the questionable legitimacy of rulers reinforce the impression of rapid change.

Perhaps, as B. P. Groslier has recently suggested, the hydraulic organization of the kingdom had already begun to falter during the reign of Suryavarman II.[49] This system of reservoirs and canals, which guaranteed one harvest a year in dry times and two with adequate rainfall, was the basis of Angkor's rice-oriented agricultural economy and allowed the concentration of large populations in the area. Groslier suggested that the system reached peak efficiency in the mid-eleventh century. The hydraulic components of Angkor Wat, a hundred years later, were much smaller than those around earlier temple-mountains. Indeed, Groslier went on, under Suryavarman II, for the first time in Cambodian history, hydraulically based cities were built at considerable distances from Angkor—at Beng Melea and Kompong Svay. Perhaps this was done because the water resources in the Angkor region, which had lasted so long, had now been tapped to the limit. Water came from a network of small streams, running south from the low hills to the north along the slight slope that extended to the shores of the Tonle Sap. As demands for water increased, these streams were diverted closer and closer to their sources. This process reduced the nutrients that the streams brought to fertilize the Angkorean plain.

Because the slope of the plain is so slight, in dry periods the canals would probably have been nearly stagnant, especially if unstable political conditions, warfare, or epidemics had drawn off the labor normally used to maintain them. Groslier suggested, as other scholars have done, that this increasing stagnation may well have coincided with the appearance of malaria on the Southeast Asian mainland, accelerating the process.[50] Here, as so often, we lack generalized statements about conditions at Angkor, or any overall statistics, that might tell us about the size and composition of the population, the condition of the hydraulic network at particular times, and the relationship—or lack of it—between particular kings and productive agricultural life.

The close relationship between water management, priesthood, and temple foundations that characterized Angkor somewhat resembles the social organization of ancient Egypt and is similar also to the Maya civilization of medieval Guatemala.[51] In all three cases, grain surpluses (of wheat, rice, or maize) were collected for the benefit of the state and its prevailing ideologues, the priests, who served as patrons of temples and advisers to the kings. In various ways, all three cultures—like the regime of Democratic Kampuchea in the 1970s—were engrossed in what Marx referred to as the Asiatic mode of production, although, as we have seen, some kings at Angkor, like Suryavarman, were more "Asiatic" than others.

CHAPTER 4

Jayavarman VII and the Crisis of the Thirteenth Century

Between Suryavarman II's death around 1150 and Jayavarman VII's coronation in 1181, no dated Cambodian inscriptions have survived. What we know about this period must be filtered through inscriptions carved at Jayavarman's behest, reflecting his view of the world as well as what he wanted people to believe about his early life. Because he was not, apparently, an entirely legitimate contender for the throne, his early years, like those of so many Cambodian founder-kings, are poorly documented.

Jayavarman's biography was pieced together by George Coedes, who saw him as a pinnacle of Cambodian history, rather than an aberration.[1] Jayavarman's inscriptions and what they tell us about his point of view make radical departures, in many ways, from what had gone before. Because of this radicalism and grandeur, Jayavarman VII has tended to dominate the historiography of Cambodia, particularly since Coedes's work in the 1930s. His reign, as we shall see, contained several mysteries and contradictions.

Jayavarman appears to have been a first cousin of Suryavarman II and the son of a royal prince, Dharanindravarman, who may have reigned briefly as king and who was certainly a fervent Buddhist. Groslier has recently cast doubts on the first of these assertions[2] because it is so poorly documented and because it places Jayavarman in the direct line of succession in a way that makes the facts we know about his life even more difficult to understand.

It seems likely, all the same, that Jayavarman as a young man served in some capacity at Yasovarman's court. His elder brother, Groslier argued, helped the king subdue the rebellion mentioned at the end of Chapter 3. From 1166 to 1177, Jayavarman appears to have lived away from Angkor, perhaps in the vicinity of the temple now known as the Preah Khan in Kompong Svay. A portrait statue of him, manifestly younger than others produced later in his reign, has been found at this location.[3] The dimensions of the temple and its carvings provide evidence of the evolution of Cambodian artistic styles and also suggest that even in semiexile, Jayavarman was able to exercise systematic control over a sizable pool of labor. Was the city of Preah Khan subservient to Angkor or a rival to it? How did Jayavarman relate to the usurper-king who followed Yasovarman to the throne? Even more important, what were his relationships with Champa to the east? It is important to ask these unanswerable questions in order to place Jayavarman's reign, following his accession in 1178, into the context of his early life and in the framework of Cambodian foreign relations.

JAYAVARMAN VII AND BUDDHIST KINGSHIP

Throughout his time of waiting to be king, Jayavarman immersed himself in the teachings of Mahayana Buddhism—the variant still followed in much of northern Asia. More than any other king, he labored to integrate Buddhist notions with Cambodian ideas of kingship. Buddhist kingship, as he practiced it, differed in several ways from the more eclectic Hindu model that had been followed for centuries at Angkor. In the traditional version, a king, alive or dead, was thought to enjoy a special relationship with a particular deity—usually Siva, more rarely Vishnu, occasionally the composite of them both known as Harihara—to whom his temple-mountain was eventually dedicated. The kings used this special relationship to explain their grandeur, while their subjects assumed that the relationship had something to do with the provision of adequate rainfall.

Because Cambodian society was hierarchically organized, and because the king was thought to centralize the kingdom, most Cambodians—like their contemporaries in medieval Europe—probably recognized the necessity for a king. Rare inscriptions—and perhaps the act of constructing reservoirs—indicated that an individual king occasionally had his subjects' welfare on his mind. In human terms, however, the king was nearly always a distant, mysterious figure concealed inside an awesome palace. The notion that he was accountable to his people—expressed, for example, in royal audiences—does not seem to have caught hold, despite the king's involvement in providing patronage for the elite. Inside his palace, and within the network of kinship and preferment relationships extending from it, the king was the master and the victim of a system whereby people clamored for his favors, for titles, for the right to own slaves or sumptuous possessions.

Buddhist kingship, of course, grew out of this Indian tradition (the Buddha had been an Indian prince), but in Jayavarman's reign these notions were modified in several ways. Jayavarman was no longer seen as the devotee of a divinity or as drawn up to the divinity in death. Instead, he was considered to be a living Buddha, or *bodhisattva,* turning back from the brink of his own enlightenment to redeem his people (a new concept in itself) from suffering. By redeeming others in this way, it was thought, a king redeemed himself.[4]

Before examining how these ideas of kingship acted themselves out during the reign of Jayavarman, it is important to stress that his program was not aimed at reforming Cambodian society or at dismantling such "Hinduized" institutions as Brahmanism, slavery, and kingship. Far from it; in his conservatism and his elitist frame of reference, Jayavarman VII was a recognizably twelfth-century king, although in Cambodian terms he was a revolutionary one. Put very starkly, the difference between a Buddhist king and a Hindu one resembles the difference between a monologue that no one overhears and a soliloquy addressed to an audience of paid or invited guests. A "Hindu" king's rule was an aggregation of statements—rituals, temples, poems, marriages, inscriptions and the like— and his grandeur and godliness. A Buddhist king made similar statements, but he addressed them, specifically, to an audience consisting of his people. This made the people less an ingredient of the king's magnificence (as his thousands of slaves had always been) than objects of his over-whelming compassion, an audience for his merit-making and participants in *his* redemption. This is, at least, what many of Jayavarman VII's inscriptions and temples appear to have been saying.

Why did Jayavarman VII choose to break so sharply with the past? Scholars have given several explanations. These include his apparent estrangement from the court at Angkor, combined with his resentment of the usurper who had proclaimed himself king in 1167; a "master plan" of buildings, ideology, and kingship that had been maturing in his mind, after years of study; and very possibly, the influence of a scholarly, ambitious wife. These proposals are helpful, but they do not identify the real key to Jayavarman's reign—the Cham invasion of Angkor in 1177. As Paul Mus and Jean Boisselier have shown, we can see Jayavarman's entire reign as a response to this traumatic event.

Jayavarman's own links with Champa appear to have been close. In the 1160s, he apparently spent several years there; his status is unclear, although we know he went without his wife. Was he a hostage, an exile, or leading a military campaign? Perhaps his absence was connected in some way with being out of favor at the Cambodian court, for he returned home only after Yasovarman II had been deposed. As the sources of our uncertainty are Jayavarman's own inscriptions, all that is clear about the prelude to the Cham invasion of 1177—and indeed about Jayavarman's early career—is that later on he found little to boast about in these obviously formative years.

Because inscriptions tend to trace the causes of war to royal ambition, treachery, and revenge—that is, to the world of the *Ramayana*—it is difficult for us to determine exactly why Champa invaded Cambodia, by land in 1177 and then by water in 1178.[5] The prospects of booty and prisoners were certainly part of the Cham rationale; so were memories of earlier defeats. Two Chinese, shipwrecked off the coast of Champa, apparently helped the Chams in both campaigns. One taught them to fire crossbows while mounted on horseback.[6] The Cham king's enthusiasm for this tactic led him to raid the Chinese mainland and the island of Hainan in search of horses. Not finding enough of them, Chinese sources assert, he decided on a second attack by sea, this time with the aid of a Chinese navigator, who piloted the expedition up the Mekong, the Great Lake, and the Siem Reap River, taking the city of Yasodharapura by surprise: "With a powerful fleet, [he] pillaged it and put the king to death, without listening to any proposal of peace."[7]

Jayavarman's whereabouts in 1177 are unknown, but he appears to have done nothing about the invasion. In 1178, however, he gathered arms and supporters for a new campaign against the Chams, defeating them in another naval battle, probably on the Mekong near present-day Kompong Cham, in 1179 or 1180. An inscription suggests that a Cambodian prince—not Jayavarman himself—killed the Cham king "with a hundred million arrows." Jayavarman's royal name, in fact, which means "protected by victory," may have derived from his success in battle, as well as from his restoration of the Cambodian capital, which in the wake of the invasion he found "plunged into a sea of misfortune" and "heavy with crimes." Some of these troubles could be traced to the unmeritorious reigns of predecessors; others perhaps to Hinduism, the religion of the Chams; and still others to the fractionalization of power inside the kingdom, referred to in an inscription written by his wife: "In the previous reign, the land, though shaded by many parasols, suffered from extremes of heat; under [Jayavarman] there remained but one parasol, and yet the land, remarkably, was delivered from suffering."[8]

Jayavarman VII was crowned in 1181, therefore, owing little to his predecessors and much, as his inscriptions tell us, to his acumen, his Buddhist faith, and his victories in battle. Over the next thirty years or so (the precise date of his death is unknown) he stamped the entire kingdom with his personality and his ideas of kingship as no other ruler was able to do before Norodom Sihanouk in the 1960s and Pol Pot in the late 1970s. Like these later figures, Jayavarman wanted to transform Cambodia; he saw himself as the instrument of the transformation.

Much of the interest in his reign, moreover, springs from the tension inherent in the words "Buddha" and "king." Using the Hinduized apparatus of kingship and the material grandeur associated with it, Jayavarman also sought in all humility—if his inscriptions are to be believed—to deliver himself and all his people from suffering. As a *bodhisattva,* he included his subjects in the process of his own redemption. As a king, he led armies against the Chams. As a *bodhisattva,* through his meritoriousness, he could prevent the Chams from attacking Cambodia again. As a king, he had roads built throughout his kingdom, perhaps to accelerate his military response to uprisings or invasions; as a *bodhisattva,* these roads were evidence of his beneficence. His program of public works, indeed, was more extensive than that of any other Cambodian king. This nationalization of kingship by a man who was arguably the most otherworldly of Cambodia's kings gave Jayavarman's reign a peculiar contradictory appearance. Sentences about the man soon fall into the pattern of "on the one hand" and "on the other."

For example, many of the bas-reliefs on the Bayon, depicting battles against the Chams, contain vivid scenes of cruelty. Similarly, some of Jayavarman's inscriptions praise his vengefulness and his skill at political infighting vis-à-vis the Chams. On the one hand, the numerous portrait-statues of him that have come down to us depict him as the Buddha, a *bodhisattva,* or an ascetic deep in meditation.[9] From his inscriptions, we learn that he "suffered from the maladies of his subjects more than from his own; for it is the public grief that makes a king's grief, and not his own."[10] And yet his roads, temples, rest-houses, reservoirs, and hospitals were thrown up with extraordinary haste, between his coronation in 1181 and, at the very latest, the second decade of the thirteenth century. There were so many of them, in fact, that workmanship was often sloppy, and by the end of the reign local supplies of sandstone and limestone for use at Angkor had run out.[11] Hundreds of thousands of ordinary people, inscriptions tell us, labored to erect and maintain these constructions built, at the ideological level, to deliver them from pain. To a twentieth-century eye, this seems ironic to say the least, but we should remember that suffering in Buddhist terms should not be taken merely in a physical sense; it must also be related to the purposes of life and to the ways that suffering of certain kinds can serve the teachings of the Buddha. Suffering to praise the Buddha by building Jayavarman's city, for example, assured the workers of less suffering and greater happiness—but in another life.

Why was Jayavarman's building program carried out with so much haste? He was an elderly man—perhaps as old as sixty—when he reached the throne; the buildings may have been parts of his race against time. A more speculative answer is that in his years away from Angkor he had conceived a Buddhist-oriented construction program that could only be completed, and *had* to be completed, at Angkor while he was still alive. The program, in a way, was for Jayavarman VII a process of redemption, although the sins for which he was atoning are not clarified by his inscriptions. What we know about the first years of his reign comes from inscriptions written at a later stage. It seems that these years were probably spent in deflecting yet another Cham attack (depicted as a naval battle in the bas-reliefs of the Bayon), in quelling a rebellion in the northwest, and in rebuilding the city of Angkor. Major shifts in population, as usual, followed these military campaigns, as the Preah Khan inscription of 1191 suggests: "To the multitude of his warriors, he gave the capitals of enemy kings, with their shining palaces; to the beasts roaming his forests, he gave the forests of the enemy; to prisoners of war, he gave his own forests, thus manifesting generosity and justice."

As with other Cambodian kings, it would be wrong to make a sharp distinction between Jayavarman's politics and his religion, between temporal and spiritual powers, and between his ideas about himself and his ideas about his kingdom. Before dismissing him as a mindless megalomaniac, however, it is worth recalling that had no one shared his vision or believed in his merit, he would never have become king, especially starting out from such a weak position, and certainly would not have been able to remain in power. High officials, brahmans, evangelical Buddhists, and military men probably saw advantages, and not entirely otherworldly ones, in the physical expansion of the kingdom, partly by means of royally subsidized religious foundations and partly by bringing previously indifferent populations under some form of Angkorean control. By the beginning of the thirteenth century, in fact, Angkor was extracting tribute from most of what is now Thailand, Laos, and Malaysia, as well as from Champa, occupying the coastal areas of central Vietnam. To these corners of the known world—and to China, to which the king sent tributary missions— the multiple half-smiling faces of Jayavarman's temple-mountain and his portrait statues addressed their benignly powerful glance.

The art historian Philippe Stern, who studied Jayavarman's reign in great detail, perceived three stages in the development of his iconography and architecture.[12] These coincide with the three phases of construction noted by Stern for earlier Cambodian kings: namely, public works, temples in honor of parents, and the king's own temple-mountain.

The public works of earlier kings, as we have seen, usually took the form of reservoirs (*baray*). Other projects, such as roads and bridges, may have been built, but they are seldom noted in inscriptions. Jayavarman's program departed from the past. His hospitals, probably established early in his reign, were built to the west of Angkor and as far north as central Laos. The Ta Prohm inscription says that these hospitals could call on the services of 838 villages, with adult populations totaling approximately eighty thousand people. The services demanded appear to have been to provide labor and rice for the staffs attached to each hospital, or approximately a hundred people, including dependents.[13] The so-called hospital inscriptions give details about the administration of the hospitals, and about the provisions and staff allocated to them.

A second set of Jayavarman VII's public works consisted of rest-houses placed at approximately 16 kilometer (10 mile) intervals along Cambodia's major roads.[14] There were fifty-seven of these between Angkor and the Cham capital and seventeen more between Angkor and a Buddhist temple-site at P'imai in northeastern Thailand. Finally, there was Jayavarman's own reservoir, known now as the northern Baray and during his reign as the Jayatataka, located to the northeast of Yasodharapura.

These innovations stemmed from what Jayavarman saw as his mission to *rescue* his subjects, as the hospital inscription says:

> Filled with a deep sympathy for the good of the world, the king swore this oath: "All the beings who are plunged in the ocean of existence, may I draw them out by virtue of this good work. And may the kings of Cambodia who come after me, attached to goodness . . . attain with their wives, dignitaries and friends, the place of deliverance where there is no more illness.[15]

THE TEMPLES OF JAYAVARMAN VII

In the second stage of Jayavarman's reign he erected temples in honor of his parents. The first of these, now known as Ta Prohm (Ancestor Brahma), was dedicated in 1186; it honored Jayavarman's mother in the guise of Prajnaparamita, the goddess of wisdom, conceived metaphorically as the mother of all Buddhas. The temple also housed a portrait statue of Jayavarman's Buddhist teacher, or guru (the word *"kru"* means "teacher" in modern Khmer), surrounded in the temple by statues of more than six hundred dependent gods and *bodhisattvas*. The syncretism of Cambodian religion is shown by the fact that Shaivite and Vaisnavite ascetics were given cells on the temple grounds alongside Buddhist monks and learned men.

The appearance of Ta Prohm today gives a poor idea of its original appearance, for unlike the other major temples at Angkor, it has never been restored; instead, it has been left to the mercy of the forest. Stern has argued that the carvings show a closer affinity to the style of Angkor Wat than to the style of Jayavarman's later monuments, such as the Bayon and Banteai Chhmar.

The next temple complex to be built by Jayavarman VII is known nowadays as the Preah Khan (Sacred Sword), an apparent echo of its original Sanskrit name.[16] As a sword probably formed a part of Jayavarman VII's regalia—as it did for post-Angkorean kings—it is possible that the temple was associated with Jayavarman's coronation. Its inscription says that it was built on the site of an important Cambodian victory over the Chams. No other inscription mentions this battle, fought so close to Yasodharapura as to suggest a second Cham invasion of the city. Groslier, however, argued that it took place and has proposed that it is depicted in bas-reliefs at the Bayon.

Preah Khan was dedicated in 1191 and housed a portrait statue of Jayavarman's father, Dharanindravarman, with the traits of Lokesvara, the deity expressive of the compassionate aspects of the Buddha. The symbolism is relentlessly appropriate, for in Mahayana Buddhist thinking the marriage of wisdom (*prajna*) and compassion (*karuna*) gave birth to enlightenment, which is to say, to the Buddha himself, the Enlightened One.[17] In this stage of Jayavarman's artistic development, Lokesvara appears more and more frequently, and throughout his reign, the triad of Prajnaparamita (wisdom), the Buddha (enlightenment), and Lokesvara (compassion) was central to the king's religious thinking, as Hiram Woodward and others have shown. The placement of the two temples southeast and northeast of the new center of Yasodharapura (later occupied by the Bayon) suggests that the three temples should be "read" together, with the dialectic of compassion and wisdom giving birth to enlightenment in the form of a Buddharaja, or Buddha-king, the central statue of the Bayon and, in another sense, Jayavarman VII himself.

The inscriptions from these two "parent temples" show us how highly developed the Cambodian bureaucracy had become, particularly in terms of its control over the placement and duties of the population, but also in terms of the sheer number of people in positions of authority who were entitled to deposit and endow images of deities inside the temple. Ta Prohm housed several thousand people, as its inscription attests:

There are here 400 men, 18 high priests, 2,740 other priests, 2,232 assistants, including 615 female dancers, a grand total of 12,640 people, including those entitled to stay. [In addition there are] 66,625 men and women who perform services for the gods, making a grand total of 79,365 people, including the Burmese, Chams, etc.[18]

Similarly, the people dependent on Preah Khan—that is to say, those obliged to provide rice and other services—totaled nearly a hundred thousand, drawn from more than five thousand three hundred villages. The inscription goes on to enumerate people who had been dependent on previous temple endowments. Drawn from thirteen thousand five hundred villages, they numbered more than three hundred thousand. The infrastructure needed to provide food and clothing for the temples—to name only two types of provision—must have been efficient and sophisticated. Coedes estimated that the annual rice consumption by people in religious foundations came to 38,000 tons.

Three interesting points emerge from the inscriptions. One is that outsiders—"Burmese, Chams, etc."—were accounted for in different ways than local people were. This is perhaps because they were prisoners of war, without enduring ties to individual noblemen, priests, or religious foundations. Another is that the average size of the villages referred to in the inscriptions appears to have been about two hundred people, including dependents—still the median size of rice-growing villages in Cambodia in the 1960s. Finally, the inscriptions indicate that the temples, although dedicated to the Buddha and serving as residences for thousands of Buddhist monks, also housed statues and holy men associated with different Hindu sects. Jayavarman VII obviously approved of this arrangement, for we know that he also retained Hindu thinkers and bureaucrats at his court.

The jewel-like temple known as Neak Po'n (Twining Serpents) forms an island in the Jayatataka and was probably completed by 1191, for it is mentioned in the inscription of Preah Khan:

> The king has placed the Jayatataka like a lucky mirror, colored by stones, gold, and garlands. In the middle, there is an island, drawing its charm from separate basins, washing the mud of sin from those coming in contact with it, serving as a boat in which they can cross the ocean of existences.[19]

The island with its enclosing wall, constructed in a lotus pattern, was intended to represent a mythical lake in the Himalayas, sacred to Buddhist thinking. Around the temple, as at the lake, four gargoyles spew water from the larger lake into the smaller ones. The temple itself, raised above the water by a series of steps, was probably dedicated, like Preah Khan, to Lokesvara, whose image appears repeatedly in high relief on its walls.

Groups of statues were also placed at the four sides of the temple. Unfortunately, only one of these, representing the horse Balaha, an aspect of Lokesvara, can be identified with certainty; two others are probably representations of Siva and Vishnu. Jean Boisselier has argued that the presence of these gods inside the enclosure can be read as a political statement, showing that the former gods of Angkor were now submitting to the Buddha. But why should they do so? Boisselier, following Mus, suggested that Shaivism and Vaisnavism were seen to have failed the

Cambodians when the Chams were able to destroy so much of Angkor in 1177. Lake Anavatapta, moreover, was sacred not only to all Buddhists but particularly to Buddhist rulers, or *chakravartin,* beginning, legend asserts, with the Emperor Asoka, who was able magically to draw water from the lake to enhance his own purity and power.[20]

Boisselier argued that the political significance of the temple goes even further, as it was known in the Preah Khan inscription as the Rajasri, translatable as "the regalia." Situated at the auspicious northeastern corner of Angkor Thom,[21] Neak Po'n probably housed palladia of the kingdom. Boisselier believed that it was torn down by the Thai when they captured Angkor in 1431 and, according to their chronicles, carried off Cambodia's regalia to their own capital city of Ayudhya. In the Thai view, the destruction of Neak Po'n delegitimized the universal kingship of Jayavarman VII and his successors. In the sixteenth century, when Ayudhya was invaded by the Burmese, these very regalia were carried off to Burma, where two Cambodian statues, perhaps from Neak Po'n, can now be seen in Mandalay.[22]

Because Jayavarman's ideology had led him to welcome his subjects as participants in the redemption of the kingdom, the statements made by inscriptions, temples, and public works (as well as by other things that have not survived, like poems, ceremonies, and royal edicts) were "legible" to everyone. A slave, for example, would not have to know much about the iconography of Lokesvara to understand the purifying aspects of water. To all people, perhaps, the Neak Po'n was not just a symbol of the Anavatapta: It actually *was* the lake, brought down to earth, like the mythical Merus of the various visible temple-mountains, from "elsewhere." Most would probably give credit for this to Jayavarman himself, for it was the "king's work" (*rajakar*) to connect different levels of merit and existence.

In this second phase of his iconography Jayavarman VII also sponsored additions to many earlier structures—notably the temples of P'imai in northeastern Thailand and Preah Khan in Kompong Svay. New constructions for this time included the massive ruin known today as Banteai Chhmar in northwestern Cambodia.[23]

The sheer size of these foundations suggests a trend toward urbanization under Jayavarman VII, or at least a tendency to herd and collect large numbers of people from peripheral areas into the service of the state. It seems likely that Jayavarman VII, like Suryavarman II before him, was attracted to the idea of increasing centralization and the related idea of bureaucratic state control. Perhaps these ideas formed part of what he perceived as a mission to convert his subjects to Buddhism or were connected with organizing people to respond swiftly to foreign threats.

The second phase was marked by several stylistic innovations. These included the motif of multifaced towers, inaugurated at the small temple of Prasat Preah Stung and carried to its apex in the entrance gates to the city of Angkor Thom and, ultimately, in the hundreds of faces that look down from the Bayon; the stone walls surrounding the entire city, apparently for the first time in Angkorean history; and the causeways of giants outside the gates of the city.

These constructions can be read in terms of both politics and religion. Boisselier, following Mus, has compared the wall-building at Angkor Thom to a fortified Maginot Line, supposedly offering an impenetrable defense against any Cham invasion. At the same time, the walls can be said to represent the ring of mountains that surround Mt. Meru or Jayavarman's temple-mountain, the Bayon.

After capturing the Cham capital in 1191, Jayavarman probably spent the rest of his reign at Yasodharapura. At this very point, his buildings began to show signs of hasty construction and poor workmanship, as well as of a shifting ideology; the temple that was to become the Bayon, for example, was radically altered at several points in the 1190s.[24] It is tempting to seek an explanation for the haste and quantity of Jayavarman's monuments in his personality or in otherwise unknown aspects of his life. Did the temples represent an attempt to impose his legitimacy and point of view on his successors? Was he attempting to purify Angkor after it had been desecrated by the Chams? Did he have personal shortcomings to atone for? Evidence to answer these questions is thin, but it is certainly true that Jayavarman, for whatever reason, tried to stamp Cambodia with an ideology drawn from Mahayana Buddhism and with his own personality as well. These two aspects of his reign overlap in his portrait statues and perhaps most dramatically in the symbolism of his idiosyncratic temple-mountain and of the city that surrounded it.

An inscription from the end of Jayavarman's reign describes the city as his bride: "The town of Yasodharapura, decorated with powder and jewels, burning with desire, the daughter of a good family . . . was married by the king in the course of a festival that lacked nothing, under the spreading dais of his protection."[25] The object of the marriage, the inscription goes on to say, was the "procreation of happiness throughout the universe"—a worthy objective for a Buddha-king.

At the center of the city was the Bayon (literally, "ancestor *yantra*," *yantra* being a magical geometric shape), with its hundreds of gigantic faces, carved in sets of four, and its captivating bas-reliefs, depicting everyday life, wars with Champa, and the behavior of Indian gods. The temple at one time housed thousands of images. Its central image, discovered in the 1930s, was a statue of the Buddha—perhaps a portrait of Jayavarman VII—sheltered by an enormous hooded snake, or *naga.*

There has been considerable controversy about the symbolism of the temple and about what was meant by the causeways leading up to it, with giants (*asura*) and angels (*devata*) engaged in what looks like a tug of war, grasping the bodies of two gigantic snakes. Some have argued that the causeways represented the well-known Indian myth of the churning of the sea of milk. Others have agreed with Mus, who saw them as rainbows, leading people out of their world into the world of the gods. At another level, the *asuras* represented the Chams and the *devatas,* Cambodians. In this respect it is tempting to perceive the city, and most of Jayavarman's works, in dialectical terms. For example, as we have seen, the pair Lokesvara (compassion/father) and Prajnaparamita (intelligence/mother) give birth to the Buddha (enlightenment, thought to be the child of wisdom and compassion), i.e., Jayavarman VII himself. We have encountered this turn of mind before, in the cult of Harihara and in the opposition and synthesis in Cambodian popular thought of divinities associated respectively with water/moon/darkness and earth/sun/brightness. Similarly, the struggle between the Cambodians and the Chams, acted out along the causeways and in the bas-reliefs at the Bayon and at Banteai Chhmar, can be seen as bringing to birth the new, converted nation of Cambodia, in which the Buddha has won over the Hindu gods of Champa. This dialectic, in a sense, is the "message" of the Bayon, which Boisselier saw as the "assembly hall of the city of the gods."[26] Once again, the message can be read in terms of the civil polity as well, and so can the half-smiling faces with their half-closed eyes that dominate the temple. As so often in Angkorean art, it would be narrow and inaccurate to interpret these haunting faces as representing only one kind of deity, performing one kind of task. In a way, for example, they serve as guardians of the Buddha and his teachings; in another, glancing out in the four directions, they oversee the kingdom and perhaps represent civil and military officials of the time. Boisselier, who argued that they are princely manifestations of Brahma, has noticed also that their tiaras resemble those worn by the Cham *asuras* along the entrance causeways. Perhaps, as Woodward has suggested, this signifies the conversion of the Chams to Buddhism.

Another extraordinary feature of the Bayon, found also at Banteai Chhmar, is that its bas-reliefs depict historical Cambodian events rather than, say, incidents in the *Ramayana* or some other literary work that coincide with or resemble historical events. The battles depicted on the Bayon are fought with recognizable weapons, and other panels depict ordinary people buying and selling, eating, gambling, raising children, picking fruit, curing the sick, and traveling on foot or in ox-carts. Nearly all the customs, artifacts, and costumes depicted in the bas-reliefs could still be found in the Cambodian countryside at the end of the colonial era. Although the voices of these people are missing from Jayavarman's inscriptions, they move across his bas-reliefs with unaccustomed freedom, citizens at last of the country they inhabit, adorning a king's temple as they never had before. Perhaps the bas-reliefs are intended to show that the people have been converted and saved—which is to say, revolutionized—by Jayavarman's example. They also exhibit the "lowest" of the worlds one traverses on the way to enlightenment; in this sense, they resemble their counterparts carved on the eighth-century Javanese Buddhist monument, the Borobudur.

Unless more inscriptions come to light from Jayavarman's reign, he will remain mysterious to us, because there are so many ambiguities about his personality and his ideas. The mystery springs in part from the wide-ranging social and ideological changes that characterized thirteenth- and fourteenth-century Cambodia and may have been due in part to forces that Jayavarman or people near him set in motion.

Another source of ambiguity can be traced to the uneasy coexistence in Jayavarman's temples and inscriptions of an overwhelming compassion and an overwhelming will, of a detachment from things of the world— symbolized by the horse Balaha at the Neak Po'n—and a detailed program aimed at transforming the physical world of Angkor, which had been so badly damaged by the Cham invasion. A third mystery is the silence— both in terms of buildings and inscriptions—that followed Jayavarman's reign and appears to have begun in his declining years. We have no way of telling if Jayavarman was in some sense to blame for this inaction. In subsequent inscriptions he is hardly ever mentioned. The patterns of continuity, stressed so often in earlier inscriptions, seem to have been broken or damaged severely by his reign.

THERAVADA BUDDHISM AND THE
CRISIS OF THE THIRTEENTH CENTURY

The largest change affecting Cambodia in the thirteenth century was the conversion of most of its people to the Theravada variant of Buddhism, discussed below.[27] What role Jayavarman VII played in this conversion is impossible to judge. The history of his reign is the story of the imposition of one man's will on a population, a landscape, and a part of Asia, ostensibly in the service of an ideal, Mahayana Buddhism, which in its allegedly "liberating" fashion bears an ominous resemblance to the ideology of Democratic Kampuchea, which was also imposed from above. The comparison, of course—including the personality cult that apparently affected both Jayavarman and Pol Pot—can be pushed too far. It is very doubtful, for example, if Jayavarman VII saw the Cambodian elite as his enemies, as Pol Pot did, or preferred "forest people" to those living at Angkor. But his break with the past, his obsession with punitive expeditions, the impetuous grandeur of his building program, and his imposition of a national religion rather than his patronage of a royal cult all have parallels with recent historical events. Interestingly, the only feature of Angkorean life singled out for praise by Democratic Kampuchea was precisely the full-scale mobilization of the people that Jayavarman VII, but very few other kings, managed to carry out.

Some writers have connected Cambodia's conversion to Theravada Buddhism to the upheaval that affected Southeast Asia in the wake of the Mongol invasions of China; others have seen it as evidence of the growing influence of Mon- and Thai-speaking peoples, who were already Theravada Buddhists, on the people of Angkor. We know that wandering missionaries from the Mon-language parts of Siam, from Burma, and from Ceylon played an important part in the process and that Cambodian pilgrims—including a son of Jayavarman VII—visited Ceylon to learn about Theravada Buddhism and to obtain clerical credentials. We know some of the agents of the change, but it is difficult to say why conversion was so rapid and so widespread. Some scholars argue that the Theravada variant, unlike Brahmanism or Mahayana Buddhism, was oriented toward ordinary people. Others have seen the conversion as a rejection of the personalized megalomania of Jayavarman VII. Perhaps the most likely explanation, advanced by Briggs,[28] is that the increasing interaction between Khmer- and Mon-speaking residents of the Thai central plain, with the Mons being devotees of Theravada Buddhism, led gradually, over half a century or so, to the conversion of Khmer-speakers further east. We have no way of telling what aspects of the sect were more attractive than others, or which segments of society were drawn most rapidly to it. The conversion in any case was by no means total, for Chou Ta-kuan, at the end of the thirteenth century, noted that Brahmanism and Shaivism, as well as Theravada Buddhism, still enjoyed the status of approved religions at Angkor.[29] Nor was it entirely peaceful, for it seems to have come after some sort of rebellion against Jayavarman VII's brand of Buddhism—exemplified by defacements of Buddha images at the Bayon and elsewhere and by clumsy attempts to change some of the images, iconographically, into Hindu ones.

In other words, it is likely that the thirteenth century—the least recorded of the Angkorean centuries in terms of datable inscriptions—was marked at Angkor by a serious religious upheaval or by a succession of upheavals, which had political causes and effects as well.

The end of Jayavarman's reign and the reign of his successor, Indravarman II, are both obscure. Inscriptions found at the Bayon have little to say about this last phase of Jayavarman's life. Those at the four corners of his city, apparently all inscribed at the time of his death, however, provide helpful references to Jayavarman's wars against the Chams and the Vietnamese. These inscriptions are written, Coedes contended, in execrable Sanskrit. Several of them (like some of the bas-reliefs at the Bayon) are unfinished, almost as if the workmen had dropped their chisels on receiving news of the king's death.[30] This hypothetical scene is brought to life by the Swedish author Jan Myrdal, writing about Angkor:

> The craftsmen were at work while the old masters sat in the shade talking. Now and then they came over, to keep an eye on the work. Then one of the apprentices comes running. He shouts: "Now he's dead!" At this the craftsmen stopped hacking at the stone wall and put down their tools . . . and went off home.[31]

Because of the grandeur of the beginning of Jayavarman's reign and the obscurity of its closing years, some authors have argued that he died of leprosy after many years of isolation. Evidence to support the argument springs from Cambodian oral tradition, already active by the end of the thirteenth century, that a leper king had reigned at Angkor, and also from the official silence of the last years of his life.

Although the contention that Jayavarman VII was a leper fits some of the evidence, it is also possible that the "leper king" was his successor, Indravarman II, whose reign is mentioned in only one inscription, which provides us with the date of his death.[32] There is some evidence to connect this monarch with the abortive Hindu revival alluded to above, but whether his leprosy was real or invented by his enemies to describe serious failures of kingship (connected, perhaps, with defeats at the hands of Thai armies in the mid-thirteenth century), we know almost nothing about events inside Cambodia between Jayavarman's death, perhaps around 1220, and the arrival of a Chinese embassy, sent by the Yuan emperor, at Angkor in 1296.

This dearth of information coincides with a critical period of Cambodian history. The thirteenth century as a whole, as Coedes has shown, was a period of crisis throughout mainland and insular Southeast Asia—a time of rapid change, significant movements of population, foreign invasions, altered patterns of trade, the appearance of new religions, and shifts in the balance of power.[33] In Burma, Siam, Laos, and Cambodia, the major change was the growth of Theravada Buddhism at the expense of state-sponsored and caste-enhancing Hindu cults. In the long run, this change had several ramifications. Brahmans retained their positions at court for ceremonial purposes but otherwise diminished in importance. In Cambodia, inscriptions came to be written in Pali (the language of Theravada) and more frequently in Khmer. The rich mythical and literary bases of Indian literature and iconography, reflected up to now in bas-reliefs, sculpture, architecture, and inscriptions, narrowed perceptibly to satisfy the more austere requirements of Theravada aesthetics, and Cambodian literature, like the local version of the *Ramayana,* came to be suffused with Buddhist values.

In terms of foreign relations, the most important development affecting Cambodia at this time was the weakening of its control over the people to the northwest of Angkor, in present-day Thailand. Although Cambodian cultural influence remained strong in the central plain (where the Thai capital of Ayudhya was to be founded in the fourteenth century), Cambodian political control diminished. Principalities that formerly sent tribute to Angkor, like Sukot'ai and Louvo, now declared their independence. So did principalities in Laos, and still others to the south. Angkor was once again vulnerable to invasion from every direction but the east, as Champa was no longer a power to be reckoned with. A major Thai invasion, in fact, occurred toward the end of the thirteenth century.

CHOU TA-KUAN'S
ACCOUNT OF ANGKOR, 1296–1297

The record by the Chinese envoy, Chou Ta-kuan, of his stay in Cambodia in 1296–1297 is the most detailed account we have about everyday life and the appearance of Angkor.[34] Chou's memoir is rich in circumstantial detail. He was not constrained by the Indian traditions that remove ordinary people from literary consideration. In his account, for example, we see them bathing, selling goods, and marching in processions. From our point of view, it is a shame that Chou devoted so much of his short manuscript to exotic revelations of "barbarian" life. In fact, although he provided us with a newsreel—or perhaps a home movie— of his stay at Angkor, our appetites are whetted for the feature film he might have made had he known (or cared about) the gaps that have persisted ever since in the historical record.

The account, in French translation, runs to only thirty-five pages, divided into forty sections. These range in length from a short paragraph to several pages and, topically, from religion, justice, kingship, and agriculture (to name only four) to birds, vegetables, bathing customs, and slaves. Many features of thirteenth-century Cambodian life he described— including clothing, tools, draft animals, and aspects of rural commerce— were still observable in the 1960s, and others—such as slavery, sumptuary laws, and trial by ordeal—endured in modified form until the nineteenth century at least.

Five of Chou's sections deserve detailed attention—those dealing with religion, slaves, festivals, agriculture, and the king's excursions. Chou found three religions enjoying official status at Angkor; they appear to have been Brahmanism, Theravada Buddhism, and Shaivism. The brahmans, Chou noted, often attained high positions as officials, but he could find little else to say about them: "I do not know what models they follow, and they have nothing which one could call a school or a place of teaching. It is difficult, also, to know what books they read." The Theravada monks, known colloquially by a Thai phrase (*chao ku*) closely resembled their twentieth-century counterparts in Theravada Southeast Asia: "They shave their heads, and wear yellow robes, leaving the right shoulder bare. For the lower half of the body, they wear a yellow skirt. They are barefoot."

Like the palace and the houses of high officials, Chou tells us, Buddhist monasteries could have tile roofs, but those of ordinary people had to be made of thatch. Chou was impressed by the simplicity of the *wats*, noting that (unlike Mahayana temples in China) they contained "no bells, cymbals, flags, or platforms," housing only an image of the Buddha made of gilded plaster. Finally, Chou described the method used to inscribe palm leaf manuscripts, which persisted well into the twentieth century, particularly in the case of religious and historical texts.

The Shaivites, whom Chou called "Taoists," inhabited monasteries that were less prosperous than Buddhist ones, in which "the only image which they revere is a block of stone analogous to the stone found in shrines of the god of the soil in China." Although monastic Shaivism declined in importance after the abandonment of Angkor and eventually disappeared altogether, Indianized cults, including the use of linga, continued into modern times, and officials calling themselves brahmans continued to work at the Cambodian court, where they were entrusted with the performance of royal rituals and with maintaining astronomical tables. When monastic Theravada Buddhism is added to these two "religions," we note that the three categories for religious activity singled out by Chou Ta-kuan survived, in modified form, into very recent times.

Chou's account makes it clear that perhaps the majority of the people living at Angkor were slaves, for he tells us that "those who have many [slaves] have more than a hundred; those who have only a few have from ten to twenty; only the very poor have none at all." He went on to say that slaves are generally taken as captives from mountain tribes, a practice that persisted into the nineteenth century. It seems likely, in fact, that this is the way Cambodian society built itself up, over time, gradually absorbing and socializing "barbarians," who figure in such large numbers in the inscriptions. In Angkorean times, moreover, slaves were set apart from other people by several prohibitions: "They can sit or lie down only underneath a house. For their work, they can ascend into the house, but then they must kneel down, join their hands together, and prostrate themselves. After that they can move forward." Slaves enjoyed no civil privileges; their marriages were not even recognized by the state. Forced to call their masters "father" and their mistresses "mother," they tried frequently to escape and, when caught, were tattooed, mutilated, or chained.[35]

Although Chou is informative about people at court and about slaves, he is vague about the proportion of society in the 1290s that was neither in bondage nor part of the elite. Clearly the people with "a few" slaves would fall into this category; so would the private landowners, discussed in an earlier context by M. C. Ricklefs;[36] and so would the Sino-Cambodians who were active in international trade. Special privileges were extended to the elite and to religious sects; special prohibitions applied to slaves; but about those in between—the people, in fact, who probably made the kingdom prosper—we know far less than we would like.

When Chou goes into detail, however, his account is often illuminating. His description of what he called a new year's festival, which occurred toward the end of November, is a good example of his narrative skill:

> In front of the royal palace, a great platform is built, capable of holding a thousand people, and decorated with lanterns and flowers. In front of it, at a distance of one hundred and twenty feet, another platform is built, one hundred and twenty feet high by laying pieces of wood end to end. This is done in the same way as a scaffolding for Buddhist *stupas*. Each night, three, four, five or six of these are built. On top of them, rockets and firecrackers are attached. The cost of these is met by the provinces and by the noble families. When night has fallen, the king is asked to watch the spectacle. The rockets are released and the firecrackers lighted. The rockets can be seen [about a mile] away . . . . The festival goes on like this for fifteen days. Every month there is a festival.

This ceremony, probably observed by Chou himself, appears to have been celebrated at the end of the rainy season, when the waters of the Tonle Sap begin to subside, setting in motion the first stages of the agricultural year. After the move to Phnom Penh in the fifteenth century, the ceremony became known as the water festival and was similarly marked by fireworks, floats, and royal patronage until the monarchy was overthrown in 1970.

As for agriculture, Chou noted that three or even four rice harvests a year were possible—a statistic singled out by Democratic Kampuchea in its efforts to revolutionize production. It is unlikely that this abundance applied throughout the country, for at Angkor, several harvests were possible only because of the water-storage system perfected in the region over hundreds of years. Another factor was the peculiarly helpful conduct of the Tonle Sap. Chou's comments on the agricultural cycles' relationship to this beneficent body of water can be quoted in full.

> In this country it rains for half of the year; in the other half, it hardly rains at all. From the fourth to the ninth month, it rains every afternoon, and the water level of the Great Lake can reach seven or eight fathoms [approximately 50 feet]. The big trees are drowned; only their tops can be seen. People who live on the shores all go away to the mountains. Later, from the tenth month to the third [of the following year], not a drop of rain falls, and the Great Lake can be navigated only by small boats. . . . The people come back down at this point, and plant their rice.

The "miracle" of the Tonle Sap amazed many subsequent travelers to Angkor. As long as the region supported a large population, the deposits left by receding water provided useful nutrients for the soil. Even after Angkor was abandoned, the lake remained the most densely populated natural fishbowl in the world, providing generations of Cambodians with much of the protein for their diet.

We would welcome the chance to interrogate Chou about the workings of agriculture at this time. For example, how was the rice surplus handled? Were cultivators for the most part freepeople or some kind of slaves? Did agriculture differ markedly at Angkor from that in other parts of the kingdom? How much land was in the hands of members of the royal family, and how much was controlled by Buddhist *wats*? What did this control imply?

As we have no answers to these questions, we must be grateful to Chou for what he gives us. His description of rural marketing, for example, could easily have been made in Cambodia in the 1960s:

> In this country, it is the women who are concerned with commerce. . . . Every day, a market takes place which begins at six in the morning and ends at noon. There is no market made up of shops where people live. Instead, people use a piece of matting, which they spread out onto the earth. Each of them has her own location, and I believe that fees are charged for these locations.

It seems likely, in view of Cambodia's trade with China, that many Chinese had by this time settled in Cambodia to engage in commerce. According to Chou, the products exported by Cambodia in the thirteenth century were those that had been exported since the time of Funan; they were to form the bulk of Cambodian exports until the twentieth century. These were such high-value, low-bulk items as rhinoceros horns, ivory, beeswax, lacquer, pepper, and cardamom. Imported products included paper and metal goods, porcelain, silk, and wicker. It is unclear from Chou's account how products were paid for, but it seems likely that some form of barter took place at the rural level, with Chinese coins and credit in circulation at Angkor and at the ports.

Chou was fascinated by the king reigning at Angkor during his visit (Indravarman III, r. 1296–1308), but he seems to have been nonplussed by the king's accessibility during his stay. Chou observed the king five times.

> Every day the king holds two audiences to deal with government affairs. There is no set agenda. Functionaries or common people who want to see him sit on the ground and wait for him to appear.

The king had reached the throne, Chou remarked, in a curious manner:

> The new king was the son-in-law of the former one [Jayavarman VIII]. Before assuming the throne, he was a general. Now the father loved his daughter, but she robbed him of his golden sword, and took it to her husband. Thus the king's true son was deprived of the succession. . . . [Indravarman] had this prince's toes cut off, and hid him in a cell.

These events, which had taken place just before the Chinese embassy's arrival, are alluded to discreetly by some inscriptions that date from Indravarman's reign. One of them refers to the "old age" of Jayavarman VIII and a "host of enemies" inside the kingdom; another mentions that Indravarman shaded the country with his single umbrella, whereas no shade had existed before, under "a crowd of [such] umbrellas."[37]

The transition between the reigns of Jayavarman VIII and Indravarman IV, in fact, probably marked a sharp transition in Cambodian history, although we do not learn of it from Chou. Under Jayavarman VIII in 1285, the last stone temple, the Mangalartha, was erected in the Angkor region. We know that Indravarman IV was careful to sponsor Theravada Buddhists as well as brahmans, and it is tempting to speculate about a religious ingredient in his apparently nonviolent coup d'état.

The king's procession, like so much else in Chou's account, gains in interest when compared with similar processions recorded in the colonial era.[38] It becomes clear in comparing the procession with the one marking Sihanouk's coronation or other twentieth-century processions for which records have survived, that ceremonial Cambodian life and the hierarchical arrangement of such events changed little between Angkorean times and our own era. In Chou's words,

> When the king goes out, troops are at the head of the escort; then come flags, banners, and music. Palace women, numbering from three to five hundred, wearing flowered cloth, with flowers in their hair, hold candles in their hands, and form a troupe. Even in broad daylight, the candles are lighted. Then come other palace women, bearing royal paraphernalia made of gold and silver. . . . Then come the palace women carrying lances and shields, the king's private guards. . . . Carts drawn by goats and horses, all in gold, come next. Ministers and princes are mounted on elephants, and in front of them one can see, from afar, their innumerable red umbrellas. After them come the wives and concubines of the king, in palanquins, carriages, on horseback, and on elephants. They have more than a hundred parasols, flecked with gold. Behind them comes the sovereign, standing on an elephant, holding his sacred sword in his hand. The elephant's tusks are encased in gold.

Chou then described a royal audience of the sort that Indravarman conducted on a daily basis and closed his account by remarking superciliously, "One can see by all this that even though it is a kingdom of barbarians these people certainly know what a ruler is."

CHAPTER 5

Cambodia's Dark Ages

Probably the least-recorded period of Cambodian history falls between Chou Ta-kuan's visit to Angkor and the restoration of some of the temples there by a Cambodian king named Chan in the 1550s and 1560s. These two centuries witnessed major, permanent shifts in Cambodia's economy, its foreign relations, its language, and probably—although this is harder to verify—in the structure, values, and performance of Cambodian society. Evidence about these shifts that can be traced to the period itself, however, is very thin. When the amount of evidence increases and becomes reliable around 1500 or so, many of the shifts had already taken place.

Evidence from the period consists largely of Chinese references to Cambodia, for almost no inscriptions appear to have been carved, on stone at least, inside the kingdom between the middle of the fourteenth century and the beginnning of the sixteenth. Other sources include a Cham inscription and some from Thailand; two Thai chronicles from the seventeenth century, one of them very fragmentary, probably contain some accurate information about events in these two hundred years.

THE SHIFT FROM ANGKOR
TO PHNOM PENH

The Chinese evidence is important, for as Michael Vickery has convincingly argued, the shifts in Cambodia's geographical center of gravity in the fourteenth century were probably connected with the rapid expansion of Chinese maritime trade with Southeast Asia, and particularly with the mainland, under the Mongols and the early Ming. More than a dozen tributary missions were sent from Cambodia to China between 1371 and 1419—more than throughout the entire Angkorean period—and although some of these may have been purely ceremonial, it seems likely that they came primarily to trade and to arrange for trade. The number of missions, and the respect accorded them by the Chinese, indicate not only that Cambodia remained active and powerful during this period, but also that the Cambodian elite, perhaps now less rigidly tied down to religious foundations and the ceremonial duties of brahmanical bureaucracy, were eager to exploit the possibility of commercial relations with China. How and why this shift in their thinking and behavior occurred is impossible to ascertain, but both Vickery and O. W. Wolters held that the shift should not necessarily be connected with the notion of "decline," for, as Wolters argued, "perhaps we have become too ready to regard the decline of Angkor in the fourteenth and fifteenth centuries as being on a catastrophic scale."[1] Indeed, throughout this period, rulers inside the present-day frontiers of Cambodia were able to compete for resources and trade with their new and prosperous neighbors in Ayudhya, to the west. They were also able to convince the Chinese of their continuing importance and were occasionally able, well into the seventeenth century, to defeat the Thai in war.

Because this shift of emphasis was accompanied by so few "Angkorean" activities (such as stone temple construction, inscriptions, and expanded irrigation works), authors have often spoken of "decline" where "change" would be more appropriate. "Decline," for one thing, fails to explain Cambodia's enduring strength; for another, the word suggests that Jayavarman VII, for example, was in some ways a more authentically Cambodian king than the Theravada one observed by Chou Ta-kuan. Some authors have connected the abandonment of Angkor—a historical event, which probably took place in the 1440s—with a national failure of nerve and certainly with major losses of population. Such losses, the argument runs, would have made it impossible to maintain irrigation works at Angkor, and the water, becoming stagnant, could have become a breeding place for malarial mosquitoes, further depleting the population in a spiraling process. Still others have argued that Theravada Buddhism was in some ways subversive of Angkorean cohesion while it invigorated the politics of Ayudhya and Pagan in Burma; the "peaceable" nature of this variant of the religion has been used to explain Cambodian defeats, but not its victories or those of the Thai, who shared the same beliefs.

What emerges from the evidence is that Cambodia was becoming post-Angkorean well before the abandonment of Angkor. Angkorean institutions—inscriptions, stone temples, a Hindu-oriented royal family, and extensive irrigation, to name only four traditions—seem to have stopped, faded, or redirected themselves soon after the conversion of the Cambodian elite to Theravada Buddhism, an event that probably took place not long after Jayavarman VII's death. It would be premature to see these changes as springing uniquely or even primarily from the ideology or content of the new religion. It is more likely that they were related to the rise of Ayudhya to the west and to the entanglement, which was to last until the 1860s, between the Thai and Cambodian courts. People, ideas, texts, and institutions migrated west from Angkor to Ayudhya, where they were modified and eventually reexported into Cambodia to survive its genuine decline from the eighteenth century onward. As this was happening, people and institutions were also migrating southward to the vicinity of Phnom Penh, where the capital of Cambodia was to remain for the next six hundred years.[2]

The suitability of Phnom Penh as a site for a Cambodian capital sprang in large part from its location at the confluence of the Mekong and the Tonle Sap. A fortified city at this point—the "four faces"—could control the riverine trade from Laos, as well as trade in rough pottery, dried fish, and fish sauce from the Tonle Sap, to say nothing of incoming goods— primarily Chinese in origin—approaching from the Mekong Delta, still largely inhabited by Khmer. Once the choice had been made to become a trading kingdom—and it is impossible to say when, how, or why this happened—locating the Cambodian capital at Angkor no longer made much sense.

It is likely that the shift of the capital also represented a momentary triumph, later legitimized and prolonged, of regional interests, and perhaps those of an individual overlord, at the expense of people lingering near Angkor or gathering strength in the Menam Basin to the west. These members of a southeastern Cambodian elite—for these interests took the form of chiefs and their followings, rather than rice farmers singly or en masse—probably took advantage of their distance from Ayudhya to trade with China on their own account. It seems likely, also, that they could rely on support from overlords long entrenched in the region, which was the heartland of Funan, an area where Angkorean writ had often been ignored.

But these are suppositions. It seems more certain that the myth connected with the founding of Phnom Penh, which tells of an old woman's discovery of a Buddha image floating miraculously downstream, was concocted after the city had come to life, under a name suggestive of its location at the crossroad of two rivers, a name that has survived into modern Khmer as Chatomuk, or "four faces"—an interesting and perhaps unconscious echo of the iconography of the Bayon.[3]

The role played by foreigners adept at trade in this new city is difficult to assess, but influential figures probably included speakers of Malay, from Champa or the Indonesian islands, who left such words behind in the Cambodian language as *kompong,* or "landing place," and *psaar,* or "market," as well as several bureaucratic titles and administrative terms. The Malay legacy may indeed have been deeper than this and needs to be explored, for seventeenth-century European descriptions of riverine

Cambodia, and the way its politics were organized, strongly resemble descriptions from this era and later of riverine Malaya.[4] Other foreigners active in Phnom Penh were the Chinese, already busily trading at Angkor in the thirteenth century; there were three thousand of them in Phnom Penh in the 1540s. It seems likely that Chinese and Malay traders and their descendants married into the Cambodian elite, just as the Chinese continued to do in the colonial era, tightening the relationships between the king, his entourage, and commercial profits.

If we view Angkor from this perspective rather than in terms of a collapse, it is not surprising that the city was not reoccupied and made a capital again, even in periods when Cambodian kings may have thought of doing so, as in the late sixteenth century.

Some of the reasons for the change have already been suggested. Another element conducive to it might be called the emulation factor, affecting both Phnom Penh (and other capitals nearby) and Ayudhya. These were newly established trading kingdoms, respectful—but perhaps a little wary—of the idea of Angkor. By the 1400s, Ayudhya and these Cambodian cities looked to each other rather than to a brahmanical past for exemplary behavior. Until the end of the sixteenth century, moreover, "Phnom Penh" (or "Lovek" or "Udong") and "Ayudhya" considered themselves not separate polities, but participants in a hybrid culture. The mixture contained elements of Hinduized kingship, traceable to Angkor, and Theravada monarchic accessibility, traceable to the Mon kingdom of Davaravati, perhaps, which had practiced Theravada Buddhism for almost a thousand years, as well as remnants of paternalistic, village-oriented leadership traceable to the ethnic forerunners of the Thai, tribal peoples from the mountains of southern China. In both societies the Buddhist *sangha,* or monastic order, was accessible, in its lower reaches at least, to ordinary people. Brought into contact with each other through wars, immigration, and a shared religion, the Thai and the Khmer blended with each other and developed differently from their separate forebears.

CAMBODIA IN THE FIFTEENTH AND SIXTEENTH CENTURIES

The narrative history of the fifteenth and sixteenth centuries, about which we know so little, can be disposed of fairly quickly. The Thai-oriented administration of the Angkor region, it seems, was overthrown by forces loyal to Phnom Penh toward the middle of the fifteenth century, that is, about twenty years after the last Thai attack on the old capital. Once the Thai were removed from the scene at Angkor, however, neither they nor the Cambodians sought to administer the area for more than a hundred years. During this period, a succession of kings, whose names and dates as reported in the chronicles are probably fictional, held power in Phnom Penh.

By the end of the fifteenth century, the chronicles suggest, conflict had developed between these new rulers, as they renewed and formalized their relations with Ayudhya and with officials or chieftains with followings rooted in the southeastern *sruk,* or districts. Some of these forces, the chronicles state, were led by a former slave; Europeans writing somewhat later stated that this new king was in fact a relative of the monarch whom he had deposed.[5] What is important for later events is that the deposed king, Chan, took temporary refuge in Ayudhya before returning with an army to depose the usurper. His restoration under Thai patronage set a precedent that many Cambodian kings were to follow, as did the fact that he was deposed by forces coming from the eastern portions of the kingdom. From the seventeenth century onward, these traditional regions of dissidence could rely on Vietnamese support, setting in motion a whipsaw between Vietnam and Siam, with Cambodia in between.

The first European to write in detail of Cambodia was Tome Pires, whose *Suma Oriental* was published in Venice in 1563 from a Portuguese manuscript written between 1512 and 1515. The kingdom is described as a warlike one, whose ruler "obeys no one," and Pires hinted at the richness of the products that could be obtained from it.[6] He was relying, however, on hearsay; the first eyewitness account comes to us from the Portuguese missionary Gaspar da Cruz, who visited Lovek toward the end of King Chan's reign in 1556. He left after about a year, disappointed by his inability to make converts, and chose to blame the superstitions of the people and their loyalty to Buddhist monks. Da Cruz was impressed, indeed, by the solidarity of the Cambodians, and in an interesting passage he remarked that they

dare do nothing of themselves, nor accept anything new without leave of the king, which is why Christians cannot be made without the king's approval. And if some of my readers should say that they could be converted without the king knowing it, to this I answer that the people of the country is of such a nature, that nothing is done that the king knoweth not; and anybody, be he never so simple may speak with the King, wherefore everyone seeketh news to carry unto him, to have an occasion for to speak with him; whereby without the king's good will nothing can be done.

He suggested that the *sangha* contained more than a third of the able-bodied men in Cambodia or, by his estimate, some hundred thousand—

a fact with clear implications for politics and the economy. These monks commanded great loyalty from the population: Da Cruz found them to be

> exceedingly proud and vain . . . alive they are worshipped for gods, in sort that the inferior among them do worship the superior like gods, praying unto them and prostrating themselves before them: and so the common people have great confidence in them, with a great reverence and worship: so that there is no person that dare contradict them in anything. . . . [It] happened sometimes that while I was preaching, many round me hearing me very well, and being very satisfied with what I told them, that if there come along any of these priests and said, "This is good, but ours is better," they would all depart and leave me alone.[7]

The absence of inherited riches cited by da Cruz provides a good example of royal interference in everyday life. When the owner of a house died, da Cruz remarked, "All that is in it returneth to the king, and the wife and children hide what they can, and begin to seek a new life." Possessions, in other words, were held by people at the king's pleasure, as were ranks, land, and positions in society. This residual absolute power, it seems, gave the otherwise rickety institution of the monarchy great strength vis-à-vis the elite. One consequence of the arrangements cited by da Cruz was that rich families could not, in theory at least, consolidate themselves into lasting antimonarchical alliances; the king's response to them (dispossessing a generation at a time) suggests that kings distrusted the elite.

Da Cruz said nothing abut Angkor, although a later Portuguese writer, Diego do Couto, reported in 1599 that some forty years beforehand (in 1550 or 1551) a king of Cambodia had stumbled across the ruins while on an elephant hunt. The story is not confirmed by other sources, but dated inscriptions at Angkor reappear in the 1560s, suggesting that the date of the rediscovery may be accurate, although it may have taken place during a military campaign, instead of during a hunt, for the Angkor region was a logical staging area for Cambodian armies poised to invade Siam.

Do Couto wrote that when the king had been informed of the existence of ruins,

> He went to the place, and seeing the extent and the height of the exterior walls, and wanting to examine the interior as well, he ordered people then and there to cut and burn the undergrowth. And he remained there, beside a pretty river while this work was accomplished, by five or six thousand men, working for a few days. . . . And when everything had been carefully

cleaned up, the king went inside, and . . . was filled with admiration for the extent of these constructions.[8]

He added that the king decided at that instant to transfer his court to Angkor; if he ever did so, in fact, it was probably for only a very brief period, for his sojourn is not mentioned in Thai or Cambodian chronicles. Two inscriptions from Angkor Wat, moreover, indicate that the temple was partially restored under royal patronage in 1577–1578. Both of these, and two more incised at Phnom Bakheng in 1583, honored the king's young son, in whose favor he was to abdicate in 1584, possibly to delay a coup by his own ambitious and more popular brother.[9] The identically worded Phnom Bakheng inscriptions, in fact, may refer to this in-fighting by expressing the hope that the king would no longer be tormented by "royal enemies." It is equally possible, however, that the phrase refers to the Thai royal family, with whom the Cambodian elite had been quarreling throughout the 1570s.

Indeed, in spite of the apparent ideological solidarity noted by da Cruz, the period 1560–1590, when Cambodia reemerges in historical documents, was a turbulent one in which Cambodian troops took advantage of Thai weakness (brought on in part by the Burmese sacking of Ayudhya in 1569) to attack Thai territory several times. According to Europeans, the Cambodian king, worried by internal and external threats, changed his attitude toward Catholic missionaries, allowing them to preach and sending gifts of rice to the recently colonized centers of Malacca and Manila in exchange for promises of military help (which never in fact arrived). Earlier, the king had apparently attempted to seek an alliance, or at least a nonaggression pact, with the Thai.

The flurry of contradictory activities in the field of foreign relations suggests instability at the court that is reflected in the frequent moves the king made, his premature abdication, and his unwillingness or inability to remain at peace with the Thai, who regained strength in the 1580s and unsuccessfully laid siege to Lovek in 1587, a date confirmed by an inscription from southeastern Cambodia.[10] If subsequent Cambodian diplomatic maneuvering is a guide, it seems likely that these sixteenth-century moves were attempts by the king to remain in power despite the existence of heavily armed, more popular relatives and in the face of threats from Ayudhya and the surprisingly powerful Lao states to the north.

By 1593, Thai preparations for a campaign against Lovek forced the king to look further afield for help. He appealed to the Spanish governor-general of the Philippines, even promising to convert to Christianity if sufficient aid were forthcoming. Before his letter had been acted on, however, the king and his young son fled north to southern Laos, while another son was placed in charge of the defense of Lovek; the city fell in 1594.

Although throughout most of the seventeenth century, Cambodian military forces were often as strong as those of the Thai and although, as we shall see, European traders were often attracted to Cambodia almost as strongly as they were to Ayudhya, Thai and Cambodian historiography and Cambodian legend all interpret this capture of Lovek as a turning point in Cambodian history, ushering in centuries of Cambodian weakness and Thai hegemony. The facts of the case as they appear in European sources are more nuanced than this, but the belief is strong on both sides of the poorly demarcated border that a traumatic event (for the Cambodians) had taken place.

The popular legend of *preah ko preah kaev,* first published by a French scholar in the 1860s, is helpful on this point and is worth examining in detail.[11] According to the legend, the citadel of Lovek was so large that no horse could gallop around it. Inside were two statues, *preah ko* (sacred cow) and *preah kaev* (sacred precious stone); inside the bellies of these statues in turn, "there were sacred books, in gold, where one could learn formulae, and books where one could learn about anything in the world; these were inside the bellies. Now the king of Siam wanted to have the statues, so he raised an army and came to fight the Cambodian king."

The legend then relates an incident contained in the chronicles as well. Thai cannon fired silver coins, rather than shells, into the bamboo hedges that served as Lovek's fortifications. When the Thai retreated, the Cambodians cut down the hedges to get at the coins and thus had no defenses when the Thai returned in the following year to assault the city. When they had won, the Thai carried off the statues to Siam. After opening up their bellies, the legend tells us,

> they were able to take the books which were hidden there and study their contents. *For this reason* [emphasis added] they have become superior in knowledge to the Cambodians, and for this reason the Cambodians are ignorant, and lack people to do what is necessary, unlike other countries.

Although keyed to the capture of Lovek, the legend may in fact be related to the long-term collapse of Angkor (insofar as this could be "remembered") and perhaps to the relationships that had developed between Siam and Cambodia by the nineteenth century, when the legend emerged in the historical record. The temptation to prefer the earlier collapse as the source for the legend may spring from the fit between the legend's metaphors and what we know to have happened—i.e., the transfer of Cambodia's regalia, documents, customs, and learned men from Angkor to Ayudhya in the period between Jayavarman's death and the Thai invasion of 1431. The statue of *preah ko* is a metaphor for Cambodia's Indian heritage; the less precisely described *preah kaev* seems to be a metaphor for Buddhist legitimacy, embodied by a Buddha image like the one taken from Vientiane by the Thai in the 1820s (and known as a *preah kaev*) to be enshrined in the temple of that name in Bangkok. The seepage of literary skills from Cambodia to Siam, and the increasing power of the Thai from the seventeenth century onward, are ingredients in the legend, which, like that of the leper king discussed in Chapter 4, may contain a collective memory of real occurrences, half-hidden by a metaphorical frame of reference. The myth, in other words, may have been used by many Cambodians to explain Cambodia's weakness vis-à-vis the Thai in terms of its unmeritorious behavior (chasing after the coins) and its former strength in terms of palladia that could be taken away.

The last five years of the sixteenth century are well documented in European sources. These years were marked by the high tide of Spanish imperialism in Cambodia, directed from the Philippines and orchestrated largely by two adventurers named Blas Ruiz and Diego de Veloso.[12] Their exploits make fascinating reading and illuminate three themes that were to remain important in Cambodian history. The first was the king's susceptibility to blandishments and promises on the part of visitors who came, as it were, from "outer space." Both Spaniards were honored with bureaucratic titles and given *sruk* to govern and princesses for wives. The second theme was the revolution in warfare brought on by the introduction of firearms, particularly naval cannon, which played a major part in all subsequent Cambodian wars. Because they were masters of a new technology, Ruiz and de Veloso were able to terrorize local people—just as their contemporaries could in Spanish America—while accompanied by fewer than a hundred men.

A third theme, linked to the others, was that by the end of the sixteenth century the Cambodian king and his courtiers had become entangled in the outside world, symbolized at the time by the multitude of foreign traders resident in Lovek and Phnom Penh. European writers emphasized the importance of these people and the foreign residential quarters at Lovek. These included separate quarters for Chinese, Japanese, Arabs, Spanish, and Portuguese, as well as traders from the Indonesian archipelago; they were joined briefly in the seventeenth century by traders from Holland and Great Britain.[13] The traders worked through officials close to the king and members of the royal family, as well as through their compatriots. In the seventeenth century, according to Dutch sources, foreign traders were required to live in specific areas of the new capital, Udong, reserved for them and to deal with the Cambodian government only through appointed representatives, or *shabandar*. This pattern may have originated in China and also applied in Siam; its presence at Lovek in the depths of Cambodia's "decline," like other bits of data, suggests, that the kingdom was by no means dead.

The Spanish missionary San Antonio left an account of the closing years of the sixteenth century, which includes the adventures of Ruiz and de Veloso. It is often illuminating and occasionally comic, as when he attributed the construction of the temples at Angkor to the Jews, echoing local disbelief in Cambodian technology.[14] He was also convinced that Spain should colonize the kingdom for religious and commercial reasons, and this may have led him, like many early explorers, to exaggerate the value of its resources, much as French visitors were to do in the 1860s. His impressions of prosperity may have sprung from the fact that visitors were forced by the absence of overland communication to limit their observations of Cambodia to the relatively rich and populated areas along the Mekong, north of Phnom Penh—an area that was still one of the most prosperous in Cambodia when it was studied four hundred years later by Jean Delvert.[15] The goods that San Antonio saw included gold, silver, precious stones, silk and cotton cloth, incense, lacquer, ivory, rice, fruit, elephants, buffalo, and rhinoceros. The last was valued for its horns, skin, blood, and teeth as a "subtle antidote for a number of illnesses, particularly those of the heart"—a reference to the Chinese belief that rhinoceros byproducts were effective as aphrodisiacs. Like Frenchmen of the 1860s, San Antonio stressed that Cambodia was prosperous because it was a gateway to Laos, which, almost unknown to Europeans, was assumed to be some sort of El Dorado. He closed his discussion of Cambodia's prosperity with a passage that might seem to have been lifted from "Hansel and Gretel":

> There are so many precious things in Cambodia that when the king [recently] fled to Laos, he scattered gold and silver coins, for a number of days, along the road so that the Siamese would be too busy gathering them up to capture him.[16]

San Antonio also remarked that the country contained only two classes of people, the rich and the poor:

> The Cambodians recognize only one king. Among them there are nobles and commoners. . . . All the nobles have several wives, the number depending on how rich they are. High ranking women are white and beautiful; those of the common people are brown. These women work the soil while their husbands make war. . . . The nobles dress in silk and fine cotton and gauze. Nobles travel in litters, which people carry on their

shoulders, while the people travel by cart, on buffalo, and on horseback. They pay to the principal officials, and to the king, one-tenth of the value of all goods taken from the sea and land.

The slave-owning, nonmercantile "middle" class, noted by Chou Ta-kuan in the thirteenth century, seems by now to have diminished in importance, although there is evidence from legal codes and at least one chronicle that it continued to exist.[17] It is possible that its place was taken in Cambodian society by foreign traders and semi-urban hangers-on, while ethnic Khmer remained primarily rice-farmers, officials, monks, and gatherers of primary produce. Another mediating "class" in Cambodian society, of course, consisted of the *sangha,* about whom San Antonio's contempt exceeded his curiosity. What emerges from his account, and from others by European visitors, is a picture of a Cambodian social structure that remained essentially unchanged from the sixteenth century to the nineteenth.

But as so often in Cambodian history, the rice farmers are omitted from the record. We see the people the visitors saw—the king, the elite, the foreign traders, and their slaves. Inland from the *kompong,* villages were linked to the trading capitals by economic relationships, by taxation, and by the social mobility provided by the *sangha;* they also led their own lives. At least, this is what we must suppose, for without such relationships, kingship and other institutions would have withered. But like the particles of subatomic physics, in terms of which atomic behavior makes sense, these major actors are invisible to the eye.

VALUES IN SEVENTEENTH-CENTURY CAMBODIA

I would not wish to suggest, all the same, that seventeenth-century Cambodian society can be understood solely in terms of timelessness. In many ways, it differed from its nineteenth-century counterpart. For one thing, nineteenth-century Cambodia had been brought to its knees by foreign powers; seventeenth-century Cambodia was still reasonably independent. Nineteenth-century Cambodia was isolated from the outside world by the same two powers—Siam and Vietnam—that dominated its internal politics; seventeenth-century Cambodia, on the other hand, traded freely with many countries. The elite Cambodian literary tradition, enshrined in the local version of the *Ramayana,* the *Reamker,* as well as in the inscriptions at Angkor Wat and other works, was, as we shall see, far more vigorous in the seventeenth century than in the nineteenth.

Saveros Pou traced this decline in part to Thai influence but more profoundly to what she referred to as a "slow degradation of values from the seventeenth century on."[18] It is easy to share her impression after reading the *Reamker* alongside some of the fatuous verse-novels composed in the 1880s or after comparing the seventeenth-century legal codes, translated by Adhémard Leclère, with the scattered and timorous documents left by nineteenth-century kings. Although the values she referred to emanated from the elite, Pou saw the decline as one that modernized the collective acceptance of traditional values. She saw these values, in turn, as linked with Buddhist notions of the cosmos (enshrined in the didactic poem known as the "Trai Phum," or "Three Worlds"), especially as these filtered into Buddhist teaching in oral form, enshrined in the aphoristic collection of "laws," or *chbab,* until very recently memorized by Cambodian schoolchildren.[19] In other words, she viewed seventeenth-century Cambodia as a nation abiding by rules that were later watered down, abused, or forgotten.

These values—seldom in fact acted out by a particular monarch—are those that delineate proper conduct for the people. This conduct has to do in large part with one's position in society and governs the way one relates to others. Everyone, of course, comes equipped with several positions, being at the same time older than some and younger than others, richer and poorer, wiser and more foolish, and so on. A more elderly "inferior" is to be addressed with respect, for example; so is a younger monk, and a monk of peasant origin, in theory at least, is to be paid homage by a king. In many cases, moreover, one person's patron is someone else's client.

The *chbab* stress several normative relationships of this kind, the most important of which are probably those with parents and teachers. In the *chbab,* these authority figures convey material to be memorized. There is nothing to discuss. The teacher's relation to his student, like so many relationships in Cambodian society, is lopsided. The teacher, like the parents, bestows, transmits, and commands. The student, like the child, receives, accepts, and obeys. Nothing changes in the transmission process, except perhaps the ignorance of the student; knowledge is passed on from student to student over generations, and if this involves little or no "progress," we should recall that the idea of progress is not especially widespread and was not well known in precolonial Southeast Asia. What kept society coherent, Cambodians thought, was the proper observance of relationships among people, as well as the shared acceptance of Buddhist ideology. The first of these involved proper language and appropriate behavior. The Khmer language, like many others in Southeast Asia (Javanese is perhaps the best example) displays differences between people in the pronouns they use in speaking to each other and, in exalted speech (used to describe royalty, or monks, for example), in many verbs and nouns as well. Except among close friends not otherwise related (for relatives, family-oriented pronouns would normally be used), no word in traditional Khmer translated readily as "you" or "I." Instead, words emphasized the status of the speaker in relation to the person addressed. Thus,"you" could be directed "up," or "down," as could "I" and the other personal pronouns.[20]

Further evidence of this grading comes from the fact that Cambodian thinkers saw the universe, too, in graded terms, with men inhabiting "middle earth." This is a familiar concept in many cultures, and so is its corollary, that behavior on earth has been prescribed to us by heroes who have passed "above" or "below" us. To those of us accustomed to expanded (or fragmented) frames of reference, this picture of the world entails enslavement or mystification. To scholars like Saveros Pou, however, and, it would seem, to the poets who composed the *Reamker* ("the Glory of Rama"), the picture offered little to complain about in moral or aesthetic terms.[21] Perhaps there is a relationship between the day-to-day dangers of a society and the energy of belief that its thinkers invest in otherworldly, or at least exceptionally beautiful, alternatives. But to say this is to suggest that the *Reamker* is essentially a vehicle by which to escape society; its authors and many of its listeners, on the other hand, might say that the poem was an excellent vehicle for understanding it.

Egalitarian ideals and the related notion of class warfare have perhaps eroded our sympathies for hierarchical societies, which in twentieth-century terms—themselves ephemeral, of course—appear to make no sense. We think of society at war with itself, or at peace, brushing up against other societies with different interests, and so on. Seventeenth-century Cambodians had no word for "society" at all; the word *sangkhum* appears to have entered the language via Pali in the 1930s. They preferred to think of themselves in terms of a king and his subjects; in terms of a spectrum of relative merit; or as people, scattered over time and space, sharing recognizable ideals that sprang, in turn, from being farmers, being lowly, being Buddhists, and speaking Khmer.

Perhaps the best way to enter the thought-world of seventeenth-century Cambodia is to look at the epic poem, the *Reamker*. The version that has survived contains only some of the events related in the Indian original, and many of these have been altered to fit into a Theravada Buddhist frame of reference and into Khmer. Although its characters inhabit a recognizably Indian, brahmanical epic (as well as half-mythical kingdoms far away, it seems, from Southeast Asia) their behavior, language, and ideals are very much those of the Cambodian people who assembled to listen to the poem or to watch it enacted by dancers, poets, and musicians. These additional dimensions resemble the way in which medieval

Reenactment of the *Ramayana,* Battambang, 1964. Photo by Jacques Nepote.

and Renaissance painters in Europe depicted Greek and Biblical figures wearing European clothes.

   The plot of the *Reamker* can be easily summarized. Sent out in disgrace from the kingdom he was about to inherit, Prince Ream (Rama), accompanied by his wife, Sita, and his younger brother, Leak (Laksmana), travels in the forest and has many adventures, until Sita is taken away by Prince Reab (Ravana), who rules the city of Langka. Aided by the prince of the monkeys, Hanuman, Ream attacks Langka, hoping to regain his wife, and wins a series of battles. Here the narrative breaks off. In terms of plot alone, it is difficult to understand the hold the *Reamker* has had for so long on the Cambodian imagination. Its language is often terse, and the development of the action is occasionally obscure. This is partly because the poem has come down to us as a series of fairly brief episodes, each suitable for mime (with the verse to be recited) and geared to a performance by dancers or perhaps, as elsewhere in Southeast Asia, by leather shadow puppets.

In modern times, episodes from the poem were often enacted by the palace dancers; in the countryside, events from the poem were acted out as part of village festivals.[22] A complete oral version, somewhat different from the printed text, was recorded in Siem Reap in 1969.[23] The relation of these Cambodian poems to other versions elsewhere in Southeast Asia is an important issue that remains to be explored.

What probably captivated so many Cambodians about the poem was its combination of elegance and familiarity. Its subject—the conflict of good and evil—is the theme of much epic literature. At one level, the poem is a statement of Theravada Buddhist values; at another, a defense of hierarchy and the status quo; and at a third, it is about the contrast between what is wild (*prey*) and what is civilized. The poem, in a sense, is itself a kind of civilizing act, just as the Javanese word for "chronicle" (*babad*) is derived from one that means to "clear the forest."[24] Goodness in the poem and its three heroes are linked to meritorious action and elegance. Evil characters are unpredictable, passionate, in disarray.[25] The contrast is by no means mechanical, however, and is worked out in the poem with considerable subtlety. The savage ruler of the forest, Kukhan, for example, is filthy and spontaneous but is redeemed by his meritorious deference to Ream. On the other hand, Reab, the prince of Langka, consumed with passion and a slave to it, is almost as royal and at times nearly as elegant as Ream and Sita.

The role played by the *Reamker* in prerevolutionary Cambodia resembles the one enjoyed by the *wayang,* or shadow-puppet theater, in Java and Bali. Many Cambodians, in their occasional encounters with the poem, found in it a completeness and balance probably missing from their everyday lives. Good and evil, as we all can see, are at war, and evil is often victorious. In the poem, however, the two are perpetually in balance, held in place, as it were , by almost equal quantities of ornamental verse. In the strophes that have survived, the major actors are never destroyed, perhaps because evil and good must survive in order to define each other. In the *Reamker,* as in many of the poems enacted in *wayang,* "nothing happens."[26] Nothing important is different from one end of the poem to

Prince Rama, aided by monkeys, battles with Ravana. Photo by Jacques Nepote.

the other. Certainly nothing changes or turns around. The poem is useless as a revolutionary text. If it is also useless, in a narrow sense, as a historical document, because we cannot locate it in a particular time and place, its verbal elegance and its austerity allow us a glimpse of the seventeenth-century Cambodian elite's range of values and of a high artistic polish that would be difficult to associate with a period of intellectual decline.

Placed against what we know of real events in the seventeenth century, the gap between ideals and reality, as expressed in the poem, is wide and deep. Chronicles and European sources, which can be used to support each other, reveal a country whose capital was isolated from its hinterland; whose royal family was murderous, intriguing, and unstable; and which was at the mercy, much of the time, of elite factions, national catastrophes, and invaders. Increasingly, invaders came from the southeast, supported by the Nguyen overlords of southern Vietnam. The persistence of Cambodian elites, however, and the continuity of overseas trade suggest that these crises, real enough at the time, were periodic rather than perpetual and affected the parts of the country that armies moved across rather than those outside their paths.

Perhaps the most revealing social document from this period is a collection of fifty anecdotes, allegedly provided by an elderly female member of the royal family when a new set of Cambodian law codes was promulgated in the 1690s.[27] These deal with the notion of *lèse majesté* and thus concern the position of royalty in Cambodian society; they also reveal the strengths and weaknesses of Cambodian kingship at this time. The king's greatest strength, it seems, sprang from his capacity to assign and revoke titles, which were permissions to exploit people less fortunately endowed. Offenders against the king could be stripped at once of their possessions. Crimes of *lèse majesté,* even at several removes, were severely dealt with. One anecdote, for example, relates how a princess ordered her advisers to find her some fish. The officials encountered a fisherman, who muttered that they had no right to take his fish without paying for them. The officials took the fish and informed the princess about him, and he was fined for disrespect. Another anecdote relates that a king, out hunting, wandered from his entourage and encountered a buffalo tender, who addressed him in ordinary language. Instead of punishing the man, the king returned to his followers to declare that he had increased his fund of merit, as he had obeyed the law that did not allow a king to punish subjects for disrespect outside the palace. "If I had shot the man when I was alone," he said, "I would have done a prohibited thing, and after my death I would have fallen into hell, because, after all, the man didn't know that I was the king." Other anecdotes reveal that the monarch was often used by ordinary citizens as the court of last resort, as Chou Ta-kuan had suggested in the thirteenth century.

These anecdotes differ from the chronicles and, of course, from the *Reamker* by providing day-to-day information about the king. They provide a picture of a variegated, conservative, and hierarchically organized society, propped up by an almost invisible wall of rice farmers, in which great emphasis was placed on rank and privilege and on behavior thought to be appropriate to one's status. The texts also reveal how perilous it was to enjoy power in seventeenth-century Cambodia. The king ruled absolutely through changeable networks of favorites and relations, and he governed in many cases, it would seem, by pique. Officials rose into favor and fell from one day to the next. A chronicle from this period, for example, relates that a royal elephant trainer was named minister of war (*chakri*) after saving the king's life while hunting. A European minister, on the other hand, fell from office for having struck a monk who had inadvertently splashed water on his cloak.[28] Although the society was permanently ranked, in other words, change was always possible and could rarely be predicted.

VIETNAMESE AND THAI INTERFERENCE IN CAMBODIA

The impression of instability was exacerbated by increasing foreign interference, particularly from the Vietnamese, whose "march to the south" (*nam tien*) had by the 1620s carried their colonists into the Mekong Delta of what is now southern Vietnam.[29] In 1626, the Nguyen overlords of the south broke off their ties with the northern Le dynasty and began governing the southern region on their own. Although the area was lightly populated in comparison with the north, Nguyen control soon had the effect of sealing off Cambodia's southeastern frontier. The Vietnamese intrusion into the region had three long-term effects. First, the takeover of Saigon (known to Cambodians even today as Prey Nokor), first by customs agents in the 1620s and seventy years later by Nguyen administrators, meant that Cambodia was now cut off from maritime access to the outside world, especially after other, smaller ports along the Gulf of Siam were occupied in the early eighteenth century by Chinese and Sino-Vietnamese entrepreneurs and later by Vietnamese troops.[30] Cambodian isolation, which lasted nearly two hundred years, was unique in precolonial Southeast Asia, with the exception of Laos. Second, the Nguyen institutionalization of control, a process that took more than two hundred years, eventually removed large portions of territory and thousands of ethnic Khmer from Cambodian control. This process produced a legacy of resentment and anti-Vietnamese feeling that has been encouraged, for various reasons, by all the Cambodian regimes since independence, except, understandably, the People's Republic of Kampuchea. Finally, by taking over the delta and extending de facto control over the Gulf of Siam (a state of affairs that lasted through the eighteenth century) the Nguyen placed Cambodia in a vise between two powerful neighbors; its capital region, moreover, was more accessible to Saigon than to Ayudhya or Bangkok.

A side effect of the advent of Vietnamese power was that the Cambodian royal family, perennially riven by factionalism, was now able to split along pro-Thai and pro-Vietnamese lines. Depending on which power supported an incumbent, his rivals would seek support from the other to overthrow him. The history of Cambodia in the eighteenth and nineteenth centuries, therefore, is one of almost continuous invasions from Vietnam and Siam, preceded and followed by ruinous civil wars. Instability at the center was repeated in the *sruk;* because loyalty to the throne was costly, perilous, and easy to avoid, by the end of the eighteenth century large areas of the kingdom were under only nominal control from Udong; this state of affairs, in turn, decreased the king's ability to respond to foreign invasions. The king's power to reward his friends and punish dissidents had been weakened by the rapid succession of monarchs, communication difficulties, and the need to withstand repeated foreign attacks. Another destabilizing factor throughout this period was the presence in the countryside of quasi-religious leaders (*nak sel*) who declared themselves endowed with magical powers and gathered supporters, whom they convinced that the millennium was at hand.

At the same time, it seems likely that a certain continuity persisted at the capital among the bureaucratic elite. Several inscriptions at Angkor from the late seventeenth and early eighteenth centuries record the careers of important officials whose graceful rise to increasing responsibility contrasts sharply with the jagged sequence of events related by the chronicles.[31] Moreover, Vietnamese and Thai accounts agree that at several points in the eighteenth century (when it would be tempting to assert that Cambodia had already been bled white) Cambodian forces managed to repel their invading armies. This suggests, at the very least, that some regional leaders, nominally officials of the crown, were able in a crisis to mobilize enough supporters to harass and defeat a foreign expeditionary force, especially when skilled in guerrilla warfare.

Evidence from the chronicles suggests, however, that one of the darkest periods of Cambodia's dark ages came in the last few decades of the eighteenth century. The ingredients—dynastic instability, foreign invasions, civil wars—were familiar ones, but this time they were on a large scale.

The 1750s and 1760s were a period of relative calm, as far as invasions from Siam and Vietnam were concerned, but they also saw a series of coups and countercoups by rivals in the royal family that involved assassinations and reprisals. In 1767, Ayudhya fell to a Burmese army. When a Thai prince and his entourage sought asylum in Cambodia and threatened to set up a legitimate kingdom there, a Thai regional overlord, Taksin, who had assumed power in Siam, launched a series of expeditions against Cambodia, beginning in 1768.[32] His aims were to reestablish Thai hegemony over the region and thus to backdate what he interpreted as his own enormous fund of merit. He also sought to avenge himself against the Cambodian king who, according to the chronicles, refused to send gifts to him because he was the "son of a Chinese merchant and a commoner," charges that appear to have been true. There is some evidence also that he wanted to put his own son on the Cambodian throne.

Thai pressure on the kingdom persisted into the 1770s, when the Nguyen were distracted by a populist rebellion, led by the so-called Tay Son brothers, which threatened to overturn institutions throughout Vietnam. Sensing weaknesses in northern Vietnam, Thai armies attacked overland via Angkor, and their naval expeditions laid waste several small ports along the Gulf of Siam, partly in order to divert Chinese traders from this region to the vicinity of Bangkok and partly to avenge an earlier expedition financed by Chinese merchants from these coastal enclaves, that had almost succeeded in capturing the new Thai capital, Thonburi. In 1772, the Thai burned down Phnom Penh. Seven years later, a Thai protégé, Prince Eng, then only seven years old, was placed on the Cambodian throne at Udong under the regency of a pro-Thai official. In 1782, the Thonburi king himself was deposed, to be replaced by his minister of war, then campaigning in Cambodia. The personal involvement of these two men in Cambodian affairs set a pattern for Thai interference in Cambodia throughout the nineteenth century, although publicly, and perhaps privately as well, their motives for intervention included the more noble one of protecting Cambodian Theravada Buddhism and related institutions against persistent and heretical Vietnamese incursions.

By the 1780s, in fact, the heir to the Nguyen throne, fleeing the Tay Son, had taken refuge in Bangkok, providing the ingredients for a rapprochement between the two nations when and if the Nguyen assumed control of all Vietnam, as they eventually did in 1802. In the meantime, the Thai aided the Nguyen in their war against the Tay Son rebels, who had in the late 1780s forced the Cambodian court—such as it was—to recognize their legitimacy.

The boy prince Eng was taken off to Bangkok in 1790 and was anointed there by the Thai before being sent back to Cambodia in 1794. His reign, which opened up a cycle of nineteenth-century history, is discussed in Chapter 6; the fact that he was crowned in Bangkok is symbolic of his dependence on the new Thai dynasty.

CONCLUSIONS

The two main features of the post-Angkorean era, then, were a shift of the capital from the rice-growing hinterlands of northwestern Cambodia to the trade-oriented riverbanks in the vicinity of Phnom Penh on the one hand and the increasing importance of foreign powers in Cambodian internal affairs on the other. It seems clear that the apparent self-sufficiency of Angkor was as much related to the absence of military rivals as to inherent strength or flexibility in Angkorean institutions. Many of these institutions, in fact, persisted into the post-Angkorean era and got in the way of rapid bureaucratic responses (supposing that this was psychologically possible or culturally rewarding) in the face of foreign and domestic pressure.

Despite this facade of continuity, many changes in Cambodian society took place between the fourteenth century and the beginning of the nineteenth. The most important of these, perhaps, was the decline in importance of a brahmanical priestly class that had effectively linked landholdings, control of slaves, religious practices, education, and the throne. Perhaps equally important, but harder to pin down, was the widespread and apparently increasing influence of the Thai on Cambodian life. Frank Huffman has shown that the transformation that occurred in the Khmer language in the post-Angkorean period, reaching its climax in the nineteenth century, amounted to the replacement of Angkorean syntax by its Thai counterpart.[33] Saveros Pou regarded this process as inimical to Cambodian identity, especially in terms of its effects on literary style, but recognized its importance in the history of the period.

Another important change—the intrusion of the Vietnamese into Cambodian life—came later on, reaching peaks in the nineteenth and twentieth centuries. Already in the eighteenth century, however, Vietnamese activities had the effect of sealing off Cambodia from the outside world at exactly the point when other Southeast Asian countries, especially Siam, were opening up.

A final change, perceptible at the end of the dark ages, was the decline in the popularity of kingship. Of all the post-Angkorean kings of Cambodia, only Duang (r. 1848–1860) and Norodom Sihanouk seem to have struck a sustained chord of popular approval. The discontinuity between the palace and the people noticeable in the legal anecdotes of the 1690s probably widened in the chaos that affected the entire country in the following century. But this "decline," like so many notions put forward about Cambodian history, is impossible to verify. After all, during the heyday of Angkor, we have only the kings' own words to support the notion that they were popular. Like the *Ramayana,* the king and his entourage had roles to play in people's thinking, but they played *central* roles only in their own. Although Clifford Geertz's phrase "theater state"— originally applied to precolonial Java and more recently to nineteenth-century Bali[34]—can be used with caution to describe Cambodian court life, most Cambodian people probably knew and cared less about it than some scholars, entranced perhaps by the exoticism of these arrangements, might prefer. In periods of stability, of course, Cambodians may well have had more time for ceremony, and more surplus to pay for ceremonies, than in periods of warfare, famine, or distress. Between 1750 and 1850, however, the king's failure to deliver protection and stability probably undermined his relevance in the eyes of the rural poor. But the texts that have survived are ambiguous and inconclusive. At the same time, the rural poor could imagine no alternative set of political or patronage arrangements, outside of easily snuffed-out millenarian rebellions, that could grant them the protection they needed to plant, harvest, and survive.

CHAPTER 6

State, Society, and Foreign Relations, 1794–1848

In the half century or so before the arrival of the French, who established a protectorate over Cambodia in 1863, Cambodian ideas about political geography did not include the notion that "Cambodia" was defined primarily by the lines enclosing it on a map.[1] Maps were rarely used, and no locally drawn map of Cambodia in the early nineteenth century appears to have survived.[2] Instead, to the people who lived there, "Cambodia" probably meant the *sruk* where Cambodian was spoken and, more narrowly, those whose leaders (*chaovay sruk*) had received their official titles and their seals of office from a Cambodian king.

Cambodians also thought of their country, metaphorically, as a walled city with several imaginary gates. One verse chronicle places these at Sambor on the upper Mekong, Kompong Svay north of the Tonle Sap, Pursat in the northwest, Kampot on the coast, and at Chaudoc, technically across the frontier in Vietnam in the Mekong Delta.[3] Fittingly, these gates were the places where invading armies traditionally swept into Cambodia. The territory they enclosed, in the form of a gigantic letter "C" (there was no eastern gate, for armies did not cross the Annamite cordillera), covered roughly half the area of Cambodia today.

Inside this imaginary wall, *sruk* varied in size and importance. Although boundaries were generally vague, some, like Pursat and Kompong Svay, extended over several hundred square miles; others, like Koh Chan or Lovea Em, were islands in the Mekong or short stretches along the river.

SOCIETY AND ECONOMY

Little information about the size and composition of Cambodia's population in this period has survived. During the period of Vietnamese suzerainty in the 1830s, a census was taken, but the Vietnamese dismissed its figures as deflated.[4] French administrators in the 1860s, working from roughly compiled tax rolls, estimated Cambodia's population at slightly less than a million.[5] The area between Cambodia's imaginary gates, therefore, may have supported about three-quarters of a million people in the 1840s, but probably fewer, for the records are filled with accounts of regions being depopulated by famine, flight, and invading armies.

This population was overwhelmingly rural. The largest town, Phnom Penh, probably never held more than twenty-five thousand people.[6] The royal capital at Udong and the villages around it supported a population of ten thousand or so in the late 1850s; and the Khmer-speaking city of Battambang, rebuilt by the Thai in the late 1830s, had three thousand inhabitants in 1839.[7] The only parts of the kingdom that were relatively densely settled before the 1860s were those to the south and east of Phnom Penh, like Ba Phnom and Bati, and to the north along the Mekong River south of Chhlong. Significantly, these relatively wealthy *sruk* were often located outside the routes of invasion and retreat chosen by the Thai and the Vietnamese.

Nearly all the people were ethnic Khmer, who occupied themselves with rice farming and with monastic and official life. Commercial and industrial tasks were handled by minority groups. Marketing, garden farming, and foreign trade, for example, were handled by Chinese or by people of Chinese descent.[8] Cattle trading, weaving, and commercial fisheries were controlled by a Muslim minority composed partly of immigrants from the Malay archipelago—misleadingly known as *chvea,* or *Javanese,* in Khmer—and partly of immigrants from Champa. The Kui people in the northern part of the country smelted Cambodia's small deposits of iron ore. In the capital, a handful of descendants of Portuguese settlers who had arrived in the sixteenth and seventeenth centuries served as translators for the king and were in charge of his artillery pieces.[9] Before the 1830s there seem to have been few Vietnamese residents. Indeed, even without accurate statistics, it seems likely that there were proportionately fewer of these various groups in the kingdom until the arrival of the French, when the numbers of Chinese and Vietnamese residents in particular increased enormously.[10]

Near the imaginary gates, in thinly populated *sruk* like Kratie, Pursat, and Kompong Svay, tribal groups, such as the Porr, Stieng, and Samre, lived in isolated villages and collected the forest products that formed the main source of a monarch's income and the bulk of the goods that Cambodia sent abroad.

By the standards of other states in Southeast Asia, Cambodia was poor. Unlike Burma and Laos, its soil contained few gems or precious metals. Unlike Siam, its manufacturing, trade, and commerce were undeveloped, and finished goods, like brassware, porcelain, and firearms, came from abroad. Unlike Vietnam, its communications were poor and its internal markets undeveloped. Agricultural surpluses were rare, savings were low, and money was used only at the palace and by minority groups. Cambodia had a subsistence economy; most of its people spent most of their time growing rice. Landholdings tended to be small—even high officials seldom had access to more than a few hectares—yields were certainly low, and irrigation works, which might have increased production, were rare.

To the Vietnamese emperor, Minh Mang, writing in 1834, Cambodia was truly a "barbarian" country because "the people do not know the proper way to grow food. They use mattocks and hoes, but no oxen. They grow enough rice to have two meals a day, but they do not know how to store rice for an emergency."[11] Villagers often maintained a common pond, or *trapeang,* to water their rice, but there were no longer any of the dams and canals that had characterized Angkorean civilization. This was partly because there were now so few mouths to feed. There were no incentives and little technology for farmers to vary their crops or increase their holdings. Communications between the *sruk* were poor; there were no roads to speak of until the 1830s, and bandits, invading armies, and the followers of local officials carried off what surpluses they could find.

Foreign trade was restricted by the fact that the potentially important entrepôt of Phnom Penh was cut off from the outside world for most of this period by the authorities in southern Vietnam. After 1808, in fact, visitors to Phnom Penh needed Vietnamese permission to go there. Ports on the Gulf of Siam, like Kampot, engaged in some coastal and peninsular trade, but they were more closely integrated into the Vietnamese and Thai economies than into the Cambodian one.[12]

A few ships traded with central Cambodia every year. Cargo lists from two of these, bound for China and Japan respectively in about 1810, have survived.[13] Their cargoes consisted of relatively small amounts of several different products—300 pounds of ivory and 200 pounds of pepper, for example, were among the goods exported to Japan; those going to China included small consignments of cardamom, hides, tortoise shells, and aromatic wood. Exports to Vietnam in the 1820s—trade with Vietnam was conducted partly in a tributary framework—included such goods as ivory, gutta percha, cardamom, dried fish, and elephant hides.

These were traditional exports. The lists are like others that have come down from the seventeenth century and even from the Angkorean period.[14] External trade—including tribute, as we shall see—was an important source of the king's revenues and probably was important to the Chinese community in Phnom Penh and to privileged members of the king's entourage. But it was insignificant as far as the rest of the country was concerned.

Most Cambodians lived in villages. These can be divided, for the early nineteenth century at least, into three broad types. The first can be called *kompong* after the Malay word meaning "landing-place," which often formed part of their names—as in Kompong Svay and Kompong Som.[15] These were located along navigable bodies of water and could support populations of several hundred people. Often they would include a *chaovay sruk* and his assistants; the *kompong* was usually enclosed in a stockade. Some of the inhabitants were likely to be Chinese or Sino-Khmer, Malay, and Cham, although minorities tended to keep to themselves in separate hamlets that formed elements of the *kompong. Kompong* were in touch with others on the same body of water, with rice-growing villages around them, and indirectly, with the capital and the court. Through trading, travel, hearsay, and invasions, people in the *kompong* had some awareness of events elsewhere.

Rice-growing villages, the second category, enclosed the *kompong,* ideally, in a broken arc. Poorer and smaller than *kompong,* rice-growing villages were numerous and more likely to be populated by ethnic Khmer. Houses were scattered around in no special order near a Buddhist monastery, or *wat,* and also near the pond or stream that provided water for the village. Rice-growing villages were linked to the *kompong* and the world beyond in irregular ways—through incursions of officials looking for recruits or rice; through the *wat,* whose monks were encouraged to travel about in the dry season; through festivals at the new year and at other points in the calendar; and through trade with the *kompong,* exchanging rice and forest products for metal, cloth, and salt.

Rice-growing villages were unstable because they lacked means of defense and because, unlike in Vietnam, no institutionalized ancestor cult anchored people to one place rather than another. The chronicles are filled with references to villagers running off into the forest in times of crisis. In times of peace, their lives were shaped by the contours of the agricultural year and the ceremonies—Buddhist, animist, and vaguely Hindu—that marked off one stage of the rice-growing cycle from another.[16]

The opposition between "wild" and "civilized," noted in the discussion of the *Reamker* in Chapter 5, persisted in the literature of the nineteenth century. An important verse chronicle from Wat Baray, in the north-central part of the kingdom, deals with this theme repeatedly while offering a chronological treatment of nineteenth-century events. The chronicle relates the fortunes of a bureaucratic family caught up in the turmoils of Vietnamese occupation and civil war. Driven into the forest, they lose their identity, regaining it only when new titles are bestowed on male members, first by a Thai monarch and later by a Cambodian one. The chronicle was composed to celebrate the restoration of Wat Baray in 1856, and the audience to whom it was recited would for the most part have recognized the events related in it as true. What gives the chronicle its literary resonance is the way in which the lives of the characters follow patterns laid down for them by the *Reamker* and Buddhist ideology. The restoration of their status accompanied the restoration of the king; demerit was seen, in some way, as associated with the forest, a lack of official titles, and misbehavior impossible to trace.

Similarly, in a poignant Cambodian folktale, probably well known in the 1800s, three girls who are abandoned by their mother become wild and turn into birds, happily crossing the border between forest and field where, as it turns out, the birds they have become are most frequently to be found.[17] Because people's grip on the things we take for granted was so precarious in nineteenth-century Cambodia—dependent on the goodwill of foreigners and overlords, on rainfall, and on health in a tropical climate—it is understandable that "civilization," or the art of remaining outside the forest, was taken so seriously by poets and audience alike.

The third type of village lay hidden in the *prei,* or wilderness, that made up most of Cambodia at this time. Here the people were illiterate and usually non-Buddhists; they spoke languages related to Khmer but owed no loyalties to the *kompong* or the capital unless these had been forced from them. The villages were frequently raided for slaves, and they were economically important because they were able to exploit forest resources that were valued at the capital and abroad. Their political loyalties, however, were to other villages in the *prei* where people spoke the same dialect and performed similar religious rites.

PATRONAGE AND GOVERNMENT

Little information has survived about the way Cambodian villages were governed in the early nineteenth century. Some French writers have asserted that Cambodian villages had no government at all,[18] and in most of them, indeed, relations with outsiders and with the state were sporadic and unfriendly. Quarrels within a village or among neighbors were settled by conciliation rather than by law, and they often smoldered on for years. Villages were usually "ruled," for ceremonial purposes and for the purposes of relations with higher authorities, by elderly men chosen for their agricultural skill, literacy, and fair-mindedness. Taxes in rice and labor seem to have been paid, irregularly, on demand. Village government was perhaps more noticeable in the *kompong,* where there were more officials and hangers-on, but there is no evidence that any villages in Cambodia were governed by formally constituted councils of elders, as was the case in nineteenth-century Vietnam.[19]

Rice-growing villages and those in the *prei* could be days apart from each other and from the nearest representative of authority. In their isolation, the villagers faced inward onto the lives and traditions they shared with one another. They identified themselves and saw their history in terms of localized religious traditions passed on from one generation to the next. Outside the villages, just past the fields in most cases, lay the *prei,* crowded with wild animals, malarial mosquitoes, and the spirits of the dead. Beyond the *prei,* where villagers seldom ventured, lay the world of the *kompong,* the capital, and the court.

French writers in the nineteenth century often denigrated Cambodian society (one of them referred to its institutions as "worm-eaten débris"[20] and compared it unfavorably with their own "rational," centralized one or with that of the Vietnamese. The trend has continued among some anthropologists concerned with Thailand, who refer to Thai peasant society as "loosely structured."[21] The phrase is helpful—whether or not one attaches values to "tight structure"—in the sense that in Thai and Cambodian villages in the nineteenth century, there were no "durable, functionally important groups" or voluntary associations aside from the family and the Buddhist monastic order, or *sangha.* When a village organized itself—for defense, for instance, or for a festival—it did so for a short time in response to a specific need.

Despite the apparent informality of these arrangements, there was considerable structural consistency in each Cambodian village and family. This arose from the fact that Cambodians always identified themselves in terms of their status relative to the person being addressed. This identification located them for the moment at a particular, but by no means fixed, point in a flexible set of dyadic relationships extending downward from the king and the *sangha* through the graded bureaucracy of the capital and *kompong* to the villages and past them to the landless debt-slaves and minority peoples living literally at the edges of the state. As with most systematic social arrangements, what mattered to the people who used it was the place they occupied. If a man's place was relatively secure, people in weaker positions sought him out and offered homage in exchange for his protection. The society, in a sense, was fueled by the exchange of protection and service implied in these "lopsided friend-ships," as they have been called.[22] In a village context, these links might be with older or more fortunate members of one's family, monks at the local *wat,* bandit leaders, government officials, or holy men (*nak sel*) who appeared from time to time, promising their followers invulnerability and riches.

In the *kompong* and the capital, where people no longer grew their own food, patronage and clientship became more important and more complex. Having a patron and having clients was connected with one's chances to survive. People with access to power accepted as many followers or slaves as they could. In many cases, these slaves had contracted debts to their patrons, which they then spent their lifetimes working off. The widespread presence of slavery in nineteenth-century Cambodia should cloud over, to an extent, the sunny notion that clients entered their "lopsided friendships" as volunteers with a variety of choices. But it is true that many people enslaved themselves to a patron, or *me* (the word can also mean "mother"), to protect themselves against the rapacity of others.

The rectitude and permanence of these relationships had been drummed into everyone from birth. Cambodian proverbs and didactic literature are filled with references to the helplessness of the individual and to the importance of accepting power relationships as they are. Both sides of the patron-client equation, in theory at least, saw their relationships as natural, even obligatory ones. "The rich must protect the poor," a Cambodian proverb runs, "just as clothing protects the body."[23]

The relationships were seldom that genteel. Throughout Southeast Asia patrons, like kings, spoke of "consuming" the territory and people they controlled, and there are few just officials in Cambodian folklore, in which officials are compared to tigers, crocodiles, and venomous snakes. Rural government was seen as an adversary proceeding. In one *sruk* at least, when a new *chaovay sruk* took office, a cockfight was held. One bird represented the newly arrived official, the other the people of the *sruk*. The outcome of the fight supposedly gave both sponsors a hint about the balance of power that was expected to ensue.[24]

Why did the people accept these demeaning arrangements? Partly it was a case of *force majeure.* The alternatives of individual flight or organized resistance were often impossible. Moreover, a man without a patron was fair game, and an unknown patron, like a foreigner, was more of a threat than one who lived nearby. Although the *chaovay sruk* often "ate" what little material wealth he could get his hands on, the social distance between him and the rest of the *kompong* was not especially great. His wives, for example, were local women. He lived in a simple house, chewed betel, and sponsored festivals at the *wat* and ceremonies to propitiate the *nak ta.* These officials shared their clients' food, their belief in magic, their vigorous sense of the absurd, and their distrust of other officials and all outsiders. Probably because they lived among the people they supposedly controlled, *chaovay sruk* were more responsive to local issues than were authorities in the capital. The fact that all these "lopsided friendships" could be renegotiated in times of stress added to the instability of the system and perhaps to its attractiveness in the eyes of villagers and slaves.

For most Cambodians, these shifting networks of subordination and control, chosen or imposed, benevolent or otherwise, marked the limits of their experience and of their social expectations. Their ideas about the king, on the other hand, and about the Buddhist *sangha* took a different form and were expressed in a different language. Although it is useful to place the king and the *sangha* at the end of imaginary chains of local and spiritual authority extending down through the officials to the people, the people saw them as operating on a different plane and on a different set of assumptions. Little is known about the *sangha* in nineteenth-century Cambodia, and it could be misleading to assert that conditions were the same as those in Siam or Burma. There is no evidence, for example, that the *sangha* played a political role vis-à-vis the royal family, although monks and ex-monks were active in the anti-Vietnamese rebellion of 1821.[25] By and large, monks were widely respected as repositories of merit, as sources of spiritual patronage, and as curators of Cambodia's literary culture. They occupied a unique and thus mysterious place in Cambodian life because they had abandoned—temporarily at least— agriculture, politics, and marriage.

People's ideas about the king tended to be grounded in mythology rather than their own experience. The relationship of the king to most of his subjects was not negotiated, was rarely enforced, and was seldom face-to-face. For most of the early nineteenth century, by choice or by circumstance, the monarch was confined to his palace or lived in exile in Siam or Vietnam. Because they never saw him and because of the weight of traditional and popular literature about him, villagers' views of the king tended to be vaguer and more approving than their views of each other, their patrons, or even the *nak ta*. The king was at once as real (and as unreal) as the Lord Buddha. People would have accepted the *Ramayana*'s description of royal duties; they were "to be consecrated, to sacrifice, and to protect the people."[26] Many of them believed that the king could influence the weather; unlike the *sauphea,* or judges, he could dispense true justice; he was often the only political source of hope among peasants. This does not mean that he was always or even often in their thoughts; but when he appeared in his capital after years of exile, like Eng in 1794 and Duang nearly half a century later, the event ignited widespread rejoicing.

There were several other segments of Cambodian society that affected people's lives in the villages and the outcome of Cambodian politics as a whole. These included minor *sruk* officials and hangers-on, who were appointed in some cases from the capital and in others by the *chaovay sruk;* ex-monks, or *achar,* who acted as religious spokesmen and millenarian

Monument to dead kings at Udong, the Cambodian capital from about 1600 to 1866. Photo by Roger M. Smith.

leaders, often in opposition to the *chaovay sruk;* itinerant traders, actors, and musicians; and poor relations of the rich, who were able to act as go-betweens. Unfortunately, the elite-centered *bangsavatar,* or chronicles, usually devote little space to these categories of people, so it is difficult to assess their power, except directly: A rice-growing village going into revolt against the Vietnamese—as many did in 1820 and 1841, for example—was unlikely to have done so merely through the exhortations of a high official.

THE *Okya*

Historical records, on the other hand, have left a good picture of Cambodia's high-ranking officials, or *okya*.[27] Included in their number were the *chaovay sruk* and the officials surrounding the king. It is impossible to say how many *okya* there were at any given time. Lists of officials assembled in the 1860s and 1870s for the French are full of gaps and contradictions. Many of the titles in these lists do not appear to have been used, and titles occur in other sources that do not appear in the lists. Roughly, however, there seem to have been about two hundred *okya* in the capital and the countryside throughout most of the nineteenth century. The number was probably smaller after defections to the Thai in the 1830s and larger after Duang's accession. For these two hundred men, about seven hundred titles were available for use. Some of these, like those carried by the king's highest advisers and by most of the *chaovay sruk,* were always filled. Others seem to have lapsed, for a while at least, after having been held by one or several incumbents.

Everything about the titles and the work associated with them, except the fact that they were conferred on the incumbent by the king, was subject to adjustment. Sometimes a title carried a rank, and sometimes it was associated with a job, such as maintaining the king's elephants, guarding his regalia, or collecting taxes. Certain titles were reserved for certain *sruk,* and the word *sauphea* when it occurred in a title often implied judicial functions. But none of these rules was rigorously applied. Favorites or people out of favor were given jobs to do or removed from them on an ad hoc basis. People went up the ladder (or fell off) quickly. For example, one official whose function was to be in charge of the throne room of the second king (hardly an arduous calling) was named to head a diplomatic mission to Bangkok in 1819. Another, whose duties were to survey the levels of rice in the royal storehouses, led an army against the Thai in Battambang in 1818; and the list could be extended.

The titles that *okya* carried usually consisted of two or three honorific words, like *ratna* ("jewel") or *verocana* ("splendor"), drawn from Pali or Sanskrit. The *okya* received them along with the seals of office and insignia of rank (which included tiered umbrellas, betel containers, court costumes, and the like) from the king's hands, in an intentionally awesome ceremony built around an oath of allegiance that had been in effect in more or less the same form for at least eight hundred years.[28] At that time, and at regular intervals, the *okya* were expected to give presents to the king. French writers equated this exchange of titles and gifts with the notion that Cambodian government was corrupt, because jobs were available only to the highest bidder. At one level of thinking this was true, but little ethical weight was given to the transaction—high bidders, after all, were people whose power had to be reckoned with. Twice a year, the *okya* assembled at the royal *wat* near the palace, where they drank the "water of allegiance"—water brought to the capital, in theory, from streams throughout the kingdom—and renewed their oaths of allegiance to the king. Failure to attend this ceremony was tantamount to treason.

Once in office, an *okya* became part of the *komlang*, or strength (i.e., entourage) of some higher-ranking person. This might be one of the king's advisers, a member of the royal family, or the king himself. A similar system was in effect in Siam. It is not clear whether these alliances were meant to check or to enhance the power of the *okya* in question— probably they served both purposes at once. The interconnections between certain regions, official posts, family ties, and particular jobs in this period remain obscure. One manuscript chronicle, dating from the early nineteenth century, suggests that the landholdings of *okya* in certain regions persisted from one generation to the next, even when the titles of one *okya* were not passed along to his son.[29] Titles among *okya* were not hereditary. Even the successor to the throne was chosen, after a monarch's death, from among several eligible candidates. A similar fluidity affected *okya* families, although high status seems to have run in particular families.

Despite these continuities, there were few certainties in Cambodian political life. Theoretically, the survival of an *okya* depended on the king, and Akin Rabibhadana cited a 1740 Thai decree that "a king can turn a superior person into a subordinate person, and vice-versa. When he gives an order, it is like an axe from heaven."[30] In reality, however, a king's power depended on how recently he had attained it and how many outstanding debts he had; it was hampered in any case by poor communications between the capital and the *sruk.*

A new king at the start of a dynasty, or after a period of exile, could often act like an "axe from heaven" and fill *okya* positions with men who had been loyal to him in his climb to power. King Duang rewarded his followers in this way in the 1840s, as we shall see, just as the first kings of the Chakri dynasty in Thailand (1782–) and Nguyen dynasty in Vietnam (1802–1945) had rewarded theirs. Under a weak king, on the other hand, or one entangled in long-standing obligations, perhaps to older people, *okya* tended to root themselves in the *sruk* and to become more or less independent. In at least one *sruk* in the late nineteenth century, the *chaovay* was selected by other officials there and given seals of office by the regional governor, or *chaomuang,* who was Thai.

Uncertainty was an occupational hazard of Cambodian life. Everyone was on the lookout against everyone else. An *okya*'s obligations toward his king, his family, and his patrons sometimes overlapped and sometimes were in conflict. The other *okya* were potential allies and potential enemies; alliances and betrayals that took advantage of existing power balances occupied a good deal of the *okya*'s time.

Cambodia was not a bureaucratic society, like China or Vietnam, and in times of peace an *okya*'s official duties were light. He had to wait upon his patron; there was little paperwork to do; and many tasks, like requisitioning supplies for the palace or raising armies for defense (there was no standing army), were farmed out among several *okya*, perhaps to keep a single official from becoming too powerful and perhaps because there were no institutional mechanisms to prevent ambitious *okya* from shouldering each other aside in search of profit.

The judgment implied in these remarks may be too strong. Some *okya*, as in Siam, were accomplished poets and musicians, and others were generous patrons of Buddhism and the arts. A few emerge from the chronicles as competent, innovative, or brave, but the uncertainty of favor, the ubiquity of rivals, and the unreliability of followers militated against an *okya*'s being active or even attracting official notice. The *okya* and the people, then, were tied to each other with bonds of terror, affection, duty, and contempt within the framework of a shared culture. In Cambodian terms, the system worked, but when the Vietnamese tried to use the *okya* as their spokesmen in Cambodia in the 1830s and 1840s, they found the *okya* incapable of governing the country in a Vietnamese way—which is to say, of *administering* regions, conducting cadastral surveys, collecting taxes, and making detailed reports.

Aside from the king's five closest advisers, who formed a kind of cabinet, the most active and visible *okya* were the *chaovay sruk,* whose role as patrons in the countryside has been discussed. These men enjoyed considerable freedom and considerable power. They were authorized to collect taxes from their *sruk,* which meant that they had access to any surplus crops they could lay their hands on; and they were authorized to mobilize manpower for warfare or public works. In practice they maintained small private armies—rather like their counterparts, the riverine chieftains of nineteenth-century Malaya. In populous *sruk,* these armies sometimes contained several thousand men; in others they seem to have acted as bodyguards for the *chaovay sruk.* Access to manpower and rice meant that in effect the *chaovay sruk* controlled the balance of power in the kingdom. In fact, they rarely acted collectively, but as individuals, responding to local interests and dyadic arrangements. This meant that a king could count on some *chaovay sruk* but not on others and that invading armies might find some *chaovay* friendly and others opposed to them.

Some *chaovay sruk* were more important than others. Five of them, called *stac tran,* or kings of the field, were the highest-ranking *okya* and were responsible, in an unspecified way, for the governance of several *sruk* at once.[31] Each grouping was known as a *dei,* or earth. Unfortunately, nineteenth-century references to the phrase *stac tran* occur only in French texts and the meaning of *tran* itself is not clear. The officials seem to have acted as viceroys, or stand-ins for the king, in the performance of annual ceremonies in the five *dei* honoring the *nak ta.* They had the power to order executions, which the other *chaovay sruk* did not. In a functional sense, they echoed the five high ministers around the king.

These five ministers in the capital were led by a first minister, sometimes referred to as the *ta-la-ha,* and included (as in Siam, where the title *ta-la-ha* was not in use) a minister of justice (*yomraj*), of the army (*chakrei*), of the navy and foreign trade (*kralahom*), and of the palace (*vang*). Each of these officials maintained his own *komlang* and probably had economic and patrimonial links with certain *sruk.* Loosely defined territorial responsibilities of these men overlapped or extended those of the *stac tran* and the *chaovay sruk,* as well as those of certain members of the royal family, who were also entitled to "consume" particular regions. In times of stress, as several chronicles reveal, *okya* retreated to their villages, where they had relatives and land. Despite these regional links, however, the high-ranking *okya* spent their time close to the king, except in war, when some of them were called on to recruit troops and act as generals in the field. Their careers were tied to the fortunes of the king. Their effect on life in the countryside is not so clear. The palace-oriented *bangsavatar* probably exaggerate the importance of these men, and so did the Vietnamese when they looked for people to help them centralize and tidy up Cambodian government in the 1830s.

The last segment of Cambodian society that came between the villagers and their king consisted of other members of the royal family. In theory, there could be hundreds of these, for kings were traditionally polygamous, but in the nineteenth century a series of deaths and coincidences had sharply reduced their number. King Eng, who died in his twenties, had no surviving brothers and only five children. The oldest of these, Prince Chan, came to the throne when he was only six. When he died more than thirty years later, he left four daughters but no sons. His three brothers (the fourth had died as a child) went to Bangkok in 1812 and stayed there, with brief exceptions, until Chan's death in 1835. This meant that for most of his reign Chan was the only male member of the royal family living in Cambodia. The factionalism and jockeying for position, a conventional feature of Cambodian court life before and since, took place off-stage, in Siam, and in the late 1830s, in the Cambodian *sruk* under Thai control.

The Cambodian king, at the pinnacle of society, was remote from his subjects. Scholars have argued that this remoteness was expected of an Asian king; he was to rule by his largely invisible example, just as the sun shone, and he was to act as the custodian of a fund of merit and power—viewed perhaps as an interlocking, expendable commodity—that he had accumulated in previous existences en route to the throne. What has sometimes been called the "purely" religious or symbolic importance of kingship in Southeast Asia, as transmitted in Indianized texts, has been overstressed. The frontiers between political and religious actions and institutions were neither sharply delimited nor especially important; in their daily lives, kings were as concerned with mere survival as with their religious roles. Nonetheless, it would be incorrect to blot out the religious importance of kingship with evidence—however easy to assemble—of a given king's fallibility. Having a king was indispensable. According to the *Ramayana*, a country without a king enjoys "neither rain nor seed, neither wealth nor wife, neither sacrifices nor festivals,"[32] and the alarm of the *okya* in 1840–1841 when Cambodia was briefly without a monarch shows how deeply ingrained these notions were. Only a king was empowered to hand out the official titles, seals of office, and insignia of rank that held the Cambodian official class together; one Cambodian law even stated that an official without a seal did not need to be obeyed.[33]

In addition to setting Cambodia's official class in motion—an action that had no consistent effect on village life—the Cambodian monarch, like his counterparts elsewhere in Southeast Asia, also presided over a series of partly brahmanical, partly Buddhist, and partly animistic ceremonies that, from the villagers' point of view, defined the boundaries of his merit and the limits of the agricultural year; these were closely related to the success of their harvests. They included ones that honored the king's ancestors and the *nak ta*, ones inaugurating and closing the rice-growing cycle, and ones that marked off stages of the Buddhist and solar calendars. In many of them the king was assisted by court "brahmans" called *baku* who also acted as guardians of his regalia—the sacred sword, arrows, and other objects that he handled once in his lifetime, at his coronation. It is impossible to decide if the regalia were "political" or "religious." Without them, a monarch could rule—handing out titles, raising armies, and so forth—but he could not reign; he had not been consecrated, as Prince Duang discovered in the 1840s when the Vietnamese withheld the regalia from him until they could extract favorable peace terms from the Thai.

The monarch's powers, then, although perhaps overstressed in the written record, remained considerable in the eyes of the *okya* and among the common people. The absence of a monarch was felt, at many points in the society, perhaps more acutely than his presence on the throne.

CAMBODIA'S RELATIONS WITH VIETNAM AND SIAM

As we have seen, the two most important characteristics of post-Angkorean Cambodia were the shift in the country's center of gravity from Angkor to Phnom Penh, with the commercial and demographic ramifications that the move implied, and the roles played by the Thai and Vietnamese in Cambodian history. Nineteenth-century Cambodia, therefore, must also be seen in part against the background of its foreign relations.

Cambodia's foreign relations were carried out with two countries, Vietnam and Siam, and occurred within a framework of rivalry between the two larger kingdoms. Rivalry sprang from the unwillingness of either court to accept the other as equal or superior; this unwillingness, in turn, can be traced in part to the traditional language of tributary diplomacy, which stressed the inequality between the sender and recipient of tribute.

A major objective of Southeast Asian diplomacy in the nineteenth century, indeed, was the ritualized expression of differential status through the ceremonial exchange of gifts. The rules for these tributary exchanges grew out of the particular system in which they occurred. The Thai and the Vietnamese, for example, had separate ones, which overlapped inside Cambodia.

Both systems owed a good deal to their counterpart in China,[34] which had been in effect since the third century B.C. and was still in operation in the 1800s. From a Cambodian point of view, the Thai variant was looser and more idiosyncratic, for the Thai made allowances for local customs and local products; the Vietnamese did not. They were rigid in copying the Chinese model. In 1806, for example, Vietnamese Emperor Gia Long, in choosing gifts to send to the Cambodian king, transmitted facsimiles of the ones he had received, at the beginning of his own reign, from the Chinese emperor in Peking. Some of these, like "golden dragon paper for imperial decrees" and Chinese bureaucratic costumes, were meaningless to the Khmer. The seals of investiture sent from Hue to Udong were irrelevant to Cambodians because they had camels carved on them, like the seals that the Chinese court sent to tributary states in central Asia and, incidentally, to Vietnam. One puzzled Cambodian chronicler referred to the animal as a "Chinese lion."[35]

From Vietnam's point of view, Vietnam was "over" Cambodia, just as China was "over" Vietnam. At the same time, of course, Cambodia was "under" Vietnam and Vietnam was "under" China. In other words, Vietnam was the master in one relationship and the servant in the other. As a by-product of this duality, the "civilized" goods sent from Hué to Udong were facsimiles of those sent from Peking to Hué, while the "barbarian" goods transmitted from Udong were the same sorts of products that Hué transmitted to Peking.[36]

In the matter of tributary gifts, the Thai were more flexible than the Vietnamese. The Chakri kings sent gifts to nineteenth-century Cambodian kings that the recipients could recognize and use. In exchange, the Thai seem to have settled for whatever products they could get. Sometimes Cambodia sent pepper, at other times lacquer and *kravanh* cardamom. There is no evidence, however, that the Cambodians ever transmitted the gold and silver ornamental trees (*banga mas*) that were a feature of tribute to Bangkok from other dependent states.[37]

Similarly, the embassies that King Chan (r. 1796–1835) sent to Bangkok and Hué obeyed different sets of rules. Embassies to Bangkok were larger, more frequent, and more informal; the differences between the two diplomatic systems, indeed, paralleled differences in Thai and Vietnamese official attitudes toward themselves, each other, and the Khmer. These differences became crucial and painful for the Khmer in the 1830s, when the Vietnamese emperor sought to administer Cambodia directly, in a Vietnamese way. From a Cambodian point of view, however, what mattered about the Thai and Vietnamese tributary systems and attitudes toward Cambodia was not that they were different and made different sorts of demands, but that they were condescending, overlapping, and expensive.

Thai and Vietnamese official relations with each other, until they soured in the late 1820s, were marked by considerable informality.[38] This arose in part from a mutual unwillingness on the part of the Thai and the Vietnamese to accept or impose authority, because they enjoyed roughly similar power and prestige. The problem of hegemony did not yet arise in their relations with the Khmer, and notions about the roles both states should play in Cambodia were quite consistent. The barbarity of the Cambodian people and the subservience of their king, for example, were taken for granted, and so was the corollary that each superior state had a sort of *mission civilisatrice* to carry out inside Cambodia. The rulers saw themselves, in their official correspondence, as destined to supervise the Khmer. As one Thai diplomatic letter put it, "It is fitting for large countries to take care of smaller ones"; others referred to Chan as an "unruly child" and to the confluence of Thai and Vietnamese policies in Cambodia as "fruit and seeds forming a single unit."

Some of this language was merely a mask for realpolitik, but these images are nonetheless suggestive. The language of diplomatic correspondence, like the languages in everyday use in Southeast Asia, was in its pronouns hierarchical and family-oriented, and relationships between states were often described by images of child-rearing. In these, the Thai and the Vietnamese became respectively, the "father" and the "mother" of the Khmer, whose king was referred to as their "child" or their "servant." In the 1860s, a French official mused perceptively that Siam was Cambodia's father because its king gave names to the monarch, whereas Vietnam was seen to be the mother because its rulers provided the Khmer with seals of office.[39] Whatever the reasons, Thai and Vietnamese statements, like those made later by the French, amounted to unilateral declarations of dependence. The family-oriented images were unjustified and far-fetched, but they give us a useful way of looking at the period— that is, as the continuing struggle between increasingly incompatible parents for the custody of a weak but disobedient child.

Although Thai political ideas were often couched in Buddhist terminology and Vietnamese ones in terms of a Sino-Vietnamese Confucian tradition, Thai and Vietnamese objectives in Cambodia, seldom voiced explicitly, were similar. Like the Nguyen emperors, the Chakri kings were vigorous men, new to power at the beginning of a dynastic cycle. Like the Nguyen, they were eager to extend their prestige along their frontiers and to amplify their self-images as universally accepted kings. The Thai rulers also wanted to link themselves as patrons of Buddhism to the *chakravartin,* or wheel-turning monarchs, who had reigned for so many centuries at Ayudhya. These ambitions led the rulers of both states to expand the land and people under their control.

After 1810, King Chan and his advisers were swept up into a game of power politics that they had little chance to change and no opportunity to win. They had no choice. In Vietnamese terms, Cambodia was a "fence," a buffer state, and a dumping-ground for colonists. To the Thai, the Cambodians were fellow-Buddhist "children" basking in a fund of Chakri merit, who could provide cardamom for the court and manpower for Chakri wars. The Thai wanted the Cambodians to be loyal; the Vietnamese wanted Cambodia's land and, incidentally, its recognition of their superiority. The Thai demanded service and friendship, but they were usually unable—given the way they organized their armies and the distance between Bangkok and Phnom Penh—to provide protection. The Vietnamese, on the other hand, provided protection of a sort, but their actions led to the disappearance of Cambodia as an independent state. By different routes, then, the Thai and the Vietnamese often came to do the same sorts of things: taking over certain *sruk,* making hostages of the ruler and his relations, and curtailing the independence of the *okya.*

To Chan and his advisers, the outcome of this game was probably not obvious at first. In the early part of his reign, his alliance with Vietnam (which may have been forced on him by both Gia Long and Rama I), was probably meant only to deflect some of the pressures on him from the Thai. Letters took so long between Bangkok, Udong, and Hué that Chan was able to buy time on several occasions by saying one thing to the Thai and another to the Vietnamese. Moreover, for most of his reign, he kept his communications open with both capitals by means of the embassies he sent them. In fact, Chan may well have been under the impression that the equilibrium that prevailed in the early years of his reign was his own creation and that he had more bargaining power with his patrons than he really did. Even if the balance of forces and the inactivity of the Thai and the Vietnamese reflected Thai and Vietnamese choices dictated by their own perceptions of national interest and if Cambodia's independence reflected what were for the moment limited Thai and Vietnamese ambitions rather than Cambodian skill, there were still advantages to Chan of blurring the lines of his allegiance. One of the chronicles, allegedly quoting Emperor Gia Long, makes this point quite clear:

> "Cambodia is a small country," the Emperor said. "And we should maintain it as a child. We will be its mother; its father will be Siam. When a child has trouble with its father, it can get rid of suffering by embracing its mother. When the child is unhappy with its mother, it can run to its father for support."[40]

Chan was not alone in playing this game. He was joined by his rivals in the Cambodian royal family, whose alternating loyalties led King Rama III of Siam, writing in the early 1840s, to say:

> The Cambodians always fight among themselves in the matter of succession. The losers in these fights go off to ask for help from a neighboring state; the winner must then ask for forces from the other.[41]

Chan's freedom of action was illusory. He survived as king only so long as one of his patrons and all of his rivals were inactive and so long as the relatively active patron provided him with military help. When either patron turned his attention fully to Cambodia, there was nothing Chan could do to deflect the destruction that ensued. Like Prince Sihanouk in the 1960s, or Pol Pot a decade later, Chan remained "neutral" as long as stronger powers allowed him to do so. Chan suffered an additional disadvantage in having no world leaders or world forums to turn to—no Mao Zedong, no Association of Southeast Asian Nations (ASEAN), and no United Nations.

CHAPTER 7

The Crisis of the Nineteenth Century

The first sixty years of the nineteenth century form the darkest portion of Cambodia's dark ages before the Armageddon of the 1970s. Invaded and occupied again and again by Thai and Vietnamese forces, the kingdom also endured dynastic crises and demographic dislocations. For a time in the 1840s, it ceased to exist as a recognizable state. Just as Jayavarman VII's ideology can be compared in some ways to the ideology of Democratic Kampuchea, the first half of the nineteenth century bears some resemblance to the 1970s in terms of foreign intervention, chaos, and the sufferings of the Cambodian people.

Fortunately for historians, there is a wide range of sources to consult in Thai, Cambodian, and Vietnamese. The record that the sources reveal, however, is incomplete. For example, the ruler of Cambodia for much of this period, King Chan (r. 1796–1835), is rarely quoted in surviving sources; none of his own writings have survived. In other words, a crucial actor has no lines. Similarly, Thai-language sources often thin out just when we might wish to have more information about the politics of Thai foreign policy in the period—as opposed, for instance, to the logistics of invasions.

The period opens and closes with Thai-sponsored coronations. Between these two events and particularly after 1810, invasions from Vietnam and Siam alternated with internal rebellions and court-sponsored resistance to invaders, while the court, especially under Chan, pursued a dangerous policy apparently aimed at preserving independence (or merely staying alive) by playing the Thai and the Vietnamese off against each other. Although the political history of the period is reasonably clear, the politics leading up to the events, and peoples' motivations, are often difficult to discern. The pattern that emerges is one in which Cambodia drifted first away from Thai control, then into the hands of the Vietnamese, and finally back to Thai protection. By the early 1840s, much of its territory, the capital region in particular, was administered as a component of Vietnam. Three events in the drift can be singled out for study. These are the Thai absorption of northwestern Cambodia in exchange for putting Eng on the throne, the anti-Vietnamese millenarian rebellion that broke out in southeastern Cambodia in 1820, and the succession crisis of 1835 following a disastrous Thai military expedition. Each of these events marked a stage in the process of Cambodia's diminishing ability to control its own affairs.

THE IMPOSITION OF VIETNAMESE CONTROL

Eng's restoration in 1794 is treated in the Cambodian chronicle as an event of miraculous significance. When he left Bangkok, the chronicles assert, "the sky did not grow dark, nor did rain fall, but thunder boomed in the noon sky, making a noise like a mighty storm."[1] The restoration was indeed dramatic, for in the preceding fifteen years Cambodia had not been governed at all. A former official named Baen had been installed in Udong by the Thai, had been given the title of *ta-la-ha,* or first minister, and had busied himself with recruiting troops to fight the Tay Son dynasty, with Thai approval, inside Cambodia and in Vietnam. In 1794, after so many years of service, Rama I seems to have felt obliged to reward him in some way.

The reward he chose to bestow, however, was hardly his to give. It consisted of the large and prosperous *sruk* of Battambang and Mahanokor (or "great city," containing the ruins of Angkor). Baen had held power in this region for part of the 1780s and had probably retained a personal following there, but in awarding the two *sruk* to him, Rama I removed them from Eng's jurisdiction without absorbing them into Siam. In the 1790s and for most of the nineteenth century, Thai suzerainty seems to have meant only that Baen and his successors were not obligated to provide laborers for Eng and had to transmit gifts—generally wild cardamom—to Bangkok from time to time.

Details about the transfer are impossible to find. Perhaps documents were never drawn up. In the 1860s, in fact, a French official in Cambodia, seeking information about the Thai claims, reported to his superiors that "[Siam] is unable to present any documentation about the cession. The present king of Cambodia [Eng's grandson Norodom], his officials, old men who have been consulted, and Eng's widow, who is still alive, are all of the opinion that none exists."[2]

In the twentieth century, however, the "loss" of the two *sruk* poisoned Thai-Cambodian relations. Siam gave up the *sruk* under pressure from France in 1907 but resumed control over most of their territory from 1941 to 1946. In the context of the 1790s, however, it is unlikely that Rama I was pursuing a long-range plan, and his grandson, Rama IV, put the matter succinctly when he wrote that "the Thai kingdom was able to enlarge itself [at this time] because it had the greater power."[3]

After building himself a palace in Udong and visiting Bangkok with a tributary mission in 1796, Eng died at the beginning of 1797. His reign had been uneventful, and his contributions to Cambodian history, although major, were almost inadvertent. By returning to Udong, which had been without a king for so long, he brought Cambodia back to life; and by fathering four sons, he founded a dynasty that was to reign in Udong and Phnom Penh until 1970. These two contributions, rather than specific actions on his part, probably account for the reverence with which he is treated in Cambodian chronicles compiled for his descendants.

The next ten years, until Chan's coronation in 1806, are poorly documented, but for reasons that remain unclear, the young prince became alienated from the Thai court at some point in this period and seems to have begun to formulate a pro-Vietnamese foreign policy. Whatever its causes—and Thai sources hint at a feud between the young prince and Rama I—the anti-Thai orientation of Chan's official behavior is a persistent theme of his long reign.[4]

As soon as he had been crowned, he hastened to strengthen Cambodia's tributary connections with Vietnam while maintaining his subservience to Bangkok, becoming, in the words of the Vietnamese emperor, "an independent country that is the slave of two."[5] The process was even more complicated, for Chan's increasing animosity toward the Thai alienated some of his own *chaovay sruk,* especially in the northwest, and his personal insecurity is indicated by his request to the Vietnamese emperor at about this time that he be allowed to recruit Vietnamese residents of Cambodia to form his personal bodyguard. The pace of his alienation from Bangkok accelerated after Rama I's death in 1809. For some reason Chan refused to attend the cremation, and when two officials who had attended the ceremony showed signs of being pro-Thai, Chan had them executed without trial.

In 1811–1812 conflict broke out inside Cambodia between Thai and Vietnamese expeditionary forces. The Thai supported one of Chan's brothers; the Vietnamese responded to Chan's requests for help. All three of Chan's brothers fled to Bangkok at this time, leaving him free for the rest of his reign to pursue a pro-Vietnamese policy, encouraged by the fact that the Thai now took advantage of him and strengthened their influence in several *sruk* bordering Siam. The campaigns of 1811–1812 were indecisive. Their net effect was to reduce Chan's freedom of action. His growing dependence on the Vietnamese, in fact, was greater than his former allegiance, so reluctantly given, to Bangkok. Twice a month, wearing Vietnamese bureaucratic costumes supplied by Hué, the king and his entourage had to visit a Vietnamese temple near Phnom Penh—where the capital had been moved in 1812—and bow before a tablet bearing the Vietnamese emperor's name. Over the next twenty years, Chan fought with decreasing success to achieve a modicum of independence.

Three events stand out from these early years of loose Vietnamese control. These are the unsuccessful Cambodian attack on the northwestern *sruk* in 1816; the excavation of the Vinh Te Canal in southern Vietnam, using Cambodian labor, around 1820; and the anti-Vietnamese uprising that broke out soon afterward in southeastern Cambodia and in Khmer-populated portions of Vietnam.

The military expedition of 1816 was the last attempt before the 1960s by a formally constituted Cambodian army to take the offensive against foreign troops.

It was a failure. Perhaps to placate the Thai, or merely because the campaign had failed, Vietnamese authorities in Phnom Penh asked Chan to discipline the *okya* who had led the expedition. Taken to Saigon afterward, the official was reprimanded and fined. The sequence of events, although not significant in itself, epitomizes Chan's helplessness in the face of Vietnamese pressure.

The Vinh Te canal, in turn, became a symbol of Vietnamese mistreatment of the Khmer, and the rebellion that followed its excavation revealed the depth of anti-Vietnamese feeling in the *sruk,* the persistence of millenarianism, and perhaps the ambiguities in Chan's subservience to the Vietnamese.[6] In 1817, Vietnamese officials in Saigon recruited several thousand Vietnamese and a thousand Cambodian workers to excavate—or perhaps merely to restore—the Vinh Te Canal, running between the Gulf of Siam and the fortified citadel of Chaudoc, a distance of perhaps 40 kilometers (25 miles). According to a Cambodian chronicle, work on the canal was arduous in the extreme: "Workers were divided into groups. One Vietnamese marched at the head of each group, another at the back, and a third in the middle. The Vietnamese would beat the Cambodians on the back, to make them hurry. . . . Everyone was exhausted, and covered with mud."[7]

This account of the excavations is followed immediately by an account of an anti-Vietnamese rebellion, placed by other sources in 1820–1821. This suggests a causal relationship between the two events, which is reinforced by the fact that the revolt broke out fairly close to the site of the canal. This site was Ba Phnom, the small mountain in southeastern Cambodia that Coedes identified with "Funan" and also with Jayavarman II's arrival in Cambodia from "Java." In the nineteenth century it was an important population center and also a religious site.[8] The Ba Phnom revolt was led by a former monk named Kai, who claimed to be a holy man capable of making predictions. As he gathered allegedly invulnerable supporters around him, he forged a political movement. Moving north and west from the vicinity of Ba Phnom, his followers attacked Vietnamese military posts. A mixed Khmer-Vietnamese force sent against him by Chan failed, one source asserts, because the *okya* in charge of it deserted with their troops and turned on the Vietnamese. A purely Vietnamese force sent from Saigon, however, eventually defeated the rebels near Kompong Cham. The leaders were executed in Saigon, and many of their followers were beheaded in Phnom Penh.

The differences between Cambodian and Vietnamese accounts of the rebellion pose interesting historiographical problems. One has to do with where Chan's loyalties lay. Chan may have known Kai as a monk in Phnom Penh, and in any case the king, whom the Vietnamese were to find "extremely superstitious" toward the end of his reign, would probably not have moved vigorously against a Khmer believed to have supernatural powers. Whatever Chan's views might have been, his response to the movement had to be restricted and discreet. There are parallels here with the situation that faced his nephew, King Norodom, in 1884, when an anti-French rebellion led by *okya* broke out in the countryside while Norodom was under French protection in Phnom Penh. Similar problems confronted his great-grandson, Norodom Sihanouk, in turn, in the 1950s and again in 1970–1975.[9]

It is unclear how large the rebellion was and how much of a threat it posed in military and territorial terms; we know little about its organization and goals beyond the assassination of Vietnamese. Vietnamese records understandably play down the rebellion; the locally oriented *bangsavatar* probably exaggerates its extent, momentum, and success. All the sources agree, however, that it was directed against the Vietnamese rather than against Chan and his *okya* and that monks, former monks, and local officials were active in its ranks.

The chronicle version tended to confirm its audiences' ideas about themselves, the Vietnamese, and history. "All" Vietnamese were cruel, *nak sel* were powerful, and Khmer could not (or at least should not) be made to fight against Khmer. The Buddhist orientation of the text can be seen when we learn that the *nak sel*'s followers were rendered invincible by prayers and amulets but lost this invincibility when they acted contrary to Buddhist law by killing people themselves. Without special powers connected with peace ability, the rebels—including former monks—were slaughtered; and when they died, "Rain fell for seven days. It fell without stopping, night and day. The unimportant and the mighty were forced to run for shelter. In the cold air, everybody shook. There was no way of knowing when the sun set or when it rose. The nation was unhappy."[10]

It would be difficult to overstress the atmosphere of threat, physical danger, and random violence that pervades primary sources like this one, and indeed so much of everyday life in nineteenth-century Cambodia. The sources are filled with references to torture, executions, ambushes, massacres, village burnings, and the forced movement of populations. The wars of the time were localized rather than national in scope, and expeditionary forces, which usually numbered only a few thousand men, were small by twentieth-century standards; at the same time, invaders and defenders destroyed the villages they came to, killed or uprooted anyone they met, and ruined the landscape they moved across. Very few prisoners of war were taken or kept alive. A seventeenth-century Cambodian law, translated by Adhémard Leclère, stated that an expeditionary force needed only three days' supply of food, because unfriendly populations that could be robbed were thought to be never more than three days' march away.[11]

One enigma of this period is Chan himself. We know very little about him except that he was timid. A Vietnamese text from 1822 states that he was ill much of the time and kept inside his palace;[12] the Vietnamese emperor wrote of him in 1834, just before his death, that a "fresh wind or the cry of a bird could make him flee."[13] At the same time, Chan retained considerable freedom of maneuver. All through the 1820s he kept his lines of communication with Bangkok open. Tributary missions went to Bangkok every year, and Chan may have used them to provide intelligence to Thai officials, to sound out Thai policies, and to remain in contact with his brothers.

Relations between the two kingdoms broke down in the late 1820s as a result of Vietnamese support for an anti-Thai rebellion that erupted in 1824–1825 around Vientiane. The breakdown also sprang from the fact that the two rulers in Hué and Bangkok in the 1830s, Rama III and Minh Mang, unlike their fathers, owed nothing to each other and were free to pursue vigorous foreign policies, one of which was to increase influence, and therefore to court conflict, over Cambodia. Minh Mang was also suspicious of the Vietnamese viceroy in Cambodia, Le Van Duyet, whom he believed—correctly, as things turned out—to be associated with breakaway sentiment in southern Vietnam.

The Thai made some tentative military probes into western Cambodia in 1830–1831, but Rama III saw no chance of success until Duyet's death in 1832. When Minh Mang attempted to replace the viceroy's entourage with officials loyal to Hué, his move ignited a full-scale rebellion led by Duyet's adopted son.

News of the revolt quickly reached Rama III, who decided to assemble an expeditionary force. He saw several advantages in doing so. First, he could humiliate Minh Mang, whose forces had been tangentially involved in the Vientiane rebellion and elsewhere in the Thai tributary states of Laos. By establishing a tributary state in southern Vietnam, moreover, Rama III may have been planning to extend Thai and Sino-Thai commercial interests and then to profit directly from trade between Saigon/Cholon and southern China. We know that Chinese merchants in Vietnam had supported the rebellion and had informed their counterparts in Bangkok. Finally, the Thai king may have been impressed by reports reaching him from Cambodia that many *okya* would now welcome the return of Chan's two brothers, Im and Duang (the third had died in Bangkok in 1825). The time was ripe, in the king's own words, "to restore the kingdom of Cambodia and to punish the insolence of Vietnam."[14]

In the short run, the campaign was a success. The Vietnamese quickly abandoned Phnom Penh and took Chan into exile in Vietnam. The Thai commander, Chaophraya (roughly, "Lord") Bodin, then occupied the capital, but soon poor communications with the naval forces attached to the expedition (they were supposed to attack the Vietnamese coast), combined with Vietnamese attacks to force him to withdraw in early 1834. The next few months were disastrous.[15]

The Thai political strategy of placing Im and Duang in power failed, because after such a long absence the two were unable to attract support. One chronicle, in fact, describes people's confusion early in the war, as Bodin's forces entered the kingdom:

> The people were surprised to see such a large army, and they shook with fear. The head of the army shouted at them: "Don't be afraid! His royal highness the king [sic] has arrived to rule over you." The people murmured about this, and sent messengers off to inform the king [i.e., Chan] in Phnom Penh.[16]

In Bodin's retreat from Phnom Penh approximately four thousand local people were carried off. Of these, perhaps a thousand managed to escape as the overburdened Thai column reached Udong. These people then "wandered trembling and afraid in the deep woods."[17] As the Thai columns moved north and west, they disintegrated. At about this time, the rebellion in Saigon was finally suppressed.

THE VIETNAMIZATION OF CAMBODIA, 1835–1840

When Chan returned to his battered, abandoned capital early in 1834, he found himself under more stringent Vietnamese control. Thai successes in their overland offensive had shown Minh Mang that he could not rely on the Khmer to provide a "fence" for his southern and western borders. With the defeat of the rebellion, he now moved to intensify and consolidate his control. To head this *mission civilisatrice* he named the general who had crushed the rebellion in Saigon, Truong Minh Giang.

Giang needed Chan and his officials to provide the Vietnamese with labor, rice, and soldiers. Chan seems to have needed the Vietnamese somewhat less in material terms, but probably counted on them to protect him from assassination and revolt. Like later outsiders operating in Cambodia, Giang probably expected too much from the king and *okya*. Before 1834 was over, he had reported pessimistically to Hué that

> we have tried to punish and reward the Cambodian officials according to their merits and demerits. We have asked the king to help us, but he has hesitated to do so. After studying the situation, we have decided that Cambodian officials only know how to bribe and be bribed. Offices are sold; nobody carrries out orders; everyone works for his own account. When we tried to recruit soldiers, the king was perfectly willing, but the officials concealed great numbers of people. When we wanted to compile a list of meritorious officials, [the officials were willing, but] the king was unwilling, because he was jealous. For the last four months, nothing has been accomplished.[18]

Giang's impatience was understandable for Cambodian politics at the time was characterized by a diffusion of power, a shortage of resources, and a negotiability of position that effectively kept anyone from becoming powerful for very long. That Cambodians should hesitate to accomplish tasks for the Vietnamese struck Giang as insulting, even treacherous, but Minh Mang urged him to do the best he could with the human materials at hand.

Bodin, in the meantime, had settled his forces in the northwest. As the 1830s wore on, the Thai increased their military presence in Battambang and Siem Reap, placing Im and Duang in somewhat ambiguous administrative control, presumably to attract indigenous support against the Vietnamese. This program was matched to the south and east by an intensive program of Vietnamization, which affected many aspects of Cambodian life. The program was set in motion in 1834 and played itself out under the threat of Thai invasions for the rest of the 1830s, the last years of Minh Mang's reign.

An early victim of Vietnamization was Chan himself. Toward the end of 1834, according to the Vietnamese annals, he came under the influence of "magicians" who allegedly encouraged him to accept bribes and "let criminals out of jail."[19] In a sense, the "magicians" were merely asking Chan to act like a traditional king, but their influence distressed Truong

Minh Giang, who had them arrested and shot. For Chan himself, the end of his struggle to stay alive and to provide for himself and his people a modicum of independence had arrived. In early 1835, after a month's illness, he died aboard his royal barge, moored opposite his ruined palace in Phnom Penh. He was forty-four years old and he had reigned, in one way or another, for nearly forty years.

Chan's death posed problems for the Vietnamese, for he had no sons, and his eldest daughter, Princess Baen, was suspected of being pro-Thai. Soon after his death, the *okya* agreed to a Vietnamese suggestion that Chan's second daughter, Princess Mei, be named as queen. To officiate at her investiture, Minh Mang sent a Vietnamese official up from Saigon, and in a hall built specially for the purpose, Mei and her sisters faced north, toward the emperor's letter authorizing her to reign, while the Vietnamese delegate and other officials faced south, as the emperor always did in his palace in Hué.[20]

The ceremony bore no resemblance to a traditional Cambodian coronation, but from the Cambodian's point of view, the queen's ability to grant titles and bestow official seals (as well as to officiate at royal ceremonies) meant that she *was* their queen. To the Vietnamese, who treated her as the ceremonial leader of a segment of Vietnam, these aspects of the question were unimportant when compared to the far-reaching administrative reforms that Truong Minh Giang, at the emperor's request, was now ready to impose. Whereas previously the Vietnamese fort at Phnom Penh had been called Annam, or pacified south, the city itself and the surrounding countryside were now renamed Tran Tay, or western commandery, and Sino-Vietnamese names were given to all of Cambodia's *sruk*. Day-to-day administrative decisions, including personnel postings, salaries, military affairs, and the control of rice surpluses were placed in Vietnamese hands, and some sixteen officials, seventy clerks, and ten schoolmasters were sent to Phnom Penh to form the core of an infrastructure for the administration. Until 1839–1840, however, the administration of the *sruk*—including the all-important matter of labor mobilization—was left to the *okya*, who operated with royal seals, even though their appointments were cleared through the Vietnamese, leading one Vietnamese official to complain in 1839 that "local people collect the taxes that are owed to us, and still rule over one another."

Minh Mang's policy of Vietnamizing Cambodia had several facets. He sought to mobilize and arm the Khmer, to colonize the region with Vietnamese, and to reform the habits of the people. He also tried to standardize patterns of measurement, mobilization, and food supply for military reasons. Control—that is, control of the adult male population and the formation of a standing army, if possible, to resist the Thai—was the essential ingredient of all the Vietnamese programs. Problems of recruitment arose because many of the *okya* were unwilling to relinquish control over their followers. The Vietnamese soon found, in fact, that Cham mercenaries were the only troops they could recruit.

Because ethnic Khmer caused so many problems, Minh Mang sought to colonize the region with Vietnamese. He justified this policy on the grounds that "military convicts and ordinary prisoners, if kept in jail, would prove useless. Therefore, it would be better for them to be sent to Cambodia and live among the people there, who would benefit from their teaching."[21]

Ironically, Vietnamese policies toward Cambodia in the 1830s fore-shadowed the French *mission civilisatrice* that was, during the colonial era, to weaken and dismantle so many Vietnamese as well as Cambodian institutions. In a lengthy memorial to Truong Minh Giang, the emperor outlined his policy:

> The barbarians [in Cambodia] have become my children now, and you should help them, and teach them our customs. . . . I have heard, for example, that the land is plentiful and fertile, and that there are plenty of oxen [for plowing] . . . but the people have no knowledge of [advanced] agriculture, using picks and hoes, rather than oxen. They grow enough rice for two meals a day, but they don't store any surplus. Daily necessities like cloth, silk, ducks and pork are very expensive. . . . Now all these shortcomings stem from the laziness of the Cambodians . . . and my instructions to you are these; teach them to use oxen, teach them to grow more rice, teach them to raise mulberry trees, pigs and ducks. . . . As for language, they should be taught to speak Vietnamese. [Our habits of] dress and table manners must also be followed. If there is any out-dated or barbarous custom that can be simplified, or repressed, then do so.[22]

The emperor closed by advising Giang to move cautiously in engineering social change: "Let the good ideas seep in," he wrote, "turning the barbarians into civilized people."[23] Speed was not essential: "As for winning the hearts of the people, and teaching them, we plan to do this rather slowly."[24] In a subsequent memorial, the emperor recognized that even this slow process might never succeed, because "the customs of the barbarians are so different from our own that even if we were to capture all their territory, it would not be certain we could change them."[25]

There is no record of Vietnamese success in altering Cambodian agricultural techniques, although the need to do so was a recurrent theme in their correspondence of the 1830s. Likewise, Vietnamese efforts to quantify and systematize landholdings, tax payments, and irrigation works came to little. What impressed the Khmer about the Vietnamese, it seems, were their persistent demands for corvée labor and their cultural reforms, which struck at the root of Khmer notions, few of them perhaps verbalized, of their own identity. One of these was the order that Khmer put on trousers instead of skirts and wear their hair long rather than *en brosse.* Other "barbarous" Cambodian customs, according to a Vietnamese writer, included wearing robes without slits up the sides, using loincloths, eating with the fingers, and greeting from a kneeling position rather than from an upright one.[26] The two peoples lived on different sides of a deep cultural divide, perhaps the most sharply defined of those in effect in nineteenth-century Southeast Asia; it was to be savagely exploited in the 1970s, first by Lon Nol and later by Pol Pot and his xenophobic armies.[27]

Within his own ideological framework, however, Minh Mang tried hard to be informed about Cambodia, to be fair to its people, and to improve their way of life. There are several references to rewards given Cambodian officials at his behest for meritorious service. On one occasion, he asked that a history of the country be sent to him, because, among other things, the Khmer "have been a nation for over 1,200 years, but we do not know precisely what year they began, in terms of the Vietnamese and Chinese dynasties that were than reigning."[28] Earlier, the emperor had asked Truong Minh Giang to send him detailed information about Cambodia's

> customs, people, and agricultural produce. I want to know whether the people are prosperous, and whether or not the Cambodian militia has been trained. [I also want to know] if the barbarian people have learned Vietnamese ways, and if they are happy.[29]

In yet another memorial, Minh Mang outlined plans for replacing Cambodian *chaovay sruk* with Vietnamese, beginning with *sruk* close to Phnom Penh. In 1839, he was annoyed to hear that the *okya* continued to use Cambodian rather than Vietnamese official titles:

> At Tran Tay [the emperor said] Cambodian officials have all been given titles from my court. However, I understand that in correspondence and conversation they still use Cambodian titles. . . . The Cambodians should be told that it is an honor to have titles bestowed on them by this court. In conversation, therefore, they should use our titles, rather than theirs.[30]

An obscure sequence of events in 1837 culminated in Duang's arrest by the Thai and his return in chains to Bangkok. The sources suggest that Vietnamese emissaries from Phnom Penh had tried to lure him down to the capital with promises that he would be given the throne. Duang's replies to them were so ambiguous as to convince both the Thai and the Vietnamese that he intended to betray them, using *okya* in the capital region to gather supporters in an effort to regain Chan's somewhat dubious independence.[31]

In the meantime, the growing apprehension of the Vietnamese about Thai mobilization, and the slow progress of their own reforms, led them to tighten their administrative machinery. Sporadic anti-Vietnamese uprisings in 1837–1839 were both a cause and an effect of these reforms. According to the Vietnamese annals, there were four parts to their revised strategy. The most innovative one was to redraw the *sruk* and to replace indigenous *chaovay* throughout the country with Vietnamese. In making selections for these posts (never actually filled, it seems) the Vietnamese ministries were urged to find "about twenty" low-ranking officials, whose educational attainments were less important than their agricultural experience and their talent as military leaders. The second element of the policy was to open more plantations, to train more indigenous soldiers, and to store more rice in an attempt to free the Vietnamese and mercenary garrisons from dependence on southern Vietnam. Third, the Cambodians were to be taught Vietnamese so as to "improve communications." Finally, the Vietnamese were to encourage further colonization of Cambodia by Chinese immigrants and Vietnamese convicts, even though Truong Minh Giang had pointed out the dangers of this policy at great length in a memorial to Minh Mang earlier in the year.

These reforms led the Thai chronicles to refer to Minh Mang's naming the Khmer "new Vietnamese."[32] The Vietnamese saw nothing harmful in this, any more than they did in changing Cambodian weights, measures, fashions, and coiffures. Of the innovations, the one aimed at replacing the *chaovay sruk* probably had the most to do with the rebellion that broke out against the Vietnamese in 1840–1841. It is significant that the *okya,* when attacked in this fashion, could easily rally followers to defend the status quo rather than what might well have been a more equitable and forward-looking Vietnamese administration. There are interesting parallels here, moreover, with the People's Republic of Kampuchea (PRK) administration in the 1980s.[33]

In December 1839 Prince Im, favored by the Thai since Duang's imprisonment, defected to Phnom Penh with several thousand men, mistakenly convinced that the Vietnamese intended to place him on the Cambodian throne. When he reached the capital, he was arrested by Truong Minh Giang and taken off to Saigon and Hué, thus removing from the scene yet another contender for the throne.[34]

One Thai response to these events, when they heard of them in early 1840, was to install a military garrison in Battambang. When Chaophraya Bodin reached the city to investigate Im's defection, he found that of three hundred Cambodians with some sort of official standing in the *sruk,* nearly two hundred had fled. His plans for a full-scale invasion of Cambodia were temporarily postponed because he was uncertain of local agrarian support.[35]

The rebellion against the Vietnamese that broke out at several points in September and October 1840 had reached the planning stage in May. Intermittent uprisings, in fact, had broken out every year since 1836, and deteriorating conditions in Cambodia, as we have seen, had led Minh Mang to tighten his administration. One of his steps was to improve the collection of taxes. Traditionally, these had been collected through the *okya;* however, the amounts of tax, paid in rice and cloth, had never been sufficient to support the Vietnamese. In an 1840 decree, Minh Mang ordered that Cambodia's arable land be remeasured and that records be maintained concerning rainfall, granaries, and irrigation works, so that Vietnamese operations in Cambodia could pay for themselves. He had been making similar demands for six years, he said, but little had been achieved.[36]

In June 1840 Minh Mang brusquely demoted Mei and her two sisters, giving them rather low ranks in the Vietnamese civil service. Following the demotion, the six highest-ranking *okya,* including the *ta-la-ha,* were placed under arrest and taken off to Saigon, accused of falsifying census records and "hiding" some fifteen thousand people otherwise liable for militia duty and corvée.[37] This was done in secret, and their followers assumed that they were dead. Their disappearance was one of the most significant causes of the revolt.

Indeed, the failure of the Vietnamese to impose a workable pattern of administration in Cambodia was connected with their willingness, in the early years at least, to work through the *okya,* whose loyalty to them was intermittent at best and whose operating styles—based on such things as fear, arrogance, patronage, local ties, and loyalties to other officials—were neither sympathetic nor conducive to the format of their kind of administration. Most of the *okya* were happy enough, it seems, to accept rewards occasionally from the Vietnamese. They showed no eagerness to become Confucian civil servants. By working with them, the Vietnamese accomplished few of their objectives, but as Vietnamese measures added up to a policy of laissez-faire, most of the *okya* had no reason to take up arms against them.

When they took over the administration of the *sruk* themselves in 1840, however, the Vietnamese reached the point at which they could impose their will at the same time that their actions perhaps inevitably ignited a revolt. With a Thai invasion imminent, however, and the failure of the *okya* to perceive that Vietnamese economic and military interests in Cambodia overlapped their own, the Vietnamese had little choice, unless they were to abandon Cambodia altogether. Minh Mang's policies failed because he was unable to understand the intransigence or ingratitude of the "barbarians" in the face of paternally administered social change. In a decree to the Cambodian people in 1838, he had stressed the irrationality of this ingratitude:

> Thanks to . . . my generosity, Imperial troops were despatched to Cambodia, costing millions of coins, and brought you security by destroying the Thai. Troops were stationed [among you] to bring peace. This action was like bringing the Cambodian people out of the mud onto a warm feather bed, and was well-known by everyone. . . . Anyone who can think for himself should be grateful to the court; why are there people who hate us and believe the rebels?[38]

The situation became worse in 1840, when wide-ranging rebellion broke out in September and marked the most significant turning point in Cambodia's history between the eighteenth century and the arrival of the French. The uprising, which was centered in the eastern and southern *sruk,* is a rare example in prerevolutionary Cambodia of sustained and coordinated political action; the only others that spring to mind are the anti-French rebellion of 1885–1886 and the so-called 1916 Affair (see Chapters 8 and 9). Smarting under Vietnam's *mission civilisatrice,* the *okya* had discussed the idea of rebellion for several months, in letters known today by their date, addresses, and general contents; the letters themselves do not seem to have survived.[39] What set the rebellion in motion was an interlocking set of provocations by the Vietnamese together with Cambodian expectations of a Thai invasion and Thai support. The uprising collapsed in the early months of 1841, when a new emperor in Vietnam and the hoped-for Thai invasion coincided with Vietnamese military successes and a shortage of supplies among the insurgents. The rest of the early 1840s were filled with seesawing warfare and negotiations between the Thai and the Vietnamese and by a gradual shift in the balance of power in Cambodia in favor of the Thai.

The immediate cause of the rebellion, from the point of view of the *okya,* was a sequence of Vietnamese actions that seemed to the *okya* to be aimed at extinguishing kingship, Buddhism, and the official class in Cambodia. The sequence began, as we have seen, with the demotion of the princesses and the reshuffling of Vietnamese officials in Phnom Penh. In June 1840 Minh Mang had instituted a Vietnamese taxation system in Cambodia. This made new demands on the *okya* by taxing additional products, such as fruit and vegetables, and by calling for a new census, cadastral surveys, and reports on water resources.

Another part of the Vietnamese program in 1840 was to call in Cambodian seals of office in at least some of the *sruk,* replacing them with Vietnamese ones that carried no indication of rank. At least one rural official was dismissed at this time for corruption, and rumors spread among the *okya* that all officials would soon be arrested by the Vietnamese.

The climax came in August, when the Vietnamese arrested Mei and her sisters in Phnom Penh. The women were lured aboard a barge after their immediate entourage had been softened up with liquor and a performance of Vietnamese opera; at this point all of them, according to an eyewitness, "laughed whenever they talked."[40] The princesses were taken secretly to Vietnam, and Cambodia's regalia, which Mei had inherited from her father, accompanied them. At this point the *okya* in Phnom Penh and the *sruk,* with rumors and the Vietnamese record toward Cambodians to rely on, assumed that *Ta-la-ha* Lung, his associates, and the four princesses (all held incommunicado) had been killed, and they thought that they were next.

To many Cambodians, the disappearance of their monarch, however restricted her authority might have been, signified the disappearance of the state. The absence of regalia with which to legitimize someone else made the situation worse. For the *okya,* the disappearance of their high-ranking patrons at court, the reformed tax system, the devaluation of seals of office, and the Vietnamese assault on their freedom of action were precipitants of revolt. Vietnamese "rational" actions, supposedly beneficial to the Khmer, struck at the roots of the identity of the *okya* and at their concepts of society as a whole. Vietnamese contempt for Buddhism and for Cambodia's language, culture, and institutions also hastened the decision of the *okya* to revolt.

The uprising was concentrated at first along the east bank of the Mekong but soon spread to Vietnamese settlements along the coast, like Ream and Kampot, to parts of southern Vietnam inhabited by Khmer, and to fortified villages inland. The news of the princesses' disappearance seems to have triggered the revolt, and the rebels' goal at this stage was the restoration of the status quo ante, personified by Mei and the exiled officials. Another objective, apparently, was the mere killing of Vietnamese. As one rebel wrote, "We are happy killing Vietnamese. We no longer fear them; in all our battles we are mindful of the three jewels [of Buddhism]: the Buddha, the law, and the monastic community."[41]

The Vietnamese were surprised by the level of coordination among the *okya* and blamed it on Thai influences, which Thai sources fail to confirm. They were also baffled by the absence of a single leader. Their estimate of rebel strength ran to thirty thousand men, operating throughout the kingdom, in "hundreds of" small bands, and occasionally larger ones, usually in territory familiar to them and commanded by people they could trust. The formidable problems of counterguerrilla warfare were summed up in one Vietnamese report in 1841:

The rebels have established posts along the river banks at strategic points. They appear and disappear at will. If our troops look to the east, the rebels escape to the west. . . . They concentrate their forces where the jungle is thick, and in swampy areas where our troops cannot manoeuver. Other regions have tall grass at eye-level and are very hot and dusty. One can march all day without finding potable water. Moreover, we have no intelligence about the enemy, and no guides.[42]

The Vietnamese also had problems moving troops and supplies against the swift river currents prevalent at that time of year, and the report adds that "not even one" rebel had surrendered, despite the "tolerant" policies of the Vietnamese court and even though the record is full of references to the Khmer fleeing like "rats and mice," or attacking like "swarms of mosquitoes." At the start of the rebellion, Minh Mang (who was to die following an accident at the beginning of 1841) thought that an adequate application of force, combined with rewards to loyal troops and local officials, would be enough to put down the rebellion, which angered him, he wrote, so much that his "hair stood on end."[43] He ordered *Ta-la-ha* Lung and others to write letters asking their relatives and clients in Cambodia to surrender, thus misreading Cambodian loyalty to unavailable and devalued patrons, and he also approved sending "monks and magicians" into Phnom Penh to undermine morale. In the last months of his reign, he demanded weekly reports from the front and suggested that Cambodian crops and orchards be burned down as a preemptive measure. "The Cambodians are so stupid," he declared, "that we must frighten them. Ordinary moral suasion has no effect."[44]

It is impossible to say what Minh Mang would have done had he survived the next seven years, but it is clear that the rebellion had begun to lose momentum before his death and also that his successor, Thieu Tri, was less committed than he had been to a victory in Cambodia.[45] The new emperor began his reign looking for a solution that would be acceptable to his court and to the Cambodians, if not necessarily to the Thai; at one stage, he brushed aside a suggestion that he negotiate directly with the Thai as being "wrong and foolish." Distance, distrust, and the momentum of the war, however, as well as the ambiguity of Thieu Tri's objectives in Cambodia, kept the conflict going until 1847, increasingly involving the Vietnamese and the Thai, rather than the Khmer, as combatants.

Despite Vietnamese reports to the contrary, Cambodian troops were often poorly supplied. At the end of 1840, a rebel *okya* complained to the Thai that "we are unable to continue fighting the Vietnamese. We lack the troops to do so, the rifles, the ammunition, and the supplies. For weapons we have only knives, cross-bows and clubs; we cannot continue to fight."[46] The shortage of manpower was confirmed by another official, who wrote that "in former times, Cambodian armies were large; nowadays, men are always lacking." In this light, and in view of Chaophraya Bodin's estimate of rebel strength as ten thousand men, the Vietnamese figure of thirty thousand seems inflated. Of course, even ten thousand men, motivated by resentment, fear, and xenophobia as the Cambodians were, would have been sufficient to terrorize and massacre Vietnamese garrisons in Cambodia and to weaken Vietnamese administrative control.

THE RESTORATION OF CAMBODIAN INDEPENDENCE

As the Vietnamese court and its officials in Cambodia sought a solution to what they saw as an internal Vietnamese problem, Chaophraya Bodin's expeditionary force, numbering some thirty-five thousand men, assembled near Battambang and then attacked the Vietnamese garrison at Pursat. After defeating the Vietnamese garrison there, Bodin prepared to attack the capital but hesitated because he was short of supplies and lacked confidence in his troops. Instead he withdrew to Battambang, where he sought to consolidate his political position. During the siege of Pursat, eighteen rebellious *okya* had sent identical letters to him pleading for Thai support and for Duang's return from Bangkok.[47] In them, the *okya* pledged allegiance to Rama III, complained about shortages of supplies, and asserted that Cambodians would be happy only if the political conditions of the early nineteenth century, before the Vietnamese had arrived, were reestablished.

Bodin transmitted the letter to Bangkok and added his own recommendation for Duang's return to some kind of political power. In January 1841 Duang reached Battambang, accompanied by Thai and Cambodian advisers and carrying elaborate gifts for his supporters, including insignia of rank and royal accoutrements, if not actual regalia, provided for him by Rama III.[48] According to one source, Bodin had urged Duang's release because "if there are no superior people to look after a population, the common people have no security."[49] The records also suggest that Bodin's motives included winning over the *okya* (he was eager that local Khmer, rather than his own inexperienced troops, should engage the Vietnamese) by promising them that Duang would rule over Cambodia. In fact, for the rest of the 1840s, Duang was to be closely watched and manipulated by Bodin. Duang's return to Cambodia and Rama III's solicitude for him opened an era in Thai-Cambodian relations that lasted until French intervention in 1863.

While Duang was conferring with potential courtiers and Bodin (to whom Vietnamese sources refer as a "Siamese tribal chief," or *xiem muc*) was complaining that the newcomers were consuming Thai supplies, Thieu Tri was attempting to understand and control Vietnamese policy toward Cambodia, with a view to thwarting a Thai invasion, pacifying rebellious provinces of southern Vietnam, and maintaining Vietnamese prestige. In late 1841, Truong Minh Giang attempted to bring Prince Im back into power, but edicts issued in his name attracted no support. It was at this point, perhaps, that Truong Minh Giang realized that he had almost no chance of restoring a favorable political balance in Cambodia. He withdrew to Vietnam, taking Im, the princesses, and the population of the city, numbering some six thousand people, with him. When he arrived in Vietnam, he sent a letter to Hué, taking the blame for "losing" Cambodia, to which he referred as the emperor's "rightful property." He then took poison and died.[50]

The Vietnamese loss did not mean that the Thai had in any sense succeeded, and by 1843 for Chaophraya Bodin, as for Giang, Cambodia had become a quagmire. As Bodin wrote Bangkok: "We have been in Cambodia for three years without accomplishing anything. We are short of supplies; people are going off into the forest to live on leaves and roots; and nearly a thousand men in our army have died from lack of food."[51] In 1844, in fact, he had to abandon Phnom Penh, where the Vietnamese soon reinstalled Princess Mei as Cambodia's "legitimate queen" while Thai forces congregated near Udong. The Vietnamese maneuver infuriated Bodin, who saw that many *okya* might now be unwilling to support the Thai. He complained to Bangkok that "all the Khmer leaders and nobles, all the district chiefs and all the common people are ignorant, stupid, foolish and gullible. They have no idea what is true and what is false."[52]

In spite of these difficulties, Vietnamese attempts to dislodge the Thai forces around Udong throughout 1845 were fruitless; by the end of the year, Thai and Vietnamese leaders had opened negotiations for a cease-fire. The talks moved forward, for they were grounded in Thieu Tri's willingness to abandon his military positions in Cambodia and, by implication, his father's policies there. They moved slowly, however, in a context of military stalemate, even though in political terms conditions were favorable to the Thai. In Prince Duang they had a seasoned, popular ruler, loyal to Bangkok and able to work through a well-established network of loyal officials in the *sruk*. But the Vietnamese still occupied a strong bargaining position, particularly as they retained Cambodia's regalia, without which Duang could not legitimately ascend the throne.

In a face-saving gesture, they demanded that a tributary mission headed by a Cambodian official travel to Hué in March 1846 and declare Cambodia's *pro forma* subservience to Vietnam.[53] When the embassy returned to Phnom Penh in June 1847, the Vietnamese handed over the Cambodian regalia and released several members of the royal family who had been in their custody, in some cases for many years. Soon afterward, they withdrew their forces from Cambodia; for the first time since 1811, there were no Vietnamese officials on Cambodian soil.

Over the next few months, in a series of ceremonial gestures, Duang reenacted the restoration of Thai-sponsored kingship that had been eclipsed for so many years. It would be a mistake to dismiss these ceremonial actions as mere protocol, because Duang, like most traditional Southeast Asian rulers, probably did not disentangle what we would call the religious and political strands of his thinking, duties, and behavior. Kingly behavior, in other words, was thought to have political results, and political actions were thought to enhance or diminish his fund of merit.[54]

Many of these ceremonies, in fact, had to do with the restoration of Theravada Buddhism as the state religion. One account relates that Duang

levelled the [Vietnamese] fortifications at Phnom Penh, and hauled away the bricks to build and restore . . . [seven] Buddhist monasteries near Udong. Broken Buddha-images were recast, and new ones were carved. Monks were encouraged to live in monasteries again, and people were encouraged to respect them.[55]

To his subjects, Duang's return to Cambodia and the restoration of Buddhism there were ex post facto proofs of his kingliness, legitimacy, and merit. An inscription from 1851 describes the electric effect of this restoration ten years before:

In that year, there was a mighty ruler, whose name was Duang. He came from the royal city [Bangkok] to Cambodia, and lived in the fortified city of Udong. With merit, skill, and masterly intelligence, the king scattered his enemies in terror; and soon the three warring states were friends again.[56]

On an auspicious day in April 1848, Duang was anointed by Thai and Cambodian brahmans in Udong and ascended the throne. He was fifty-two years old. His reign, which lasted twelve years, can be seen as a Cambodian renaissance. For most of these years, the kingdom was at peace; and although Thai political advisers and some Thai troops lingered at Udong, Duang was relatively free to make political decisions, such as those connected with awarding titles to *okya*. The chronicles of his reign place much emphasis on its restorative aspects. A wide range of institutions and relationships was involved. The chronicle points to linguistic reforms, public works, sumptuary laws, and new sets of royal titles. From other sources, we know that Duang was an accomplished poet and presided over the promulgation of a new law code and the compilation of new chronicle histories.[57]

Chroniclers in both the 1880s and the 1930s, looking back to those few years of Cambodian independence prior to French control, may have considered Duang's reign to be a kind of golden age. The king himself seems to have been cautious after so many years of semicaptivity in Bangkok. His relations with Rama III and Rama IV (King Mongkut) were extremely subservient, as his letters to these monarchs show.[58] He seems to have made no attempt to improve relations with Vietnam in the hope of gaining some freedom of maneuver, perhaps because he was frightened by the precedent of the 1830s and because from the Vietnamese point of view any improvement in relations would only have intensified his dependency on them. Instead, in 1853 he appears to have somewhat clumsily sought French protection by sending gifts and offering his "humble homage" to the emperor of France, Napoleon III, via the French consulate in Singapore. Duang was probably put up to this by French missionaries who were active near Udong. His gifts included four elephant tusks, two rhinoceros horns, and sizable quantities of sugar and white pepper. A French diplomatic mission to his court, bearing a draft treaty of friendship (see Chapter 8) was not allowed to proceed to Udong by the Thai, who had swiftly brought their client monarch to heel.

Duang seems to have sought French help not so much to escape Thai protection, which would have been impossible to manage, as to defend himself against the Vietnamese. In letters to the French, he referred to them, as Pol Pot was to do in the 1970s, as Cambodia's "traditional enemies." Ironically, as we shall see, in the 1860s France took over Vietnam's patronage of Cambodia and eliminated Vietnamese influence. After his attempt to make friends with France had failed, Duang explained himself to a French missionary, saying, "What would you have me do? I have two masters who always have an eye fixed on me. They are my neighbors, and France is far away."[59] Clearly, many conditions had to change before Cambodia could emerge from this dual dependency, which had lasted with brief interludes for more than fifty years.

CHAPTER 8

The Early Stages of the French Protectorate

There are several ways of looking at the years of French hegemony over Cambodia. One is to break them into phases and to trace the extension and decline of French control. Another would be to examine the period and its ideology and practice—political, economic, educational, and so forth—from a French point of view; and a third would be to treat the period as part of Cambodian history, connected to the times before and after French control.

The French are gone, and the third perspective now seems the most attractive. Although there are serious gaps in the sources and useful primary material in Cambodian, aside from royal chronicles, is very scarce, in this chapter I will attempt to see the French as often as possible through Cambodian eyes.

In the meantime, if we look at the colonial era in terms of the waxing and waning of *French* control (the first of the three perspectives), the years break fairly easily into phases. The first phase lasted from the establishment of the protectorate in 1863 to the outbreak of a national rebellion (supported, clandestinely, by the Cambodian king) in 1884. The second phase would extend from the suppression of the rebellion in 1886 to King Norodom's death in 1904, when a more cooperative monarch, Norodom's half-brother, Sisowath, came to the throne. The third phase lasted until Norodom Sihanouk's coronation in 1941 and spans the reigns of Sisowath (r. 1904–1927) and his eldest son, Monivong (r. 1927–1941). This period, it can be argued, was the only systematically *colonial* one in Cambodian history, for in the remainder of the colonial era (1941–1953) the French were concerned more with holding on than with systematizing their control.

From a Cambodian perspective, however, it is possible to take the view that the colonial era falls into two periods rather than four, with the break occurring at Sisowath's coronation in 1906. From that point on, Cambodians stopped governing themselves and the westernization of Cambodian life intensified every year. What would have been recognizable in a *sruk* in 1904 to a Cambodian official of the 1840s had been modified sharply by 1920, when French government, particularly at the local level, had been organized as part of a total effort in Indochina.

But until the late 1940s, I suspect, few Cambodians would have seen these somewhat mechanical changes, and indeed the French presence as a whole, as having a deleterious effect on their lives or on their durable institutions of subsistence farming, Buddhism, and kingship. The political stability that characterized most of the colonial era can be traced partly to French patronage of the king and the king's patronage of the *sangha,* which tended to keep these two institutions aligned—politically, at least—with French objectives; partly because kings, monks, and officials had no tradition of innovation; and partly because popular methods of questioning their authority—heresy and rebellion—had been effectively smothered by the French since the 1880s. In terms of economic transformations, the significant developments that occurred in the technology of rice farming tended to be limited to the northwestern part of the kingdom, where huge rice plantations had come into being. In the rest of the country, as Jean Delvert has shown, the expanding population tended to cultivate rice in small, family-oriented plots.[1]

Because of this stability, perhaps, the French in many of their writings tended to romanticize and favor the Cambodians at the expense of the Vietnamese. At the same time, because in their terms so little was going on, they tended to look down on the Cambodians as excessively "lazy" or "obedient." An ambiguous and not very thoughtful romanticism suffuses a great many French-language sources composed in the colonial era, especially in the twentieth century, when clichés about the people were passed along like heirlooms from one official (or one issue of a newspaper) to the next. At the same time, until the early 1940s, no Cambodian-language sources questioned the efficacy of French rule or Cambodia's traditional institutions.

For these reasons, it is tempting to join some French authors and skip over an era when "nothing happened." To do so would be a mistake, because what was happening, especially after the economic boom of the 1920s, was that independent, prerevolutionary Cambodia (with all its shortcomings, intellectual and material) was being built or foreshadowed in spite of large areas of life that remained, these French writers would say, part of the "timeless" and "mysterious" Cambodia of Angkor.

It is tempting also to divide French behavior in Cambodia into such categories as "political," "economic," and "social." The terms give the false impression that they are separable segments of reality, but in fact what the French meant by them in the context of the colonial situation tended to be idiosyncratic. "Politics," for example, meant dissidence and manipulation rather than participation in a political process. Ideally, in a colony there should be no *politics* at all. "Economics" meant budgets, taxes, and revenues—in other words, the economics of bureaucratic control. On the rare occasions when French writers looked at Cambodia's economy as a whole, they related it to the rest of Indochina, particularly in terms of export crops and colonial initiatives, like public works, rather than to Cambodian needs and capabilities. By the 1920s, in the eyes of French officials, Cambodia had become a sort of rice-making machine, producing revenue as well in exchange for "guidance." This meant that the essence of government—*rajakar,* or royal work—remained what it had always been, the extraction of revenue from the peasants. As for "social" the word as the French used it did not refer to solidarity among people, or relationships that added up to political cohesion. Instead, "society" meant a conglomeration of families, obediently at work.

The chronological perspective and the analytical ones just dealt with may be helpful in looking at the period 1863–1953; looking at these years in terms of *Cambodian* history means looking at them in terms of continuity and change. From this angle, the alterations to Cambodian society and the thinking of the Cambodian elite are as important as the apparently timeless life in the villages, which was also changing after all.

THE ESTABLISHMENT OF THE FRENCH PROTECTORATE

The beginnings of French involvement in Cambodia are to be found in the eighteenth century, when missionaries from time to time took up residence in the kingdom, especially in the vicinity of Udong. Involvement did not become political, however, before the late 1850s, coincidentally with French involvement in Vietnam. In the mid-1850s King Duang had sought French support in an attempt to play off the Thai against the Vietnamese, but a French diplomatic mission to Cambodia in 1856, armed with a draft treaty of cooperation, failed to reach the Cambodian court, which was frightened away from welcoming it by Thai political advisers. The draft treaty, incidentally, contained several clauses that passed into the operative one concluded in 1863: The French wanted teak for ship-building, for example, freedom to move about the country, and freedom to proselytize for the Roman Catholic faith.[2]

French interest in Cambodia deepened with its involvement in Vietnam and also after a French naturalist, Henri Mouhot (1829–1867), visited

Duang's court and then proceeded to Siem Reap, where he "discovered" the ruins of Angkor. Mouhot suggested in a book about his travels that Cambodia was exceptionally rich and that its rulers were neglecting their patrimony.[3] Duang's openness to Mouhot and to other European visitors in this period stemmed in part from his friendship with a French missionary, Monseigneur Jean Claude Miche, whose mission headquarters was located near Udong and who had actively supported the 1856 diplomatic mission. Miche convinced the king that there could be advantages in being free from Thai control and Vietnamese threats. In the last two years of his reign, moreover, Duang saw French expansion into Vietnam as an opportunity for him to regain territory that Cambodia had lost to the Vietnamese over the preceding two hundred years.[4]

Bogged down in guerrilla warfare in Vietnam, and unsure of support from Paris, the French administrators in Saigon were slow to respond to Cambodia's assertions of friendship. The matter lapsed when Duang died in 1860 and Cambodia was plunged into a series of civil wars. Duang's designated heir, Norodom, was unpopular in the eastern *sruk* and among Cham dissidents, who had almost captured Udong while Duang was alive. Norodom had spent much of his youth as a hostage at the Thai court. Unable to rule, he fled Cambodia in 1861, returning with Thai support at the end of the following year. But he returned on a probationary basis, for his regalia remained in Bangkok. Angered by Thai interference, and attracted by French promises of gifts, Norodom reopened negotiations with the French. According to a contemporary, the French admiral in charge of southern Vietnam, "having no immediate war to fight, looked for a peaceful conquest, and began dreaming about Cambodia."[5]

The colonial era began without a shot and in a very tentative way. A delegation of French naval officers concluded a treaty with Norodom in Udong in August 1863, offering him protection at the hands of a French resident in exchange for timber concessions and mineral exploration rights. Norodom managed to keep the treaty secret from his Thai advisers for several months. When they found out about it and notified Bangkok, he quickly reasserted his dependence on the Thai king, declaring to his advisers that "I desire to remain [the Thai king's] servant, for his glory, until the end of my life. No change ever occurs in my heart." The Thai, in turn, kept Norodom's change of heart a secret from the French, who learned of it only after his earlier declaration of faith had been ratified in Paris in early 1864.[6]

What Norodom wanted from the French vis-à-vis the Thai is unclear. He seems to have been playing for time, and the method he chose resembled that of his uncle, King Chan, with the French in the role of the Vietnamese. He wanted to be crowned, and by the middle of 1864, the Thai and the French had agreed to cosponsor his coronation. The unintentionally comical aspects of the ceremony are recounted by several French sources. Thai and French officials quarreled about precedent, protocol, and regalia, while Norodom, using time-honored filial imagery, proclaimed his dependence on both courts. For the last time, the Cambodian king's titles were chosen and transmitted by Bangkok; for the last time, too, the Cambodian king claimed to draw legitimacy from two foreign courts. For the first time, a Cambodian king accepted his crown from a European. The next three Cambodian monarchs followed suit. From this point on, Thai influence in Cambodia began to wane, fading even more sharply and more or less for good after King Mongkut's death in 1867.[7]

The imposition of French protection over Cambodia did not end the dynastic and millenarian rebellions that had plagued the earlier years of Norodom's reign, although French military forces were helpful in quelling these rebellions by 1867. The most important of these was led by Pou Kombo, an ex-monk who claimed that he had a better right than Norodom to be king. A year before, Norodom had shifted his palace to Phnom Penh. He had been urged to do so by the French, just as Chan had been encouraged to move by the Vietnamese earlier in the century, and for similar tactical reasons. In the French case, commercial motives were also at work, for Phnom Penh was more accessible from Saigon than an inland capital would have been, and the exploration of the Mekong River under Commandant E. Doudart de Lagrée (1823–1868) hoped to bring back data about the river's northern reaches that would justify French pipe dreams of Phnom Penh as an important commercial city.[8]

For the French, the 1860s and 1870s were a heroic period. This was partly because government remained in the hands of young naval officers hungry for glory, eager for promotion, and entranced by the exotic setting in which they found themselves. By and large, these pioneers of colonialism—men like Doudart de Lagrée, Francis Garnier, Jean Moura, and Etienne Aymonier—possessed great energy, sympathy for the Cambodians, and intellectual integrity. They explored the Mekong, translated Cambodian chronicles, deciphered inscriptions, and arranged for the shipment of tons of Cambodian sculpture to museums in Paris, Saigon, and eventually Phnom Penh. The grandeur of their exploits and of Cambodia's distant past formed a sharp contrast in their minds with the "decay" of the Cambodian court and the "helplessness" of the Cambodian people.

And yet there was probably little difference between the way Cambodia was governed in the 1860s and the way Angkor had been governed almost a thousand years before. In both cases, perhaps, and certainly for most of Cambodia's dark ages, government meant a network of status relationships whereby peasants paid in rice, forest products, or labor to support their officials. The officials, in turn, paid the king, using some of the rice, forest products, and peasant labor with which they had been paid. The number of peasants one could exploit in this way depended on the position one was granted by the throne; positions themselves were for sale, and this tended to limit office-holders to members of the elite with enough money or goods on hand to purchase their positions.

In the nineteenth century, as we have seen, the destabilization of rural society pummeled the infrastructure of these arrangements, but they persisted into the colonial era. The king's personal demands on the system were now—in the colonial era—taken care of increasingly by French and Chinese entrepreneurs, who frequently tempted him into unwise investments.

THE TIGHTENING OF FRENCH CONTROL

Within the palace, Norodom governed in what the French considered to be an arbitrary, authoritarian way. The French, however, offered him no alternative style, and throughout his reign, Norodom was drawn less by the idea of a sound administration than by the imperatives of personal survival. Revolts against his rule (and implicitly against his acquiescence to the French) broke out in 1866 and in the 1870s. Both attracted considerable support, and both were put down with difficulty by the French. Unwilling to blame themselves for this state of affairs, the French blamed Norodom and were increasingly drawn to support his half-brother, Sisowath, who had led troops alongside the French in both rebellions.

Under French pressure, while another half-brother, Siwotha, was in revolt against him, Norodom agreed in 1877 to promulgate a series of reforms. Although these were never carried out, they are worth noting as precursors of more extensive French control and as indications of areas of French concern. The reforms sought to dismantle royal involvement in land ownership, to reduce the number of *okya,* to rationalize tax collection, and to abolish slavery. Had they been enacted, they would have worn away the power bases of the Cambodian elite. What the French disliked, as Minh Mang had in the 1830s, was the Cambodian way of doing things, which interfered with their ideas of rational, centralized control. Institutions like slavery and absolute monarchy, moreover, went down poorly with officials of the Third Republic, less charmed by the romantic operetta aspects of Cambodia than Napoleon III and his entourage had been.

In the early 1880s, as the French tightened their grip on Vietnam, it was only a matter of time before they solved Cambodia's "problems" and imposed their will on the Cambodian court. The comedy in Phnom Penh had gone on too long and cost too much. The Cambodians had not seen the importance of paying for French protection. The French became impatient and assumed for this reason that time was running out. The "riches" of Cambodia remained untapped. What had seemed exotic and quaint in Cambodian society in the 1860s and 1870s was now seen by a new generation of officials as oppressive; it was time for protection to become control.

In early 1884 the French succeeded in getting Norodom to agree to siphon off customs duties, especially on exports, to pay for French administrative costs. Norodom sent a cable to the president of France protesting against French pressure and was chided for doing so by the governor-general of Cochin China, Charles Thomson, who had been negotiating secretly with Sisowath to arrange a transfer of power should Norodom prove resistant to the reforms.[9]

The blow fell in June 1884, when Thomson sailed from Saigon to Phnom Penh and confronted Norodom with a wide-ranging set of reforms encased in a treaty that went much farther than previous documents to establish de jure French control. Thomson arrived at the palace with the treaty, traveling aboard a gunboat that was anchored within sight. As Norodom reviewed the document, Thomson's armed bodyguards stood nearby. Aided by a complaisant interpreter, Son Diep, who rose to bureaucratic heights after Norodom's death, the king signed it because he saw that doing so was the only way to stay on the throne; he undoubtedly knew of Sisowath's machinations. Perhaps he thought that the document's provisions would dissolve when the French encountered opposition to them among the Cambodian elite. This is, in fact, what happened almost at once, but Article 2 of the treaty nevertheless marked a substantial change in the style and intensity of French control: "His Majesty the King of Cambodia [it read] accepts all the administrative, judicial, financial and commercial reforms which the French government shall judge, in future, useful to make their protectorate successful."[10]

It was not this provision, however, that enraged the Cambodian elite, who by this time probably saw Norodom as a French puppet in any case. The features that they saw as revolutionary (and that the French saw as crucial to their program of reforms) were those that placed French *résidents* in provincial cities, abolished "slavery," and institutionalized the ownership of land. These provisions, of course, struck at the heart of traditional Cambodian politics, which were built up out of entourages, exploitation of labor, and the taxation of harvests (rather than land) for the benefit of the elite, who were now to become paid civil servants of the French, administering rather than "consuming" the people under their control.

Although few French officials had troubled themselves with studying the nuances of slavery in Cambodia, and although their motives for abolishing it may have included a cynical attempt to disarm political

opposition in France to their other reforms, it is clear that the deinsti-
tutionalization of servitude was a more crucial reform, in Cambodian
terms, than the placement of a few French officials in the countryside
to oversee the more numerous Cambodian elite. Without this reform, the
French could not claim to be acting on behalf of ordinary people, and
more important, they could do nothing to curb the power of the elite,
which sprang from control over personnel. Without abolishing slavery,
moreover, the French could not proceed with their vision—however
misguided it may have been—of a liberated Cambodian yeomanry responding rationally to market pressures.

By cutting the ties that bound masters and servants—or more precisely,
by saying that this was what they *hoped* to do—the French were able
to justify their interference at every level of Cambodian life. Their proposal
effectively cut the king off from his entourage, and this entourage, in
turn, from its followers. What the French wanted to administer in Cambodia
was, in fact, an extension of Vietnam, with communal officials responding
directly to the French, even though government of this sort and at this
level was foreign to Cambodia, where no communal traditions—had they
ever existed—had survived into the nineteenth century.

In the short run, the Cambodian reaction to the treaty was intense
and costly to the French. In early 1885, a nationwide rebellion, under
several leaders, broke out at various points.[11] It lasted a year and a half,
tying down some four thousand French and Vietnamese troops at a time
when French resources were stretched thin elsewhere in Indochina. Unwilling
to work through Norodom, whom they suspected of supporting the
rebellion, the French relied increasingly on Sisowath, allowing him a free
hand in appointing pro-French officials in the *sruk* and thereby further
undermining Norodom's authority. It seems likely that Sisowath expected
to be rewarded with the throne while Norodom was still alive, but as the
revolt wore on, the French found that they had to turn back to Norodom
to pacify the rebels. In July 1886 the king proclaimed that if the rebels
laid down their arms, the French would continue to respect Cambodian
customs and laws—in other words, the mixture as before. The rebellion
taught the French to be cautious, but their goals remained the same,
namely, the rationalization of Cambodian government and control over
the economy of the kingdom. It was at this stage that the French began
to surround Norodom with Cambodian advisers who were loyal to them
rather than to the throne. These were drawn, in large part, from the
small corps of interpreters trained under the French in the 1870s; the
most notable of them, a Sino-Khmer named Tiounn, was to play an
important role in Cambodian politics for more than fifty years.

The issue at stake in the rebellion, as Norodom's chronicle points out,
was that the "Cambodian people [were] fond of their own leaders,"

especially because alternatives to them were so uncertain. A French writer in the 1930s blamed the French for their hastiness in trying to impose "equality, property, and [an] electorate,"[12] for Cambodians were supposed to choose their own village leaders under an article of the treaty. He added aphoristically that in fact "the masters wanted to keep their slaves and the slaves their masters"; people clung to the status quo.

Faced with the possibility of a drawn-out war, the French stepped back from their proposed reforms, and although the treaty was ratified in 1886, most of its provisions did not come into effect for nearly twenty years, after Norodom was dead.

At the same time, it would be wrong to exaggerate the Cambodian "victory," or to agree with some recent Cambodian writers who have seen the rebellion as a watershed of Cambodian nationalism, with Norodom cast as a courageous patriot cleverly opposing French control. The evidence for these assertions is ambiguous. Norodom, after all, accepted French protection in a general way but attacked it when he thought his own interests—especially financial ones—were at stake. There is little evidence that he viewed his people as anything other than objects to consume. Certainly the French distrusted him more after 1886; they spent the rest of his reign reducing his privileges and independence. But it would be incorrect to endow the rebellious *okya* with systematic ideas about the Cambodian nation (as opposed to particular, personal relationships).

With hindsight, we can perceive two important lessons of the rebellion. One was that the regional elite, despite French intervention in Cambodia, was still able to organize sizable and efficient guerrilla forces, as it had done against the Thai in 1834 and the Vietnamese in 1841; it was to do so again in the more peaceable "1916 Affair," discussed in Chapter 9. The second lesson was that guerrilla troops, especially when supported by much of the population, could hold a colonial army at bay.

The next ten years of Norodom's reign saw an inexorable increase in French control, with policies changing "from [ones] of sentiment . . . to a more egotistic, more personal policy of colonial expansion."[13] All that stood in the way of French expansion was the fact that Norodom still made the laws, appointed the officials, and controlled the national economy by farming out sources of revenue (such as the opium monopoly and gambling concessions), by demanding gifts from his officials, and by refusing to pay his bills. By 1892, however, the collection of direct taxes had come under French control; two years later, there were ten French *résidences* in the *sruk*. The 1890s, in fact, saw increasing French consolidation throughout Indochina, culminating in the governor-generalship of Paul Doumer (1897–1902).

In Cambodia, this consolidation involved tinkering with fiscal procedures and favoring Sisowath rather than any of Norodom's children as the successor to the throne. French officials were eager for Norodom to relinquish control but were frightened by the independent-mindedness of many of his sons, one of whom was exiled to Algeria in 1893 for anticolonial agitation. The king's health was poor in any case and was made worse by his addiction to opium, which the French provided him, in ornamental boxes, free of charge. As French officials grew more impatient with Norodom, and as he weakened, they became abusive. After all, there were fortunes to be made by *colons* in Cambodia, or so they thought, and Norodom barred the way. The climax came in 1897, when the *résident supérieur,* Huynh de Verneville, cabled Paris that the king was incapable of ruling the country; de Verneville asked to be granted executive authority instead. Paris concurred; the *résident* was now free to issue royal decrees, appoint officials, and collect indirect taxes. As Milton Osborne has pointed out, high-ranking Cambodian officials, previously dependent on Norodom's approval, were quick to sense a shift in the balance of power.[14] By the end of the year, the king's advice—even though he had now regained his seals, and de Verneville had been dismissed—was heeded only as a matter of form; the new *résident supérieur* was in command, answerable to authorities in Saigon, Paris, and Hanoi.

In the meantime, long-postponed royal decrees—such as one allowing French citizens to purchase land—had produced a real estate boom in Phnom Penh. The effect of the reforms in the *sruk,* as far as we can tell, was less far-reaching. Throughout the 1890s, French *résidents* complained officially about torpor, corruption, and timidity among local officials, although one of them, sensing the tune he was now expected to play, reported to his French superiors that "the population of all the villages in my province is happy; [the people] have not even the slightest complaint about the measures that have been taken."[15] The Cambodian countryside, however, as many French officials complained, remained a *terra incognita.* No one knew how many people it contained, what they thought, or even who held titles to land. Although slavery was abolished, servitude for debts—often lasting a lifetime—remained widespread. Millenarian leaders occasionally gathered followers and led them into revolt; gangs of bandits roamed the countryside at will. At the village level, in fact, conditions were hardly more secure than they had ever been.

And yet high-ranking French officials still saw their role in the country in terms of a "civilizing mission" and of rationalizing their relationships with the court. In the countryside, ironically, Sisowath was more popular than Norodom, partly because the people had seen him more often, on ceremonial occasions, and partly because Norodom's rule had been so rapacious and unjust. Sisowath, in fact, looked on approvingly at developments in the 1890s, for by 1897 or so he had been formally promised the throne by French officials.

Norodom took seven more years to die. The last years of his reign were marked by a scandal involving his favorite son, Prince Yukanthor, who sought to publicize French injustice in Cambodia when he was in France by hiring a French journalist to press his case with French officialdom. Officials paid slight attention, except to take offense. Yukanthor's accusations were largely true, if perhaps too zealous and wide-ranging, as when he declared to the people of France, "You have created property [in Cambodia]; and thus you have created the poor."[16]

Officials in Paris persuaded Norodom by cable to demand an apology from his son. It never came, for Yukanthor preferred to remain in exile. He died in Bangkok in 1934 and until then was viewed by French colonial officials with slight, but unjustified, apprehension.

The two last prerogatives that Norodom surrendered to the French were the authority to select his close advisers and the right to farm out gambling concessions to Chinese businessmen in Phnom Penh. Little by little, the French encroached on his freedom of action. Osborne has recorded the battles that Norodom lost; but the last pages of the royal chronicle (compiled during the reign of Sisowath's son, King Monivong, in 1934) say almost nothing about the confrontation, leaving the impression that the reign was moving peacefully toward its close.

SISOWATH'S EARLY YEARS

Norodom, like millions of people of his generation, was born in a village and died in a semimodern city, graced at the time of his death with electricity and running water. The modernization of the edges and surfaces of his kingdom, however, spread very slowly, partly because communications inside Cambodia remained so poor; partly because monks, royalty, and officials—i.e., the people held in most respect—resisted institutional change; and partly because the "modernizing" segment of the society was dominated by the French, aided by immigrants from China and Vietnam. The "modernizers," interestingly, thought in Indochinese terms, or perhaps in capitalist ones, while members of the traditional elite saw no reason to widen their intellectual horizons or to tinker with their beliefs.

Norodom's death, nonetheless, was a watershed in French involvement and in Cambodian kingship as an institution. The next three kings of the country were hand-picked by the French. Until 1953, except for a few months in the summer of 1945, Cambodian officials of high rank played a subordinate, ceremonial role, while those at lower levels of the administration were underpaid servants of a colonial power. At no point in the chain of command was initiative rewarded. While Norodom lived, the French encountered obstacles to their plans. After 1904, with some exceptions, Cambodia became a relatively efficient revenue-producing machine.

The change over the long term, easy to see from our perspective, was not immediately perceptible in the *sruk,* where French officials found old habits of patronage, dependence, violence, fatalism, and corruption largely unchanged from year to year. Offices were still for sale, tax rolls were falsified, rice harvests underestimated. Credulous people were still ready to follow sorcerers and mountebanks. As late as 1925, in Stung Treng, an ex-monk gathered a following by claiming to possess a "golden frog with a human voice";[17] banditry was widespread; and there were frequently famines and epidemics of malaria and cholera.

The contrast between the capital and the *sruk,* therefore, sharpened in the early twentieth century, without apparently producing audible resentment in the *sruk,* even though peasants in the long run paid with their labor and their rice for all the improvements in Phnom Penh and for the high salaries enjoyed by French officials, fueling the resentment of anti-French guerrillas in the early 1950s and Communist cadres in the independence era.

When Sisowath succeeded his brother in 1904, he was sixty-four years old. Ever since the 1870s he had been an almost fawning collaborator with the French. He seems to have been a somewhat more fervent Buddhist than Norodom and more popular among ordinary people, some of whom associated him with the ceremonies that he had sponsored (and that they had paid for) rather than the taxes charged by his brother or by the French. According to one French writer, he was so frightened of his brother, even in death, that he refused to attend his cremation. The first two years of his reign, according to the chronicle, were devoted largely to ceremonial observances and to bureaucratic innovations (such as appointing an electrician for the palace and enjoining officials to wear stockings and shoes in Western style).[18] On another occasion, Sisowath harangued visiting officials—probably at French insistence—about the persistence of slavery in the *sruk;*[19] throughout the year, like all Cambodian kings, he sponsored ceremonies meant to assure good harvests and rainfall. Each year, for the rest of his reign, the French provided Sisowath (as they had Norodom) with an allowance of high-grade opium, totaling 113 kilograms (249 pounds) per year.[20]

This early stage of his reign culminated in Norodom's cremation in 1906, which was followed almost immediately by Sisowath's coronation. For the first time in Cambodian history, the ceremony is described in detail in the chronicle (as well as by French sources). It lasted for several days. One of its interesting features was that the French governor-general of Indochina was entrusted with giving Sisowath his titles and handing him his regalia; another was that *chaovay sruk,* summoned to the palace for the occasion, solemnly pledged to the king "all rice lands, vegetable fields, water, earth, forest and mountains, and the sacred boundaries of the great city, the kingdom of Kampuchea."[21]

Almost immediately after being crowned, Sisowath left Cambodia to visit the Colonial Exhibition at Marseilles, in the company of the royal ballet troupe.[22] His voyage is scrupulously recorded in the chronicle, which makes it sound like an episode in a Cambodian poem. The king's progress through Singapore, Ceylon, and the Indian Ocean is reverently set down, and so are gnomic comments about the sights farther on (three-story buildings in Italy; the coastline of the Red Sea consisting of "nothing but sand and rock"). At Port Said, people eagerly came to pay homage to "the lord of life, and master of lives in the south." In Marseilles, when the king made a speech, "All the French people who were present clapped their hands—men and women alike." The chronicle gives the impression that the king *decided* to visit France; in fact, his visit was forced on him by the requirement of the exposition officials that the royal ballet perform.[23] From the French point of view, unofficially at least, this visit by an aged potentate and his harem told them what they already "knew" about his exotic, faintly comic little country.[24]

After exchanging visits and dinners with the president of the Republic, and a trip to Nancy to observe "the 14th of July in a European way," the king returned to Cambodia. Although the chronicle makes no mention of discussion of substantive matters, Sisowath's visit to Paris coincided with Franco-Thai negotiations there that culminated, a few months later, in Siam's retrocession to Cambodia of the *sruk* of Battambang and Siem Reap.[25] The trip received little publicity at home and is mentioned in French reports from the *sruk* only in connection with a rumor that Sisowath had gone to France to plead with the French to legalize gambling in Cambodia.

The number of pages in Sisowath's chronicle devoted to the return of Battambang and Siem Reap suggests that the compilers, like the French, considered this to be the most important event of the reign, even though the king had little to do with it beyond providing the *résident supérieur,* in 1906, with a "history" of Thai occupation. The importance of the retrocession was probably connected with the importance that Angkor, and especially Angkor Wat, retained for the Cambodian monarchy through-out Cambodia's dark ages.[26] In 1909 a copy of the Cambodian translation of sacred Buddhist writings, the *Tripitaka,* was deposited in a monastery on the grounds of Angkor Wat; and for another sixty years Cambodian monarchs frequently visited the site and sponsored religious ceremonies there.

The retrocession apparently was less painful to the Thai than the loss of the Lao states, which occurred at roughly the same time. As we have seen, the northwestern *sruk* had come under Thai control in 1794 in exchange for Thai permission for Eng to rule at Udong. Over the next hundred years, except for a brief period in the 1830s, the Thai had made little effort to colonize (or depopulate) the region, choosing to govern it at most levels with ethnic Khmer. Although they did nothing to restore the temples at Angkor, they left them intact; revenue from the two *sruk*—in stipulated amounts of cardamom and other forest products—was not especially high; and the region was more defensible by water from Phnom Penh than overland from Bangkok.[27]

For these reasons, but primarily to avoid further friction along its border, the Thai decided in 1906 to cede the *sruk* to France. King Chulalongkorn's foreign affairs adviser, an American named Stoebel, supported the move and persuaded the Thai king to approve it. The final agreement was signed by the French and the Thai in April 1907, and the *sruk* came under French control toward the end of the year. Sisowath was not encouraged to visit the area, however, until 1909, for reasons that the chronicle fails to make clear.

And yet the king and his subjects were overjoyed at the restoration of Angkor. In the *tang tok* ceremonies of October 1907, when officials traditionally offered gifts to the monarch, widely attended celebrations occurred throughout the kingdom to "thank the angels" (*thevoda*) for the return of the *sruk,* and local officials assigned to the region came to Phnom Penh to pay homage to the king.

Over the next half century, French scholars and Cambodian workers restored the temples at Angkor. In the long run, this was probably France's most valuable legacy to Cambodia. Battambang, especially in the 1920s, developed into the country's most prosperous *sruk,* providing the bulk of Cambodia's rice exports and sheltering, idiosyncratically, by far the greatest number of landlords in the country, as well as the highest number of immigrants from elsewhere in Cambodia and from the Cambodian-speaking portions of Cochin China.[28]

By 1909, typewriters had been installed in all the *résidences;* automobiles came into use on a national scale at about the same time. These two "improvements" in French administration had several unintentional effects. For one thing, the volume of reports required by *résidents,* and consumed by their superiors in Phnom Penh, Saigon, Hanoi, and Paris, increased dramatically. *Résidents,* more than ever, were tied down to their offices, presiding over a two-way flow of paper; they were seldom in contact, socially or professionally, with the people they were intended to protect.

In automobiles, tours of inspection became speedier and more superficial, for *résidents* and their aides were confined to passable roads. In fact, the intensification of French economic and political controls over Cambodia, noticeable throughout the 1920s and after, was accompanied, ironically, by the withdrawal of French officials from many levels of Cambodian life. The "government" that a Cambodian peasant might encounter in these years was composed of a minority of Cambodians and of a great many Vietnamese, brought into the protectorate because they could prepare reports in French. This interplay between Cambodians and Vietnamese had important effects on the development of Cambodian nationalism, especially after World War II.

CHAPTER 9

Cambodia's Response to France, 1916–1945

Two events of major political importance stand out from the last ten years or so of Sisowath's reign. These are the so-called 1916 Affair and the murder of a French *résident,* Félix Louis Bardez, in rural Kompong Chhnang in 1925. The first of these revealed how little the French knew about communications and social organization in Cambodia after more than fifty years of control. The second, perhaps because it was the only incident of its kind in the colonial era, shocked the regime and was blown out of proportion in postcolonial times by Cambodian nationalist writers and speech-makers.

THE 1916 AFFAIR

To understand the 1916 Affair, we must remember that the French financed almost all of their activities in Cambodia, including public works and the salaries of French officials, by a complex and onerous network of taxes on salt, alcohol, and opium, on rice and other crops, and on exported and imported goods and by levying extensive fees for all government services. Of those too poor to pay their way out, the French could require ninety days per year of corvée, but people who paid their way out were still liable in many cases to other labor requirements. The cash to pay rice-taxes came only when peasant householders had sold their harvests for cash or had been able to earn enough cash to pay the taxes by hiring themselves out in the off-season. There was a certain amount of flexibility in the system, because tax records were poorly kept and local leaders tended to underestimate the number of people they controlled in order to spread the tax burden more evenly through the population and, incidentally, to increase their opportunities for profit.

During World War I, the French increased this burden throughout Indochina by floating war loans to which local people, especially "the leisure classes" (presumably Chinese merchants), were rather forcefully urged to subscribe; by levying additional taxes; and by recruiting volunteers for military service abroad.

In late November 1915, some three hundred peasants from the area northeast of Phnom Penh arrived in the capital with a petition to Sisowath, asking him to reduce taxes, which, although levied by the French, were collected by Cambodian officials. The king met the delegation and ordered its members to go home, promising vaguely that some adjustments would be made.[1]

News of the confrontation apparently spread in the *sruk* to the east of Phnom Penh—long a hotbed of antidynastic sentiment in any case— and larger and larger delegations, sometimes numbering as many as three thousand peasants, began walking into the capital and assembling outside the palace to place their grievances before the king. French *résidents,* reporting on these movements, registered their surprise not only at the magnitude of the delegations, but also, as one wrote, that they had "been set in motion with such disconcerting speed." Another mentioned that "no one had predicted" the affair, although "the entire population was involved." French police estimated that some forty thousand peasants passed through Phnom Penh in the early months of 1916 before being ordered back to their villages by the king. Other estimates run as high as a hundred thousand. Scattered incidents in the *sruk* later in the year claimed half a dozen Cambodian lives, and at the same time Sisowath toured the eastern *sruk* by automobile, exhorting peasants to remain peacefully in their homes and canceling any further corvée for 1916.

In the long run, the 1916 Affair had little effect on the way the French ran Cambodia or on Cambodian responses to the French. In fact, it is unclear that the demonstrations were against the French at all; French administrators were sidestepped by the petitioners, who sought justice directly from the king. What is extraordinary about the demonstrations is the speed and efficiency with which they were organized by leaders whose identity and motives remain obscure. The incident undermined French mythology about "lazy" and "individualistic" Cambodians, supposedly impervious to leadership or ideology. Some French officials, panicked by the size of the delegations, blamed the affair on "German agents"; still others saw evidence of deep-seated antimonarchic feeling, citing in evidence a manifesto that had circulated earlier in 1915, which stated: "The French have made us very unhappy for many years by keeping bad people as the king and as officials while treating good people as bad."[2]

Hanuman, the sacred monkey, to the rescue aboard a steam engine, Wat Damrei So, Battambang (early twentieth century). Photo by Jacques Nepote.

Interestingly, the 1916 Affair coincided with serious anti-French demonstrations in Cochin China. The possibility of links between the two was noted by some French officials, but the speed with which Cambodian disaffection died down suggests that people there had been demonstrating to relieve local wrongs.

In the nine years that passed before the assassination of *résident* Bardez, the French so tightened and rationalized their control over Cambodia—and especially over the organization of revenue collection and day-to-day administration—that some "aged" Cambodian officials complained to them that "too many changes" were taking place. In 1920, for example, the French arranged for rice taxes to be collected by local officials rather than by officials sent to the *sruk* from Phnom Penh. A year later, the French experimented with a "communal" reorganization of Cambodia along Vietnamese lines, only to drop it after a year or so. The French extended their supervisory role to cover local justice in 1923; expanded *wat* education from 1924 onwards; and used corvée labor to build an impressive array of public works, particularly roads and a mountain resort at Bokor, favored by the king, which was built by prisoners (with a tremendous loss of life) and opened in 1925. The first rice mills had opened in Cambodia in 1917—previously, unmilled rice had been shipped to Saigon—and the period 1916–1925 (with the noticeable exception of 1918–1919, a year of very poor harvests and, in some *sruk,* famine conditions) was one of increasing prosperity in Cambodia, especially for the French.[3]

The gap in income between the French and the Cambodians—with the rare exceptions of a few favored officials and the royal family—was very wide. A French official could earn as much as 12,000 piastres a year; with exemptions for his wife and two children, such an official would pay only 30 piastres in tax. Cambodian officials were paid less for similar jobs and were the first to have their wages cut during the depression of the 1930s. A Cambodian farmer, on the other hand, with no salary other than what he could earn (at 30 cents per day, or 90 piastres a year) or what he could sell his crops for (seldom more than 40 piastres a year), was saddled with a range of taxes that totaled in the 1920s as much as 12 piastres per year. He was taxed individually and in cash payment in lieu of corvée; his rice was taxed at a fixed percentage; he paid high prices for salt, opium, and alcohol and paid abattoir taxes when his livestock went to slaughter.

What did the peasant receive in exchange? Very little, despite French rhetoric to the contrary. Monthly reports from French *résidents* show widespread rural violence and disorder, which, because it made no direct challenge to French control, seldom rose into the "political" portions of the reports. It is clear, however, that to most villagers the perpetual harassment of bandit gangs, especially in the dry season, was far more real than any benefits brought to them by the French.[4]

Before the 1930s, moreover, the French spent almost nothing on education. A French official in 1922 accurately characterized efforts in this field as a mere façade; medical services were derisory; electricity and running water were also almost unknown outside Phnom Penh. Cambodia's money, in other words, went to finance French officials and the things they wanted to build. In exchange, Cambodia was protected from control by anyone else, as well as from the perils of independence. The French succeeded in keeping the nineteenth century from repeating itself while keeping the twentieth century at bay. A royal ordinance of 1918, for example, prohibited monks "from teaching reforms or . . . from spreading among the faithful modern ideas which conflict with traditional religion." This fear of "modernity" runs through a good deal of French writing about colonial Cambodia, even though the French in another context perceived their role as one of transmitting modernity to the Khmer. Because what they were supposed to be doing was not allowed to take place, the French took refuge in beliefs about the "innate" characteristics of the Cambodians, which kept them immune from modern ideas or inherently hostile to them.

These beliefs were based on less and less direct experience with the Cambodians themselves. The most articulate critic of French colonialism at this time, A. Pannetier, remarked that competence among Frenchmen in the Khmer language declined steadily as the twentieth century wore on.[5] Ironically, as the adventure and romance of serving in Cambodia wore thin, the clichés with which French bureaucrats described the Cambodian people became increasingly fuzzy and romantic. The process came to a climax of sorts in 1927, when former Governor-General Paul Doumer, by then president of France, unveiled a group of statues on the staircase that links the railroad station in Marseilles with the city below. One of these, entitled "Our Possessions in Asia," depicts a half-naked teenaged girl, decked out in approximately Angkorean garb, lying on a divan being waited on by smaller, half-clad girls representing Laos and Vietnam. As the "easiest" and oldest of French protectorates in Indochina, Cambodia was rewarded in the statue by being portrayed as the oldest child and as receiving tribute of a kind from the other two. The notion that Cambodians lay around receiving tidbits, of course, may also have been at the back of the sculptor's mind.[6]

THE ASSASSINATION OF *RÉSIDENT* BARDEZ

In late 1923, the acting French *résident* in Prey Veng, a vigorous and ambitious official named Bardez, reported his belief that there were three reasons why tax receipts were so low: "the complete inactivity of Cambodian officials, the lack of supervision [over the officers expected to collect the taxes], and shortcomings in collection procedures."[7] In the course of 1924, Bardez improved the procedures for tax collection in the *sruk* to the extent that all eighteen categories of tax yielded more revenues than in 1923. He showed that the system could be made more productive by working harder himself. Indeed, the two categories of tax in which revenues rose the most—rice taxes and Chinese head taxes—were precisely those that could be increased by a vigorous *résident* on the spot, eager to expose the compromises, doctored books, and exaggerations of local officials.

Bardez's success in Prey Veng attracted the attention of his superiors, and in late 1924 he was transferred ahead of many more senior officials to be *résident* in Kompong Chhnang, long bedeviled by banditry and low tax revenues. Bardez's arrival coincided roughly with the promulgation of a supplementary tax to pay for the mountain resort of Bokor, but money was hard to come by, as Bardez admitted to a friend, and receipts were slow in coming. One Cambodian official trying to collect them was severely beaten by villagers in early 1925.

On April 18, angered by reports that another village, Krang Laav, was delinquent in its payments, Bardez visited the village himself, accompanied by an interpreter and a Cambodian militiaman.[8] Summoning delinquent taxpayers to the village hall, or *sala,* he had several of them handcuffed and threatened to take them to prison, even though they would not be subject to fines for their delinquency for three months. His refusal to let the prisoners have lunch while he was eating himself destroyed the patience of the large crowd of people looking on, who lacked food or shelter. In a confused melee, Bardez and his companions were set upon by twenty to thirty people. Within half an hour, Bardez, the interpreter, and the militiaman had been beaten to death with chairs, fence palings, ax handles, and the militiaman's rifle butt. The corpses were then mutilated, and according to some witnesses, the murderers danced around them. Soon afterward, incited by local leaders who were never brought to trial, seven hundred Cambodians—the crowd that had gathered to listen to Bardez—began marching on Kompong Chhnang to demand remission of their taxes. After a few hours, however, their fervor died down, and the marchers broke up or were dispersed by armed militia before they reached their destination.

The news of Bardez's murder shocked the French community in Phnom Penh, largely because it was the first case in which villagers had killed a high-ranking French official on duty; other officials had been killed by bandits or by their servants, but none while collecting taxes. The precedent obviously was a dramatic one. Moving swiftly through their puppets in the royal family, the French saw to it that Sisowath sent his eldest son, Prince Monivong, to the area with a French political counselor to communicate his discontent. This took the form of a royal ordinance changing the name of the village from Krang Laav to Direchan ("Bestiality").[9] The ordinance forced the villagers to conduct expiatory services for Bardez on the anniversary of his murder for the next ten years. The most interesting feature of the ordinance was its insistence on collective guilt. This was the line pursued by the defense in the trial of the eighteen men arrested for Bardez's murder, but it was dismissed by the prosecution, which saw danger in linking the murder with any kind of political discontent. Interestingly, one of the men arrested for the murder was still alive in 1980, when he told an interviewer that "everyone in the village" had beaten Bardez and his companions.[10]

The trial of the men accused of the murders opened in Phnom Penh in December 1925 and was widely reported in the press, in which it was fitted into a pattern of increasing anticolonial feeling elsewhere in Indochina. At the trial, the prosecution tried to prove that the defendants were "pirates" from outside the village and that robbery had been their motive. In fact, although the taxes collected by Bardez disappeared in the melee, his own billfold was untouched. More to the point, his diary was confiscated by the prosecution and classified as confidential because of the "political" material it contained. Testimony by several of Bardez's friends suggested that the diary may have recorded his pessimism about collecting any extra taxes; to one of them, he had remarked shortly before his death that there was simply not enough money in the *sruk* to meet the newly imposed demands. High-ranking French officials interfered with witnesses for the defense; at one point, the defense attorney's tea was apparently poisoned by unknown hands, and a stenographer hired by the defense was forced by her former employers to return to her job in Saigon. What the French wanted to keep quiet, it seems, was the fact that emerged at the trial, namely, that on a per capita basis the Cambodian peasants paid the highest taxes in Indochina as a price for their "docility."

The Bardez incident resembles the 1916 Affair and the 1942 monks' demonstration, discussed below, in that nothing like it had happened in the colonial era. It exposed the mechanics of colonial rule and the unreality of French mythology about the peaceable "Cambodian character." One aspect of the widening distance between the French and the Cambodians was the fact that Bardez, after fifteen years of conscientious service in Cambodia, was still incapable of speaking Khmer. Without knowing the language, how accurate could his assessments be of what ordinary people were thinking? It is as if a great deal of Cambodian life in the colonial period was carried out behind a screen, invisible and inaudible to the French. Another French *résident,* writing at about this time, made a perceptive comment in this regard: "It's permissible to ask if the unvarying calm which the [Cambodian] people continue to exhibit is not merely an external appearance, covering up vague, *unexpressed feelings* [emphasis added] . . . whose exact nature we cannot perceive."[11]

Résidents would reply to this by saying that they were paid to administer the population, not to understand it. Every month, they were required to complete mountains of paperwork, to sit for days as referees in long, often inconclusive legal cases, and to supervise the extensive programs of public works—primarily roads—which the French used to perpetuate corvée and to justify their presence in the kingdom.

COLONIAL RULE AND THE
BEGINNINGS OF NATIONALISM

The Bardez incident also offers us a glimpse of Cambodian peasants entering the historical record. Before 1927, in fact, there were no Khmer-language newspapers or journals in the kingdom. Cambodian literature, when it was printed at all, consisted almost entirely of Buddhist texts and nineteenth-century verse epics. The first novel in Khmer, *Tonle Sap*, was published in 1938, two years after the appearance of the first Khmer newspaper, *Nagara Vatta* [Angkor Wat].[12] Although these statistics are not especially surprising in view of French inactivity in Cambodian education, they contrast sharply with the quantity of printed material produced in the Vietnamese components of Indochina. Literacy in Cambodia had been linked since Angkorean times with the study and promulgation of religious texts. In the colonial era, literacy in Khmer was almost entirely in the hands of the Buddhist monkhood. Before 1936, in fact, the only Khmer-language periodical, *Kambuja Surya* [Cambodian sun] had been published on a monthly basis under the auspices of the French-funded Institut Bouddhique. With rare exceptions, the journal limited itself to printing folklore, Buddhist texts, and material concerned with the royal family. Even Cambodian chronicle histories in Khmer were not yet available in print.[13]

Because of these conditions, the picture that emerges from the 1930s is a peculiarly unbalanced one. The reading of French novels, official reports, and newspapers allows us to reconstruct Cambodian history with much of the population left out or merely acted upon by events. The manuscript chronicles of King Sisowath and his son, King Sisowath Monivong (r. 1927–1941) are not especially helpful, for they limit themselves to the formulaic narration of events in which the king himself was involved, although Monivong's chronicle "opens up" a little to cover such events as the 1932 coup d'état in Siam, the Italo-Ethiopian war, and the French surrender to Germany in 1940. The requirements of the genre have removed individual voices from the texts; even the kings are rarely quoted.[14] Because archival sources from the *sruk* themselves for the colonial era are not available for study, it is difficult to gauge the style and extent of social change and intellectual upheaval, the extent to which they can be traced to French initiatives, and Cambodian responses to them in the period before World War II. Arguably, change in Cambodia did not filter into the villages until the 1950s; and yet the face of Cambodia was already very different in the 1930s from what it had been when the French arrived, or even at the beginning of the century.

Overland communications had changed dramatically. From 1900 to 1930, some 9,000 kilometers (5,400 miles) of paved and graveled roads had been built by corvée labor throughout the kingdom. Between 1928 and 1932, moreover, a 500-kilometer (300-mile) stretch of railroad was built between Phnom Penh and Battambang; it was later extended to the Thai border. These changes meant that thousands of rural Cambodians were now able to move rapidly about the country by bus; visits to Phnom Penh and district capitals became easier and more frequent. These developments also favored French penetration and Chinese exploitation of the rural economy. The commercial development of Cambodia—especially in terms of rice exports and rubber plantations—benefited primarily the French and the Chinese entrepreneurs, who monopolized the export trade. In fact, as W. E. Willmott has shown, Chinese immigration into Cambodia, which remained steady at around two thousand a year until the 1920s, rose to five thousand a year during the boom years.[15] The Chinese population of the kingdom rose accordingly—from perhaps one hundred seventy thousand in 1905 to three hundred thousand at the beginning of World War II. Almost invariably, these immigrants went into petty commerce, already dominated by Chinese and Sino-Cambodians. Because many Vietnamese immigrants to Cambodia, aside from those recruited to work in the rubber plantations, also preferred urban employment, cities in Cambodia, as so often in colonial Southeast Asia, were enclaves dominated by foreign bureaucrats and entrepreneurs. This fact was not lost on the Cambodian elite, but the elite was unable or unwilling to do much about it.

And the elite itself, although relatively small, was gradually increasing in importance. An interesting coincidence occurred in 1930. As the first stretch of track on the railroad went into service, the first Cambodian students—including two princes and four men destined to be ministers in the 1940s and 1950s—graduated from a French lycée in Saigon. Cambodia had to wait until 1936 for a lycée of its own, named after Sisowath and occupying the site of his former palace. Primary education, for the most part, remained in the hands of the *sangha,* and the French sponsored, at very little cost, a network of some five thousand extant *wat* schools, in which students learned traditional subjects in time-honored ways.[16]

These developments were played out against the economic boom that affected most of Indochina in the 1920s. In Cambodia, the greatest beneficiaries were the firms engaged in the export of rice and in the newly opened rubber plantations near Kompong Cham. The rubber plantations, staffed largely by Vietnamese, had little economic impact on the Cambodian countryside, but rice production rose sharply to meet international demands, and new funds generated by the widening tax base were diverted into even more extensive public works, including the beautification of Phnom Penh, the electrification of provincial towns, the road-building mentioned above, and the construction of seaside resorts and mountain hotels, which benefited the French and the embryonic tourist industry. The Bardez incident, in other words, barely ruffled the surface of French complacency.

The world depression of the 1930s, however, reversed or suspended many of these trends, as the local price of rice plummeted from 3 piastres to 1 piastre a *picul* (about 68 kilograms, or 150 pounds). The Cambodian peasants' reaction, as it can be gauged from *résidents'* reports, was to reduce rice hectarage (which dropped by a third throughout the country from 1928 to 1933), to seek postponement or remission of taxes, and to find solace, in some areas, in millenarian religious cults, such as the recently inaugurated syncretic cult of Cao Dai in neighboring Cochin China.[17]

The period was marked by several uprisings against the French in the Vietnamese components of Indochina, but Cambodia remained quiet; in their reports French *résidents* frequently complimented the Cambodian peasants for the "stoicism" with which they continued to react to the highest and most variegated tax burden in Indochina; one of them traced this obedience to Cambodians' "reverence for authority." Nonetheless, the level of rural violence—with Khmer victimizing Khmer—appears to have risen slightly, only to decline when the economic crisis faded in the mid-1930s. Tax delinquency in rural areas reached 45 percent in 1931 and more than 60 percent in the following year, when remissions were granted by the *résident supérieur.* As Cambodia reverted to subsistence farming, Phnom Penh's population, unsurprisingly, rose only slightly— from 96,000 in 1931 to barely 100,000 in 1936. Throughout this period, and indeed until the 1970s, the capital was informally divided into three residential zones, with Vietnamese and Cham to the north, Chinese and French in the commercial center, and Cambodians to the south and west of the royal palace, which faced the Mekong River.

In an effort to increase tax revenue, in 1931 the French encouraged King Monivong to tour the *sruk,* where he admonished audiences supplied by local officials on the virtues of frugality and hard work. The king himself continued to live well, and his grandson, Norodom Sihanouk, later recalled that Monivong spent very little of his time attending to official business, preferring the company of his numerous wives and concubines.[18] One of these, it seems, was an elder sister of Saloth Sar, who was to emerge in the 1970s as Pol Pot, the secretary of the Cambodian Communist party. In the midst of the depression, new palace buildings were built for Monivong by the French. In 1931 he entertained the French minister of colonies, Paul Reynaud, who had come to Indochina to investigate the aftermath of the Vietnamese uprisings of the previous year. In Cambodia, the visit was entirely ceremonial and stage-managed by the powerful Cambodian official, Tiounn, who by now held the portfolios of finance, palace affairs, and fine arts. He had governed the country under the French since the beginning of Sisowath's reign. Several of his descendents were to become prominent members of the Cambodian Communist party.

When the economy of Indochina recovered slowly in the mid-1930s, rice exports, particularly from Battambang, reached 100,000 metric tons a year, and new crops—especially maize—were grown in large quantities for export. Administratively, the last part of the decade saw increased Cambodian participation in administration, especially in the *sruk,* where many who became officials of independent Cambodia—including Nhek Tioulong, Lon Nol, and Pho Proeung—were beginning their careers. In political terms, the French were pleased to notice that disturbances in Cochin China, arising in part from conflicts between Trotskyite and Communist supporters of the Popular Front government in France, aroused no echoes in Cambodia, whose late but well-mannered "awakening" was the subject of a tendentious French brochure published on the occasion of a governor-general's visit in 1935.[19] By "awakening," the French referred to economic advances and administrative participation by the Khmer rather than to any increased awareness of the colonial situation. The roots of postwar Cambodian nationalism, nonetheless, can be found in the 1930s, at first in a cooperative and well-mannered guise, while the French were looking for the sorts of "revolutionary" politics they had encountered in Vietnam. Confidential French political reports throughout the decade registered "none" under the obligatory rubric "revolutionary activities"; and latter-day Cambodian historians, looking for the roots of the Cambodian Communist movement, cannot find them in this period, supposedly the heyday of the Communist party of Indochina.[20]

And yet an awakening of a sort was taking place, primarily among the newly formed Cambodian elite in Phnom Penh, and especially among those educated at the kingdom's first high school, the Collège (and after

1936, the Lycée) Sisowath. Earlier in the decade, students at the college had appealed to the king against the favoritism allegedly shown to students of Vietnamese extraction. By 1937, an association of graduates had more than five hundred members.

This association was the first of its kind in Cambodia, where voluntary associations along professional lines had always been slow to develop and had in any case been discouraged by the French. For years, the French had lamented the Cambodian aversion to solidarity, while opposing any Cambodian attempts—by veterans of World War I, for example, or by adherents of the Cao Dai—to form associations. The fear of solidarity, in fact, appears to have dominated the French reaction to the Bardez affair, as we have seen. For administrative purposes, the French preferred to deal with a society that was, theoretically at least, arranged vertically rather than horizontally. A similarly bureaucratic turn of mind, perhaps, made many French officials suspicious of new developments in the countryside—whether they were sponsored by Protestant missionaries, the Cao Dai, or any other external agent—while doing little themselves to change the status quo of widespread poverty, poor health, and no modern education.

The three key channels for Cambodian self-awareness in the 1930s, in fact, were the Lycée Sisowath, the Institut Bouddhique, and the newspaper *Nagara Vatta,* founded in 1936 by Pach Chhoeun and Sim Var; both men, in their thirties, were soon joined by a young Cambodian judge, born in Vietnam and educated in France, named Son Ngoc Thanh.[21] The three, in turn, were closely associated with the Institut Bouddhique, to which Son Ngoc Thanh was later assigned as a librarian. This brought them into contact with the leaders of the Cambodian *sangha,* with Cambodian intellectuals, and also with a small group of French scholars and officials, led by the secretary of the Institut, Suzanne Karpelès, who were eager to help with Cambodia's intellectual renaissance.

The editorial stand of *Nagara Vatta* was pro-Cambodian without, for the moment, being anti-French. It objected to Vietnamese domination of the Cambodian civil service, Chinese domination of commerce, and the shortage of suitable employment for educated Khmer. Editorials also condemned the usury of Chinese rural merchants, French delays in modernizing the educational system, the shortage of credit for Cambodian farmers, and the low pay of Cambodian civil servants. More important, the paper sought to increase the distance between Cambodian history and aspirations on the one hand and those of the Vietnamese on the other. One editorial even went so far as to compare Hitler's territorial aggrandizement in Europe to that of Vietnam in nineteenth-century Cambodia. A thread of anti-Vietnamese feeling gradually emerged in the paper. It was to run through the ideology of every Cambodian government after independence until the Vietnamese invasion of 1978–1979.

But in terms of its own historical context, what was important about *Nagara Vatta* was that for the first time since 1863 a conversation had opened up between the French and their allegedly "dormant" clientele as well as among the Cambodian elite. The paper's circulation, as early as 1937, rose to more than five thousand copies per issue, and readership was undoubtedly far higher.

Who were its readers? Who were the new elite? Primarily, they seem to have been young Cambodian men in the lower ranks of the civil service, educated at least partially in the French educational system. Undoubtedly, they were concentrated in Phnom Penh. In his memoirs of this period, Bunchhan Muul, by that time a high official in the Khmer Republic, stated that the paper saw as its mission the awakening of the Cambodian people—an image that persisted after World War II, when Son Ngoc Thanh returned from exile and founded another nationalist paper entitled *Khmer Krok,* [Cambodians awake!]. The paper was important because it gave thousands of Cambodians a chance for the first time to read about events in the outside world in their own language.

Nevertheless, the emerging Cambodian elite, defined in terms of educational qualifications, was very small. By 1939, the number of *bacheliers* graduated from the Lycée Sisowath was barely half a dozen and perhaps a dozen Cambodians had been trained in tertiary institutions abroad. The gap between political awareness and technical proficiency, which persisted into the postcolonial period, can be blamed initially on French inertia in the field of indigenous education, itself traceable to French unwillingness to pay the bills.

Before the fall of France in the summer of 1940, none of the officials in Indochina had openly voiced doubts about the permanence of the French presence in Asia. There were no moves in Cambodia, for example, to widen the electorate, to introduce representative government on anything other than a consultative basis, or to train Cambodians to replace Frenchmen in the administration. In the *sruk,* however, some devolution took place in the 1930s whereby experienced and senior local officials, rather than Frenchmen, were allowed to prepare local budgets and write periodic reports.[22] The sense of irony of French officials, it seems, was not highly developed; in 1939, elaborate ceremonies were sponsored in Phnom Penh to honor the hundred-and-fiftieth anniversary of the French Revolution; the venue was the Place de la République.[23]

THE IMPACT OF WORLD WAR II

World War II—or, more precisely, the period between June 1940 and October 1945—must be seen as a watershed in the history of Indochina. This is particularly true of Vietnam, but French policies in Cambodia, springing from weakness, and Cambodian responses to them differed sharply from what had gone before. By the end of 1945, Cambodian independence, impracticable and almost unthought of in 1939, had become primarily a matter of time.

Much the same state of affairs applied throughout Southeast Asia, and particularly in Burma and the Dutch East Indies (now Indonesia): the development of nationalism in Indochina differed in that France was the only colonial power in the region to retain day-to-day control of its possessions for the greater part of World War II. The French managed to do so by making substantial concessions to the Japanese and by not declaring war on them. Elsewhere in Southeast Asia, between 1942 and 1945, the Japanese jailed colonial officials and ruled through local leaders, usually recruited from the ranks of opponents of colonial rule. In Indochina, on the other hand, the French sought to defuse nationalist thinking and activity by maintaining secret police surveillance, by opening up their administration to local people, and by liberalizing some of their policies. In the Cambodian case, it can be argued that this liberalization, and several events associated with it, gave birth to elite Cambodian nationalism in the form it assumed until the 1970s.[24]

Five events in this period are worth examining in detail: the Franco-Siamese war of 1940–1941; the coronation of Monivong's grandson, Norodom Sihanouk, in 1941; the so-called monks' demonstration of July 1942; the romanization crisis of the following year; and finally, the Japanese *coup de force* of March 9, 1945, which dismantled French control throughout Indochina.

These events were played out against the background of Vichy rule in Indochina, from July 1940 to March 1945 in the hands of Vice-Admiral Jean Decoux.[25] Vichy rule in some ways was more flexible, in others more repressive and certainly more ideological than the governments provided by the Third Republic had ever been. This was partly because to appease the Japanese, and following ideological preferences of their own, officials tended to follow the pro-Axis, anti-British line in force in Vichy and partly because, perceiving their vulnerability in Southeast Asia, they sought to retain control while using very little of their depleted military forces.

Examples of their flexibility in Cambodia included raising the salaries and widening the responsibilities of indigenous officials; encouraging an enhanced sense of national identity, linked to an idealization of the Angkorean era and Jayavarman VII in particular; and the organization of paramilitary youth groups along Vichy lines. These groups gave thousands of young Cambodians their first taste, outside the *sangha,* of membership in an extrafamilial group.

The regime was repressive as well. In late 1940, elected bodies (of some importance in southern Vietnam in particular) were abolished throughout Indochina. As it grew more openly anti-French, *Nagara Vatta* was suppressed in 1942; more than thirty Cambodians were imprisoned for long terms following the monks' demonstration. These moves had their greatest impact on the people who were to lead Cambodia's nationalist movement in the 1940s and 1950s; they had little effect in the countryside, as far as we can tell.

What the French were trying to do in France and in Indochina was to endure the war, hoping to reemerge even after an Axis victory with some identity and much of the French empire intact. In Cambodia and Vietnam, part of the process involved harking back to better days and to warlike heroes and heroines like Joan of Arc, the Trung sisters, and Jayavarman VII. In Cambodia, the French chose to work through the institutions of the monarchy, whereas those who opposed them became in the course of the war increasingly antimonarchical, setting the stage for factions that have endured in Cambodian politics ever since.

The Franco-Siamese war broke out in late 1940 because the pro-Japanese government of Phibul Songgram, aware of French military weakness, seized the opportunity to regain territories in Cambodia and Laos that the Thai had ceded earlier in the century to the French. These actions fitted into their irredentist nationalism of the period. On land, poorly equipped French forces suffered a series of defeats. At sea, however, French aircraft and warships scored a major victory over the Thai fleet in January 1941. Frightened by the possibility of further embarrassments to the Thai, the Japanese forced the French to negotiate in Tokyo; the upshot of these negotiations was that Battambang, most of Siem Reap, and parts of Laos—a total of slightly more than 65,000 square kilometers (25,000 square miles)—were ceded to the Thai for the derisory sum of 6 million piastres.[26] The French managed to retain Angkor for their Cambodian protégés, but the humiliating loss of territory so embittered King Monivong that for the few months remaining in his life (he died in April 1941) he refused to meet with French officials or to converse with anyone in French.

Monivong's death posed a problem for French officials concerned with the possibility, however faint, of dynastic squabbling so soon after their military defeat.[27] Throughout the 1930s, Monivong's son, Prince Monireth (b. 1909), had been favored for the throne, although French officials had also proposed the candidacy of Prince Norodom Suramarit, a grandson of Norodom's who was married to Monivong's daughter. Rivalry between Norodom's and Sisowath's descendants had surfaced occasionally in the colonial era, largely because many members of the royal family had little to do besides quarrel with each other. In the aftermath of the war with

Thailand, the French governor-general, Decoux, favored the selection of Suramarit's son, Norodom Sihanouk (b. 1922), then a student at a French lycée in Saigon. His ostensible rationale for preferring Sihanouk to Monireth was the need to heal the rift between the Norodom and Sisowath branches of the family; it is also likely that, of the two candidates, Sihanouk seemed more malleable and less independent-minded.

The shy young man who came to the throne in April 1941 and was crowned in October seemed an unlikely candidate to dominate Cambodian politics for so many of the next forty years. He was an only child whose parents were estranged; in *Indochine vue de Pékin,* as well as in his recently published memoirs, he has recalled his lonely, introverted child-hood.[28] Although an excellent student and a good musician, he had received no training for the throne and for the first few years of his reign worked closely with his French advisers—a period of dependency that Cambodian nationalists, then and later, were to criticize vociferously.

In the first few months of his reign, Sihanouk made modest efforts at reform, apparently intended to bolster his image with the Cambodian people and to compensate for the reclusiveness of his grandfather's last months. The annual gift of opium from the French was canceled; Palace Minister Tiounn was encouraged to retire; and the prince became active in Vichy-oriented youth groups.[29] His freedom of action was limited not only by French advisers, but also by the fact that by August 1941 eight thousand Japanese troops had been posted to Cambodia. No one knew what the Japanese intended to do.

French military weakness and Japanese sympathy for certain anticolonial movements—evident throughout Southeast Asia by 1942—had not passed unnoticed among the intellectuals—many of the members of the *sangha*—who were associated with *Nagara Vatta* and the Institut Bouddhique. Between 1940 and 1942, the paper took an increasingly pro-Japanese and anticolonial line. During these years, at least thirty-two issues of the paper were censored. In ten issues the lead editorial was suppressed. Perhaps in some cases the censorship involved overreaction on the part of the French; and nothing has yet been published about Japanese financial support for the Cambodian nationalists at this early stage. Some colla-boration, however, can be assumed and was actively sought by Son Ngoc Thanh and his associates. The climax of the confrontation between this group of Cambodians and the French occurred in July 1942, in the monks' demonstration.[30]

Throughout the twentieth century, the French had looked somewhat wearily at the Buddhist *sangha* in both Cambodia and Laos, noticing that it offered the Lao and Khmer an alternative value system to the colonial one. In Cambodia, as in Thailand, the *sangha* was made up of two sects, the larger known as the Mahanikay and the smaller, which enjoyed royal patronage, as the Thammayut. Jurisdictional quarrels between the two, which differed on no doctrinal matters but on several procedural ones, were frequent, and because of the Thammayut's palace connections, monks with antimonarchical ideas tended to gravitate to the Mahanikay.

One of these monks, Hem Chieu (1898–1943), a teacher at the advanced Pali school in Phnom Penh, was implicated in an anti-French plot when he proposed to several members of the Cambodian militia vague plans for a coup. A pro-French militiaman apparently informed on him and he was arrested with a fellow monk on July 17, 1942. Hem Chieu was an important member of the *sangha,* and the manner of his arrest—by civil authorities, who failed to allow him the ritual of leaving the monastic order—affronted his religious colleagues while giving nationalists of the *Nagara Vatta* clique a cause célèbre. Over the next three days, the nationalists engaged in secret conversations with the Japanese, seeking their cooperation in sponsoring an anti-French demonstration in support of the arrested monks. According to Son Ngoc Thanh, Japanese authorities in Saigon (who had jurisdiction over their colleagues in Phnom Penh) agreed in some fashion to sponsor the Cambodian rally, now planned for July 20.[31]

On that morning, more than a thousand people, perhaps half of them monks, marched along Phnom Penh's principal boulevard to the office of the French *résident supérieur,* Jean de Lens, demanding Hem Chieu's release. The demonstrators were trailed by French, Cambodian, and Vietnamese police agents, who took photographs of them. The editor of the recently suppressed *Nagara Vatta,* Pach Chhoeun, enthusiastically led the march and was arrested as he presented a petition to a French official inside the *résidence.* Along with other civilian demonstrators rounded up over the next few days, Chhoeun was quickly tried. The sentence of death imposed on him was commuted to life imprisonment by Vichy— the same sentence meted out to the murderers of Bardez only seventeen years before. Son Ngoc Thanh, who later admitted his involvement in planning the demonstration, apparently hid in Phnom Penh for several days before escaping to the Thai-controlled city of Battambang. By early 1943, he had been offered asylum in Tokyo, where he remained for the next two years, writing forlorn, infrequent letters to nationalist colleagues in Battambang, pleading that they keep the nationalist flame alive and assuring them of continued discreet Japanese cooperation.

The collapse of the demonstration suggests that Thanh and his colleagues overestimated Japanese support and underestimated French severity. The French, in any case, were eager to demonstrate that they remained in charge. Despite their censorship, however, the march and Hem Chieu's name, like the 1916 Affair and the Bardez incident, passed into Cambodian anticolonial folklore, resurfacing in 1945 during the anti-French resistance and again, among different groups, following the anti-Sihanouk coup of 1970. In 1979, after the Vietnamese invasion, a boulevard in Phnom Penh, formerly named after Sisowath Monivong, was renamed in Hem Chieu's honor. The ex-monk had died of illness on the French penal island of Poulo Condore in 1943.[32] In the short term, the demonstration accomplished nothing. Sihanouk in his memoirs dismissed it as "tragi-comic." At the time, he apparently accepted the view of his French advisers that it was foolish and unjustified.

THE GROWTH OF NATIONALISM
AND THE RETURN OF THE FRENCH

The remaining three years of World War II are important for Cambodian history, but they are difficult to study. French archives for the period remain closed for the most part, and the French-controlled press for the period, like Sihanouk's unpublished chronicle history, is largely ceremonial and bureaucratic in emphasis. Nationalists fell silent, fled to Battambang, or spent the years in prison. For these reasons, the so-called romanization crisis of 1943 is difficult to assess.

In 1943, the French *résident,* Georges Gautier, announced his intention to replace Cambodia's forty-five-letter alphabet, derived from medieval Indian models, with the roman one. The transliteration was worked out by George Coedes; available samples show that the system retained the phonetics of spoken Khmer quite well. Gautier and his colleagues saw the reform as a step toward "modernization," seen unequivocally as a good thing. In a pamphlet devoted to explaining the reform, Gautier attacked the "Cambodian attitude to the world"—as if there were one—as "out of date (*demodée*)," and compared the Cambodian language to a "badly tailored suit."[33] The addition of a "rational" French vocabulary to romanized Khmer, Gautier thought, would somehow improve Cambodian thought processes. Citing the example of romanization in Turkey, while remaining diplomatically silent about the romanization of Vietnamese, Gautier seems to have believed that the virtues of the reform were as self-evident as the primitiveness of the "Cambodian mind."

Many Cambodians, however, and especially the *sangha,* saw the reform as an attack on traditional education and on the high status enjoyed by traditional educators in Cambodian society. Cambodians in civil life were less affronted by the reform, although Sihanouk has claimed that he was on the point of abdicating over the issue. Despite these objections, the reform was pushed vigorously by the French in 1944–1945, especially in government publications and in schools; the romanization decree did not apply to religious texts. Nonetheless, when the French were pushed aside by the Japanese, one of the first actions of the newly independent Cambodian government was to rescind romanization; since then, no attempt has been made by any Cambodian government to romanize the language.[34] Once again, as so often in Cambodian history, what the French saw as a self-evident improvement in the status quo was seen by the Cambodians as an attack on the essential character of their civilization, defined in part as what had been passed down from Angkorean times. Indeed, the decree abrogating the reforms mentioned that for Cambodia to adopt the roman alphabet would be for the society to become "a society without history, without value, without mores, and without traditions."

On March 9, 1945, romanization became, literally, a dead letter when the Japanese throughout Indochina disarmed French forces and removed French officials from their posts. The move was intended to forestall French armed resistance. It also fitted into Japanese plans to equip local forces throughout Southeast Asia to resist Allied landings, expected later in the year. On March 13, in response to a formal Japanese request, King Sihanouk declared that Cambodia was independent and changed its name in French from "Cambodge" to "Kampuchea," the Khmer pronunciation of the word.[35] Sihanouk's decree, as it appears in the manuscript chronicle for this period, invalidated Franco-Cambodian agreements, declared Cambodia's independence, and pledged Cambodia's cooperation with the Japanese.

Two weeks after this declaration, Vietnamese residents of the city rioted against the French, on the basis of a rumor that the French intended to kill—or at least imprison—all Vietnamese residents in France. Disturbed by the violence of these demonstrations, the Japanese intervened on the side of the French, whom they herded into protective custody for the remainder of the war. In early April, speaking to the newly reinforced Cambodian militia, Sihanouk condemned French forces, which had been unwilling to help Japan defend Cambodia against an unspecified "enemy"; he urged Cambodians to "awaken" also. It is likely that the speech reflected the views of a Japanese political adviser, Lieutenant Tadakame, assigned to the palace at about this time.[36]

Other steps toward independence taken in this period included reinstituting the Buddhist lunar calendar at the expense of the Gregorian one and using Khmer instead of French to identify government ministries. "Independence," of course, was a relative thing; the Japanese remained in Cambodia in force. At the same time, the summer of 1945—like those of 1970 and 1975 in certain ways—allowed a clique of Cambodian intellectuals to interpose themselves between the monarchy and the colonial or neocolonial power.

The period March–October 1945 represented the first time during which Cambodian patriotic ideas could receive an open airing, as well as the first time Cambodians were encouraged to form politically oriented groups. On July 20, Sihanouk presided over a rally commemorating the monks' demonstration of 1942; he was joined on this occasion by Pach Chhoeun, just released from jail, and Son Ngoc Thanh, who had returned to Cambodia from Tokyo in April.[37] A speaker at the rally—not the king—regaled the crowd with a litany of Cambodian patriotism, citing antimonarchic rebellions in the 1860s, the 1884–1886 revolt, the 1916 Affair, the Bardez incident, and the 1942 monks' demonstration. The speaker failed to mention that on only one of these occasions—in 1884–1886—had the Cambodian monarch chosen the "right side," but the message was not lost upon Sihanouk, and these examples of nationalism—suppressed for the rest of his reign—in the late 1940s and 1950s passed into the folklore of the Cambodian Communists and that of the antimonarchical Democratic party.

Another strand of postwar Cambodian nationalism consisted of officially sponsored antipathy to the Vietnamese; clashes apparently took place, in this stirring if disorderly summer, between Khmer and Vietnamese inhabitants of Indochina. At the same time, few steps were taken by Sihanouk, other than that of forming a paper alliance with the Vietnamese regime in Saigon, to formulate a joint strategy to resist the French when they returned. Sihanouk's mind at this time is difficult to read. It is likely, however, that the obscure antiroyalist coup of August 9–10, 1945, sponsored by some hotheaded members of Cambodian youth groups, deepened the king's hostility toward such figures as Pach Chhoeun and Son Ngoc Thanh.

Of seven participants later arrested by the French, five soon became active in the anti-French guerrilla movement. Of these, three joined the forerunner of the Cambodian Communist party. At the end of August, after the Japanese surrender, Sihanouk's chronicle reports that a nationalist demonstration attracted thirty thousand people, including armed members of the militia and members of various youth groups. Four days later, a referendum engineered by Son Ngoc Thanh allegedly drew 541,470 votes in favor of independence, with only two opposed. There is no evidence that a full-scale referendum ever took place; in fact, a proposal for one seems to have been circulated as a memorandum to officials, for their approval. The figures represent an attempt by Son Ngoc Thanh to bolster his bargaining position vis-à-vis the French, who had begun to filter back into southern Indochina, under British auspices at first. Throughout September, Thanh urged his colleagues to join him in an alliance with the Vietnamese to resist the French. Many of these men disagreed with Thanh (himself half-Vietnamese, according to most reports) and sought to gain Cambodia's independence independently from Vietnam's. Some even preferred the return of the French to Thanh's continuing in power. For these reasons, when French officials arrested Thanh on October 12, 1945, in Phnom Penh, no one objected. Thanh himself seems to have been surprised; that very morning, he had presided, as the prime minister of Kampuchea, at the reopening of the Lycée Sisowath. He had lunch in the Saigon Central Prison.[38]

With Thanh removed from the scene (he was to spend most of the next six years in comparatively comfortable exile in Poitiers), King Sihanouk opened negotiations with the French, who appeared to many to have been ready to reimpose their control, as in 1940–1941. The modus vivendi signed by French and Cambodian delegates in early 1946, however, was a vaguely promising document, diluting French control and offering Cambodia membership in two nonexistent confederations. One of these, the Indochinese Federation, seems to have been little more than "Indochina" with somewhat increased indigenous participation at the top. The other, the French Union, was an even vaguer brotherhood of peoples who had been colonized by France, based on the shared experience of French civilization. The agreement promised Cambodia a constitution and the right to form political parties, but French control remained in such fields as finance, defense, and foreign affairs. In other words, the French of early 1946 had replaced the Japanese of the summer of 1945. They had not, however, reconstituted the previous status quo.

CHAPTER 10

Roads to Independence and Revolution

It is easy enough with hindsight to argue that French rule in Indochina came to an end in the summer of 1945. This did not appear to be the case, however, to the new breed of French officials sent out by General de Gaulle's government to replace the people who had looked after the region up to 1945. De Gaulle, in fact, had made the recovery of the French empire, and Indochina in particular, an important goal of his government in exile.

In Cambodia, the French were forced in October 1945 to make conciliatory gestures to the members of the indigenous elite whom they needed to run the kingdom's day-to-day affairs. These were the people whose "awakening" the French had celebrated in the 1930s. They had become patriots in the meantime and, from the French point of view, intellectually belligerent. Many of them interpreted the summer of 1945 less as a humiliation of the French that had to be avenged than as a victory for the Cambodians themselves. Cambodia, they argued, needed to *regain* its independence. A leading convert to the cause, although he was quieter than most, was King Sihanouk.

Once the modus vivendi had been signed, the French began to tidy up their colony; for example, in Phnom Penh they restored the street names honoring French colonial heroes and French events that had been changed to Cambodian ones in 1945.[1] Another step was to abolish the newly instituted national holidays that honored Sihanouk's declaration of independence in 1945 and the monks' demonstration of 1942. A third was to place Son Ngoc Thanh on trial for treason, charging him with collaboration with the Japanese (against whom, incidentally, the French had never declared war).

THE DEVELOPMENT OF POLITICAL PARTIES

In this atmosphere of business as usual, the electoral act that came into effect in the summer of 1946 opened up deep and unexpected fissures in the Cambodian elite. For the first time in their history, Cambodians were allowed to form political parties. Three sprang rapidly to life. As V. M. Reddi has pointed out, all of these "were led by princes, all of them shared the fear of neighboring countries, and all professed loyalty to the monarchy."[2] The first and third of these characteristics should come as no surprise, but the phrase "fear of neighboring countries" may need an explanation.

In 1946–1947, Thailand was still governed by the relatively radical civilian regime that had been financing anti-Japanese, and subsequently anti-French, guerrillas along the Cambodian frontier since the fall of the Phibul government in the summer of 1944. In 1945, these groups formed into the Khmer Issarak (Free Khmer) and a government in exile was hastily assembled in Bangkok. Throughout this period, moreover, the Thai retained control of the *sruk* that they had taken over in 1941. These regions offered sanctuary to four of the twelve persons implicated in the August 1945 coup, as well as to others, like Bunchhan Muul, who had participated in the monks' demonstration and were now unhappy with the return of the French. The new political parties in Phnom Penh were fearful of Thai intrusions into Cambodian politics. They were probably even more frightened, however, by developments inside Vietnam, where Communist guerrillas in the south were threatening French rule and a Communist government in the north enjoyed de facto independence.[3]

There were, all the same, significant differences between the two leading parties, the Democratic party (Krom Pracheathipodei) led by Prince Sisowath Yuthevong, and the so-called Liberal party (Kanaq Sereipheap; literally, "Freedom Group") led by Prince Norodom Norindeth. The difference between these princes encapsulated the differences between two wings of Cambodian opinon. Prince Yuthevong (1912–1947) had just returned from higher education in France; his wife was French; he wanted Cambodia to practice the kind of democracy he had so admired there. His party's program called for negotiating Cambodia's independence as quickly as possible. Prince Norindeth, on the other hand, was a conservative. As one of Cambodia's largest landowners, he believed that Cambodian politics should involve educating the people—rather slowly—and maintaining for the moment at least a dependent relationship with France. This was a view shared, understandably enough, by many members of the royal family. The third party, the Progressive Democrats, led by Prince Norodom Montana, was insignificant and quickly faded from the scene, but it was certainly as conservative as the Liberals, and it may have enjoyed a measure of support from the king and his advisers.[4]

The Democratic party attracted people who had been drawn in the early 1940s to *Nagara Vatta* and the ideas of Pach Chhoeun and Son Ngoc Thanh. Its strength came in large part from the Mahanikay sect of the *sangha,* from younger members of the bureaucracy, from supporters of the Issarak movement, and from Cambodia's "intellectual" class. Elements within the party (particularly those affiliated with the clandestine "Black Star" fraternity, dating from the Japanese period) favored violent action, an alliance with Issarak guerrillas, and perhaps, at this early stage, with the Communist Viet Minh as well.[5]

The Liberal party, on the other hand, was dedicated to the maintenance of the status quo, and its policies appear to have been less articulate. The party drew its strength from elderly members of the government, wealthy landowners, the Cham ethnic minority, and the Sino-Cambodian commercial elite. The party had strong provincial roots, it seems, among *chamkar* (riverbank plantation) owners near Kompong Cham. Its strength could be traced in large part to patronage networks in particular regions.

Sihanouk in his memoirs related that he was drawn to neither of these groups, and neither sought him out. Many Democrats, indeed, seem to have seen Sihanouk as a puppet of the French, and much of his conduct in the 1946–1949 period appears to bear this out. At the very least, Sihanouk seems to have felt that the only way to regain his country's independence was to seek it peacefully, by negotiating with the French in a friendly, diplomatic way. The king's distrust of the Democrats probably sprang from his dislike of Son Ngoc Thanh, his generalized suspicion of ideology, his traumatic experiences in the summer of 1945, and perhaps from the feeling that he was being disrespectfully upstaged.

In September 1946, soon after the parties had been formed, elections for the Consultative Assembly were held to form a group to advise the king about a constitution for the country. More than 60 percent of the newly enfranchised voters went to the polls (a far higher percentage than did so in elections in Thailand). The Democrats won fifty of the sixty-seven seats, the Liberals won fourteen, and independent candidates, three.

These results revealed the popularity of the Democratic party among Cambodian authority figures who were in a position to "deliver the vote." In this election, as in others over the next twenty years or so, many peasants voted as they were told to vote by people whom they habitually obeyed.[6] As in the 1916 Affair, moreover, Cambodians—in this case, the Democrats—showed a disconcerting ability to organize their followers. In the case of the Democrats, these patrons would be local officials, teachers, and members of the *sangha;* those who voted for Liberal candidates were often, in fact, endorsing their traditional economic patrons. At the same time, the sub rosa connections between some Democrats and the Issarak, and the connections that others made between the party and Cambodian patriots, like Hem Chieu, probably appealed to many voters more strongly than the Liberals' "program" of supporting the landowning elite. Indeed, the effects in the countryside of the disappearance of French control between March and October 1945 have never been examined. It would seem likely that bandit gangs, the principal target of the French-controlled Cambodian police in the colonial era, grew in number and importance. Many of these by early 1946 were referring to themselves as "Issarak," and many peasants, especially at a distance, probably thought of the bands as patriotic.[7]

Sihanouk appears to have been distressed by the Democrats' overwhelming victory, which he interpreted as a rebuff although he had no party of his own. In his memoirs, he is scathing about the party and particularly about Prince Yuthevong, suggesting that his own unformed political ideas were preferable, even in 1946, to Yuthevong's. After more than thirty years, he was still unable to respect Yuthevong, referring to him and his followers dismissively as "demos."

Because the Democrats now assumed that they had a mandate to impose a constitution on the kingdom, rather than merely to advise the king about one, and because the constitution they drafted in 1946–1947 reduced the powers of the king, Sihanouk soon became even more estranged from the constitutional process. Indeed, the 1947 Constitution, to his alarm, was modeled closely on the Constitution of the Fourth Republic in France. In this document, real power devolved to the National Assembly and thus to the Democrats, who held the majority of Assembly seats.

But what did "power" amount to? The Democrats, like everyone else in the kingdom, were handicapped because independence could no longer be *declared,* as it had been in the summer of 1945. It had to be *granted* by the French. Before the middle of 1949, however, the French made few concessions to anyone in Indochina. Unable to deliver independence, the Democrats began to squabble among themselves. This trend was exacerbated by the death of Prince Yuthevong from tuberculosis in July 1947 and by the assassination of his successor, Ieu Koeuss, in 1949.[8] Even after the so-called treaty of 1949, discussed below, French police arrested a dozen leaders of the party on charges, later dropped, that they were conspiring with Issarak forces. The Democrats could do nothing about it; Cambodia's "independence," as many of them had charged since 1946, was a façade.

The Issarak armed struggle against the French, which had caused serious disruptions to the Cambodian economy in 1946–1947, slowed down after Battambang and Siem Reap were returned to Cambodian control in 1947 and a regime unsympathetic to Issarak aspirations assumed control in Bangkok. In 1949, moreover, several thousand Issarak, particularly those opposed to the Viet Minh, took advantage of an amnesty offered them by Prime Minister Yem Sambaur. As noncommunist resistance to the French decreased, moreover, the Democrats were in less of a position to reply to spurious French charges that they supported the Viet Minh.

Another factor that handicapped the Democrats was that the people who held economic power in the kingdom—the French, members of the royal family, Chinese, and Sino-Cambodians—opposed the kinds of disorder that a real struggle for independence would entail. Most of them were doing well. If they were in politics at all, they supported the Liberal party; so did the French administration, in its quiet way. This meant that the Democrats were short of funds with which to influence officials, win elections, or finance an armed insurrection. The Democrats, forming the majority of the National Assembly (and thus theoretically enjoying political power) were in fact powerless to impose their will on the elite, the French, or their electorate—whose views, in fact, were rarely if ever sought.

Ensconced in the National Assembly and hampered by a constitution that encouraged factional splits, the Democrats were cut off intellectually, economically, and physically from Cambodia's ordinary people. The only weapon available to them was to try to impede the orderly procedures of government by refusing to pass bills or to ratify agreements. As cabinet followed cabinet through a series of revolving doors—for unlike in the British system, no elections followed the crises—Cambodia's government ironically came more and more to resemble the government of the Fourth Republic from which its members were so eager to liberate themselves. Moreover, governments in Paris often held power so tenuously and for such short periods that Cambodians of any political persuasion, as Sihanouk was to discover in 1953, seldom encountered coherent French policies to oppose or experienced ministers qualified to negotiate. In fact, for reasons that are not entirely clear (although financial motives were important) no French governments before the mid-1950s showed any willingness to take France out of Indochina.

By the end of 1949, all the same, the French appeared to cave in. A treaty signed at the end of the year granted what Sihanouk was later to call "50 percent independence."[9] The treaty allowed Cambodia some freedom of maneuver in foreign affairs, as well as an autonomous military zone embracing Battambang and Siem Reap. Control over finance, defense, customs, and political resistance remained in French hands, but as Sihanouk has asserted, a process had begun that would be difficult to reverse. The Democrats opposed the treaty as inadequate, but it came into force all the same.

The French had several reasons for compromising at this point with Cambodia. The war throughout Indochina had intensified, and the Communist victory in China now provided the Viet Minh with an arsenal, an ally, and a sanctuary. The Soviet acquisition of nuclear arms in 1949 was to be followed in early 1950 by the conclusion of a thirty-year pact with the People's Republic of China. Beginning in 1948–1949, the French sought increased military aid from the United States on the grounds that they were no longer engaged in a colonial war in Indochina but were fighting a crusade against communism. To many in the United States and France, the outbreak of the Korean War in June 1950 "proved" this line of argument. U.S. aid, in any case, flowed into Indochina in ever-increasing amounts beginning in early 1950, shortly after the United States had extended recognition to the "independent" regimes of Laos, Cambodia, and noncommunist Vietnam.

THE GROWTH OF THE LEFT

The history of the next four years is crucial in an understanding of what has happened to Cambodia ever since. Three trends need to be discussed. The first is the waning of the Democratic party and the eclipse of the National Assembly. The second, related to this, is the flowering of comparatively right-wing political groupings and anticommunist military forces, which often enjoyed the favor of the king. In fact, officials concerned with these groupings (e.g., Nhek Tioulong and Lon Nol) reappeared in several of Sihanouk's cabinets in the independence period. More important, perhaps, the consolidation of left-wing resistance to the French inside Cambodia, a process that began in 1950 and concluded in 1951 with the foundation of a recognizably Cambodian Communist party, also dates from this period. In a sense, these three pieces remained on the board throughout Sihanouk's rule.

The fading of the Democrats can be traced to French reluctance to negotiate with them, the king's growing hostility to them, and a shift by some opportunistic members of the party to a more royalist stance in order to gain favor and preferment. Moreover, even their traditional disruptive role in the Assembly was curtailed for much of the period because Sihanouk saw to it that the Assembly was almost never in session.

Nonetheless, in 1951 he yielded to pressure to elect a new Assembly in accordance with the Constitution. The Democrats, perhaps sensing a trap, said they were unwilling to go to the polls because of increasing insecurity in the countryside. When the Liberals and several hastily formed right-wing parties (one of them led by a middle-echelon bureaucrat, Lon

Nol) threatened to contest the elections without them, the Democrats changed their minds. In the ensuing campaign, the Democrats were aided by Pach Chhouen, recently released from nearly five years of house arrest.

The results resembled those of 1947, at least on the surface, for the Democrats captured fifty-five of the seventy-eight contested seats. Ominously, from the Democrats' point of view, some 498 different candidates had presented themselves for these seats, with little hope of winning, and had siphoned off tens of thousands of votes. For this reason, as well as the persistent strength of Liberal candidates, the Democrats attracted less than half of the total vote, polling 148,000 while the Liberals attracted 82,000 voters and the various new parties attracted nearly 100,000. It was clear, as Michael Vickery has pointed out, that "any movement which could unify the right could immediately cut the ground from under the Democrats."[10]

With victory, the Democrats asked Sihanouk to request that the French release Son Ngoc Thanh, who had been living pleasantly enough in France since 1947, earning a law degree and becoming a minor celebrity in the provincial city of Poitiers. In his memoirs, Sihanouk belittled the role of the Democrats in this affair, claiming that he had repeatedly asked that Thanh be released because of Thanh's friendliness with members of the royal family, including Sihanouk's father.[11] In any case, Thanh's return to Cambodia on October 29, 1951, was melodramatic. Thousands of people greeted him when he arrived at Phnom Penh airport, and thousands more lined the route into the city. It took the 300-car cortege almost an hour to cover the 10 kilometers (6 miles) involved. French intelligence officials estimated the crowds at more than half a million—an almost incredible indication of the organizational capacities of the Democrats and of the extent of popular support, partly for Son Ngoc Thanh himself and partly for an early solution to the problem of continuing dependence.

On the very day of Thanh's return, the French commissioner, Jean de Raymond, was murdered in his sleep. The two events have never been publicly linked by scholars of the period, although the coincidence is remarkable; blame soon focused on one of de Raymond's servants, a Vietnamese. A clandestine Communist broadcast, two weeks later, managed to touch all the bases by asserting,

For the French, the death of Raymond means the loss of a precious collaborator. For the puppets, it means the loss of a generous master. For the Cambodian people, Raymond's death means the end of a great enemy. For Buddhism, his death means that a devil, who can no longer harm religion, has been killed.[12]

Thanh was apparently politically inactive for the remainder of 1951, even refusing several cabinet posts. At the beginning of 1952, however, for reasons that remain obscure, he decided to mount a full-scale attack on the French, the 1949 agreement, and the dependent status of the Cambodian government. The occasion he chose was a provincial tour to the south of the capital, accompanying his old associate, Pach Chhoeun, recently named minister of information. His intemperate remarks on this occasion infuriated the French, all the more because they were overheard and applauded (but not understood, as they were in Khmer) by a U.S. diplomat accompanying the tour.[13]

Soon after returning to Phnom Penh, Thanh founded a newspaper called *Khmer Krok* [Cambodians awake!], explaining the title in his first issue: "We know that the Cambodian people, who have been anaesthetized for a long time, are now awake. . . . No obstacle can now stop this awakening from moving ahead."[14] The paper survived for about a month before being shut down by the Cambodians at the request of the French. As Thanh had been careful to attack the French rather than the Cambodians, this action showed him that his countrymen were puppets of their colonial masters.

Soon afterward, on March 9, 1952, the seventh anniversary of the Japanese *coup de force,* Son Ngoc Thanh fled the capital with a radio transmitter and perhaps a hundred followers, some of whom were armed. The most eminent was a leftist intellectual named Ea Sichau. Within a month, Thanh had set up his headquarters along the Thai border in the northern part of Siem Reap, joining forces with an Issarak band under the leadership of Kao Tak. Between 1952 and the Geneva Conference in 1954, Thanh and his supporters were aided to an extent by Thai intelligence agencies. Within his own "zone," he experimented with a loosely regimented ideology that he labeled "national socialism," traceable in part to his admiration for the Japanese political institutions he had observed in exile in World War II.[15] It is unclear if he believed that by going into exile again in the Cambodian mountains he could remain in command of the independence movement, as he had seemed to be on his triumphal return to Phnom Penh. In any case, very few people followed him into the maquis, and as an active force in Cambodian politics, he faded sharply after 1953. In the late 1950s and 1960s, he eked out a shadowy existence working for the Thai and the Vietnamese in their efforts to destabilize Sihanouk's regime. His nationalism through 1957 or so is difficult to question, but his motives for abandoning Phnom Penh in 1952 are difficult to figure out. Perhaps he overestimated the extent of his support among the noncommunist Issarak (or, conversely, underestimated Communist support among the guerrillas). French intelligence reports assert that he still enjoyed the support of some of the older politicians in Phnom Penh;

perhaps he hoped for international support as well. To all intents and purposes, however, he was no longer a force to be reckoned with, either by Sihanouk or by the French.[16]

At this point it is appropriate to study the growth of left-wing radicalism in Cambodia. By 1952, Communist-controlled guerrilla bands, operating in cooperation with the Viet Minh, were able to control perhaps a sixth of Cambodia's territory and to tie down several thousand French troops. Two years later, at the time of the Geneva Conference, some estimates suggested that they controlled more than half of the kingdom.

Where had they come from? When the Indochinese Communist party (ICP) was founded in Hong Kong in 1930, it included no Cambodian members, and indeed only a handful of ethnic Khmer had joined the party before the end of World War II.[17] In 1945–1947, however, Viet Minh forces made an effort to support "liberation struggles" in Laos and Cambodia; at the same time, as we have seen, the Thai government had a policy of aiding all anti-French guerrillas in Indochina, and the Khmer Issarak, operating along the Thai frontier and in the Thai-controlled *sruk* of Battambang and Siem Reap, included men who later formed right-wing and left-wing factions. Left-wingers included the pseudonymous Son Ngoc Minh (in fact a former monk, Achar Mean), Sieu Heng, and Tou Samouth. On April 17, 1950, twenty-five years to the day before the Communist "liberation" of Phnom Penh, the First National Congress of the Khmer Resistance was held in the southwestern part of the kingdom under the leadership of Son Ngoc Minh. The congress, in turn, established the Unified Issarak Front, dominated by ethnic Cambodian members of the ICP. According to a subsequent history of the Cambodian Communist party, prepared in 1973, there were only forty of these at the time; as Ben Kiernan has pointed out, however, hundreds more had already been trained in communist political schools set up under Vietnamese auspices as early as 1947; the most famous of these, founded in 1950, was named after the monk Hem Chieu.[18]

The ICP dissolved itself in early 1951, and separate Communist parties were formed in Laos, Cambodia, and Vietnam. The Khmer People's Revolutionary Party (KPRP) was founded in September 1951. Its statutes, unsurprisingly, were drawn from those of the "newly constituted" party in Vietnam. According to Party records, the KPRP at this stage had as many as a thousand members; French intelligence in 1952 estimated Communist-controlled Issarak forces as numbering about five thousand.[19] This latter figure, like many from the period, is probably an underestimate, because the French appear to have been unable to infiltrate the party and because it was in their interests, and in those of their client, King Sihanouk, to play down estimates of Communist popularity, especially in public statements. As impatience with French control increased among many segments of the population and as Vietnamese guerrillas elsewhere in Indochina moved from strength to strength, these pro-Vietnamese forces in Cambodia grew in numbers, efficiency, and cohesion. So did the KPRP. By July 1954, eight months after independence, the party had an estimated two thousand members. Nearly all of these were to seek refuge in Vietnam following the Geneva Accords. Another index of the party's growth was the fact that French authorities in 1952 believed that taxes and contributions levied by revolutionaries among the population amounted to the equivalent of half the national budget.

Although the Vietnamese cadres in these guerrilla units gradually relinquished their positions to ethnic Khmer, who were always in control of the KPRP, it is clear that these leaders in the anti-French resistance differed in several ways from their counterparts in the Democratic party and elsewhere along the political spectrum. For one thing, they saw their struggle as part of an international movement, connected with Marxist-Leninist laws of history. At another level, the liberation of Cambodia from the French did not mean, for them, the continuation of the status quo among Cambodians or the intensification of a supposedly "traditional animosity" between Cambodians and Vietnamese. Liberation from the French, in other words, was a stage in the Cambodian revolution rather than a goal. Moreover, without being puppets of the Vietnamese, these radical leaders in the early 1950s accepted Vietnam's leadership in the struggle to liberate Indochina from the French and in the formation of socialist parties throughout the region. In terms of relative power, such a policy made sense. Seen from another perspective, both the French and Sihanouk tried hard to equate anti-French resistance (as opposed to a policy of negotiated independence) with a pro-Vietnamese, procommunist, and therefore un-Cambodian betrayal. What was betrayed, of course, was the social arrangements that had characterized Cambodia throughout its history. In 1952–1953, in fact, Sihanouk and his entourage frequently and absurdly labeled Son Ngoc Thanh a communist. A decade later, he reached for the fascist label to describe his former prime minister, now allegedly in the pay of the United States.

The interplay between nationalism and internationalism inside the Cambodian Communist movement, as in many others elsewhere in the world, has plagued the party since the early 1950s. Should "Cambodian" interests (whatever they were) come first? What is "Cambodian" socialism? And how does this, in turn, fit into the history and the alignments of the Vietnamese? Without any socialist or internationalist component in Cambodian nationalism, one could proclaim Cambodia's *intrinsic* greatness, referring repeatedly to Angkor and making racist slurs against the Vietnamese. This was the route that Sihanouk chose to follow in the later 1960s. It was followed by Lon Nol and at several points by the Pol

Pot regime. It was also employed occasionally by radicals in the early 1950s. In a speech delivered in November 1951, for example, a Communist spokesman asserted that

> the Cambodian race is of noble origin. It is not afraid of death, when it is a question of fighting the enemy, of saving its religion, and of liberating its fatherland. The entire race follows the Buddhist doctrine [sic] which places death above slavery and religious persecution. King Yassovarman [sic] is a remarkable example.[20]

By seeking legitimacy in the Cambodian past, in antimonarchic heroes, and in aspects of the Buddhist religion, radicals cast a far wider net than the people around King Sihanouk, who saw independence as a goal in itself, having little effect on the structure of Cambodian society or on their own place inside it. After all, these men saw little value in mobilizing the Cambodian people or in destabilizing the regime. For these reasons, heroes like Siwotha, Hem Chieu, and Pou Kombo—favored by the Issaraks, by some of the Democrats, and by Communist propaganda at this early stage—quickly disappeared from official ideology. The fate of these heroes under successive regimes forms an interesting leitmotif in Cambodian history. After years of neglect, they reemerged under the Khmer Republic, alongside many former Democrats, only to vanish again under Pol Pot, whose official ideology, while retaining a pro-Angkorean slant, also stressed the impersonality of the regime's organization. Heroes, it was thought, were ephemeral; the organization (*angkar*) endured. To complete the cycle, some of the discredited heroes reemerged in 1979 under the Heng Samrin regime, providing new names for Phnom Penh streets.[21] So did a five-towered depiction of Angkor Wat on the Cambodian flag, favored by the Issarak in the 1950s, replacing the three-towered one favored by previous "legitimate" (and anti-Vietnamese) regimes. The government of the People's Republic of Kampuchea (PRK), in other words, places some of its roots where the Democrats, the Issarak, and Lon Nol did, i.e., in the summer of 1945 and in the antimonarchical heroes venerated at that time.

SIHANOUK AND THE ACHIEVEMENT OF INDEPENDENCE

Throughout the first few months of 1952, the Democrats in the National Assembly continued as best they could to thwart Sihanouk's policies; Son Ngoc Thanh remained a threat, although at a distance. French intelligence sources estimated that almost two-thirds of the kingdom was no longer under the day-to-day control of the Phnom Penh government.

To Sihanouk, and to his conservative advisers, the time had come for a dramatic series of gestures to gain the country's independence forcibly from France and to maintain themselves in power.

In a scathing speech to the Assembly in early June 1952, Sihanouk declared: "All is in disorder. Hierarchy no longer exists. There is no rational employment of talent. . . . If it is right to be dissident, this means that all the best patriots will seek refuge in the forest."[22] Two weeks later, Sihanouk assumed power as prime minister, appointing his own cabinet and leaving the Democratic-controlled Assembly to wither on the vine. At this point, he demanded a mandate from his people, promising to deliver complete independence within three years—i.e., before June 1955. Although no referendum was carried out at this time, Sihanouk acted as if his mandate had been granted and began what he was later to call his crusade for independence.

His dramatic gesture had little effect on the French, who were worried by Thanhist pressures and by the intransigence of the Democrats, among whom, naturally enough, antimonarchic feelings were becoming more intense. Feeling ran especially high in the lycées, whose students frequently went on strike. Their elite background and antimonarchic posturing tended to confirm and intensify Sihanouk's distrust of intellectuals, which characterized his years in power. Cambodian students in France—including several who later held office in Democratic Kampuchea, such as Pol Pot himself (then known as Saloth Sar)—also referred to Sihanouk as a "traitor to the nation" at this time. In a vituperative manifesto issued to the king on July 6, 1952, the students called on him to abdicate, blaming him for recent French military attacks, for dissolving the Assembly and for negotiating with the French instead of fighting them.[23] The manifesto went on to accuse Sihanouk's ancestors Sisowath and Norodom of collaborating with the French against "national heroes." The remainder of 1952, it seems, was a trying time for Sihanouk, as the French in effect decided to call his bluff.

He was aided by the Democrats' intransigence. The Assembly refused to approve his government's budget in January 1953. Declaring the nation to be in danger, Sihanouk dissolved the Assembly, promulgated martial law, and ordered the arrest of several Democratic assemblymen, who were, of course, now deprived of parliamentary immunity. As V. M. Reddi asserted, Sihanouk showed no hesitation in acting out what was obviously a well-planned scenario and justified it informally by telling a French correspondent: "I am the natural ruler of the country . . . and my authority has never been questioned."[24] He was appealing to the people over the heads of the elected officials, just as he now planned (without saying so at the time) to appeal directly to the French.

The king's newly acquired political energy and his insistence upon independence shocked many Frenchmen and members of the royal family. Some journalists came to terms with the king's awakening by labeling him "insane," because he had been "comical" and "exotic" (i.e., cooperative) for so long.

In February 1953, Sihanouk announced that he was traveling to France for his health—a tactic he was often to employ during the remaining years of his reign. In fact, as he revealed in his memoirs, he departed with meticulously prepared dossiers, listing outstanding matters to be discussed and negotiated with the French. His illness was "political," but the stakes were high. When he arrived in France, he wrote immediately to the aged and constitutionally powerless president, Vincent Auriol, warning him that "I have based my future as king and that of my dynasty on the policy of adhesion to the French Union and collaboration with France, to which I am and shall be loyal."[25] He added that if the Communists invaded Cambodia, he could not guarantee that his subjects would act to defend French interests.

Auriol's advisers apparently thought that Sihanouk's long letter, and another that followed soon afterwards, were alarmist, and Auriol waited two weeks to answer. When he did, he said only that he had studied the letters with care and asked Sihanouk to lunch. At that point, officials in the French government concerned with Indochina more or less told the king to return home, hinting that he might even be replaced as king.[26]

For the next month or so, Sihanouk traveled slowly homeward, pausing to give press and radio interviews in Canada, the United States, and Japan in which he publicized Cambodia's plight and the intransigence of the French. He has used this tactic of publicizing supposedly confidential discussions, when it was in his own interest to do so, ever since. In 1953, however, it was a bold course for him to follow, for he was gambling not only with the French and potential foreign allies, but also with opposition politicians at home, with the Vietnamese, and with the KPRP.

He returned to Phnom Penh in May and dramatically offered his life in exchange for Cambodia's independence. Negotiations in Paris proceeded slowly, so in June the king went into voluntary exile, first to Thailand, where he was not welcomed, and then to the autonomous military region of Siem Reap, where he took up residence at his villa near Angkor and refused to speak with French officials in Phnom Penh. In Vietnam, the war was going badly for the French. Sihanouk's increasing resistance to them, and the prospect of increased fighting in Cambodia, caused them to consider his demands more seriously than they had planned.

In October, the French caved in and granted the king authority over Cambodia's armed forces, judiciary, and foreign affairs. Their economic hold on the kingdom, however—particularly in the import-export sphere and in the highly profitable rubber plantations—remained intact (and was to do so until after the Lon Nol coup of 1970). In spite of these remnants of colonial rule, Sihanouk is correct, on balance, in interpreting the French collapse at this point as a personal victory. Using the same communications network that, in 1916 and again in 1951, had frightened French authorities, Sihanouk now ordered officials in the *sruk* between Siem Reap and Phnom Penh to organize demonstrations in his favor. As he drove back to his capital, on the second anniversary of Son Ngoc Thanh's return from exile, hundred of thousands of people lined the road, uncertain perhaps what independence would mean but at this stage happy enough to applaud their king and what they hoped would be an end to fighting. Soon afterwards, he was officially proclaimed a national hero.[27]

In the short term, France's departure from the scene had three effects. In the first place, Cambodia's independence and the relatively low level of fighting in the kingdom between November 1953 and the middle of 1954 strengthened the hand of Sihanouk's delegation to the Geneva Conference in the summer of 1954. The delegation, led by Nhek Tioulong, took a stubborn view of indigenous Communists, who were allowed no part in the deliberations and were also frozen out by Vietnamese Communist delegates eager to earn concessions for Vietnam and, to a lesser degree, for pro-Vietnamese Pathet Lao forces in Laos.[28] Surprisingly, perhaps, many Cambodian radicals continued to accept leadership from Vietnam throughout the 1950s and 1960s. For several thousand of them, 1954 marked the beginning of a "Long March" that would take them to exile in Hanoi, not to return to Cambodia until the early 1970s, where almost all of them were killed by U.S. bombing, Lon Nol's army, or particularly by internal Communist purges under the leadership of Pol Pot. A few hardy survivors from this group have been given important positions in the post-1979 regime in Cambodia, known as the People's Republic of Kampuchea (PRK).[29]

Another consequence of Sihanouk's so-called crusade was that the Democratic party and Son Ngoc Thanh, who had failed to deliver independence, lost some of their appeal. At the same time, figures further to the right who had remained loyal to the king, like Lt. Col. Lon Nol, Nhek Tioulong, and Penn Nouth, now gained in stature and were favored for government posts throughout the Sihanouk era.

Perhaps the most lasting consequence of independence in 1953 was that Sihanouk now felt that he had obtained a mandate to govern Cambodia as he saw fit. The subsequent decimation of the KPRP and the eclipse of the Democrats by 1955 gave him the impression (encouraged by many foreign correspondents and by his entourage) that his crusade had been not only successful but also astute and that the suffusion of Cambodia the state by Sihanouk the man was a salutary political

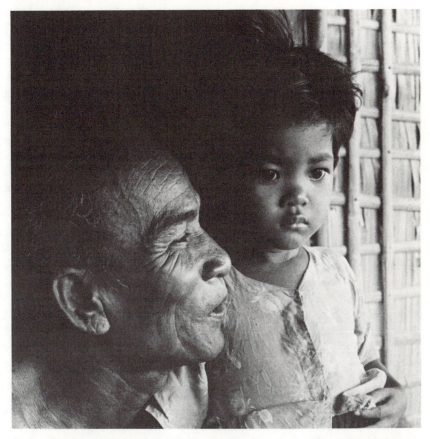

A rice farmer and his granddaughter near Kompong Speu, 1962. Author's photo.

development. A consequence of this, especially visible after 1960 or so, was that Sihanouk felt under no obligation to be at peace with his powerful neighbors, Thailand and South Vietnam, or to grant much authority to people he disliked. Just as he had "gone it alone" in 1953 and won, so Cambodia could be "independent" by courting the friendship of faraway powers like China, France, and Yugoslavia.

While this was going on, the forces that had been unleashed in the summer of 1945 fell into disrepute. Sihanouk and his advisers, never partial to social change, correctly saw that these forces endangered the stability of the country. And, as we have seen, the "inherent" stability of Cambodia, even if it has often been the subject of absurd romanticism among colonial writers, has rested throughout nearly all of Cambodian history on the acceptance of the status quo as defined by those in power.

What, then, did "independence" really mean? The removal of the French probably meant little to most Cambodians, who continued to pay taxes to finance an indifferent government in Phnom Penh (or Udong or Angkor) whose "royal work," almost by definition, removed it from contact with the people and made officials, for the most part, self-centered, concerned with status, and ill at ease with anyone else's aspirations. It was certainly just, in other words, to remove the Cambodian elite and the comparatively small intellectual class from French control. The removal left these people free not to govern themselves so much as to govern others without seeking their consent. Because the people in the country-side had never been asked to play a part in any government, they saw few short-term rewards in resisting those in power, who were at least Cambodians rather than French or Vietnamese.[30]

And yet there were important differences between Cambodia after 1953 and the kingdom that had existed before the end of World War II. In the 1940s and 1950s, hundreds of thousands of pupils passed through a greatly expanded educational system, staffed increasingly by teachers (drawn to a large extent from France) who were persuaded by Marxist-Leninist interpretations of history and experience. Hundreds of others who had been active in the Democratic party and the Issarak movement resented Sihanouk's cashing in on what they regarded as their own more painful struggle for independence. While many teachers now taught ordinary people that Cambodian society was unjust, some older people in the government or in opposition to it sought for many years to try to bring the summer of 1945 back to life and to make Cambodia a republic.

In 1953, radicals and republicans faced a long struggle and many years in the dark before they could accomplish what they had in mind. For the next seventeen years, King (after 1955, Prince) Sihanouk played the keyboards of politics, publicity, and foreign relations in such a way as to deny the press, the media, and overseas observers any access to Cambodian ideologies different from his own. Nonetheless, these alternative proposals for Cambodia survived this period, in spite and perhaps because of Sihanouk's monopolistic style of rule. But opposition to the prince before the late 1960s was neither visible nor dangerous. Cambodian Communist party histories compiled in the 1970s refer to the years 1955–1967 (the heyday of Sihanouk's rule) as a period of "political struggle," but they are evasive about what the party, restructured in 1960, was able to achieve. Similarly, republican thinkers were jostled and discredited throughout these years, and most were willing to support Sihanouk for opportunistic reasons. The previous alternative to the prince, Son Ngoc Thanh, was forced in the later 1950s to seek financial support from foreign countries, including Thailand, South Vietnam, and in all probability, the United States. He lost his following, and Sihanouk was able to call him, shrilly but with some justice, a traitor to Cambodia, which he had not been, perhaps, when he worked alongside the Japanese in the early 1940s.

CAMBODIA IN CHAOS

The debate between radicals and republicans, stifled in the 1950s and 1960s, reemerged on a small scale after 1967 when Communist insurgency against Sihanouk began and took the form of a full-scale civil war after Sihanouk was overthrown, in large part by remnants of the Democratic party, in the spring of 1970. For the next five years, while Phnom Penh and a few other urban centers were governed by the Khmer Republic, the Cambodian landscape was laid waste by U.S. bombing and by a civil war, fought with the uncompromising ferocity of Jayavarman's campaigns against Champa and the wars of the nineteenth century. When the Communists under Pol Pot came to power in 1975 as the government of Democratic Kampuchea, millions of Cambodians were displaced, and hundreds of thousands starved to death or were assassinated by supporters of the new regime. From that point on, the entire society was mobilized, under frequently fearsome conditions, to "build and defend" the country, first against class enemies, "feudal remnants" of the Lon Nol period, and then against the outside world, in particular against Cambodia's "traditional enemies," the Vietnamese.

Despite its sweeping revolutionary claims, the Pol Pot regime resembled the Cambodian governments that had immediately preceded it in three important ways. First, it showed no patience with or compassion toward political opponents, including or perhaps especially those with socialist credentials. Thousands of these people were tortured to death at the interrogation center at Tuol Sleng on the outskirts of Phnom Penh in 1976–1978. Second, the regime did little to alleviate shortages of food or to remedy the inadequacies of education and hygiene among Cambodia's rural poor, in whose name the revolution was allegedly being carried out. This is because the authorities in charge of Democratic Kampuchea (DK) were interested in power, organization, warfare, and ideology but paid little attention to the costs or consequences involved. Neither, as we have seen, did Jayavarman VII. Finally, the regime made no attempt to live in peace with its immediate neighbors.

It is tempting, indeed, to seek some parallels to this behavior in the actions of rulers throughout Cambodian history.[31] Those in command in the Pol Pot years were a kind of ruling family; they had been in clandestine association for more than twenty years; they were convinced that they had, in a sense, been born to rule the Cambodian people. But their time together, and the behavior of the regimes they successively opposed, intensified what may have been a shared suspiciousness among them. Ironically, their suspicions increased with victory. From 1975 to 1978, politics at the center came to resemble the factional politics of the eighteenth century, mixed with the kind of impositions favored by Jayavarman VII. Was the DK government strong or weak?

Like nearly all the governments that had preceded it, it was too weak to trust itself to the people it "consumed." Like very few of them, it was strong enough, right up to the end, to impose its will on the *sruk,* assassinating hundreds and perhaps thousands of cadres who urged, or were thought to believe in, a compromise with Vietnam. It was not, like Hitler's Third Reich, a popular dictatorship, except among "liberated" segments of the society and then only for a couple of years. At the same time, it commanded sufficient loyalty among the armed forces and cadres to keep the entire country at work, without pay or material incentives, on what was often a starvation diet for three and a half years. Had war not broken out with Vietnam, it is conceivable that the DK regime would have lasted a good deal longer.

Relations between Democratic Kampuchea and Communist Vietnam were never good, and with hindsight it appears that the war that broke out between the two countries in 1977–1978 was more or less inevitable. Pol Pot's regime often boasted that it had brought to an end "two thousand years" of Cambodia's history. Spokesmen for Democratic Kampuchea claimed that liberated peasants and workers owed nothing to Cambodia's past. Interestingly, however, the regime chose to pursue an anti-Vietnamese foreign policy that closely resembled policies followed by Lon Nol's ill-fated Khmer Republic and by Sihanouk in the 1950s and 1960s. Pol Pot chose to stress this continuity for many reasons, including his alliance with China, which was also anti-Vietnamese, but largely because the leaders of Democratic Kampuchea were fearful of the "special relationship" that the Vietnamese claimed to perceive between the Vietnamese Communist party and its counterpart in Cambodia. Moreover, the ideology of Democratic Kampuchea was ferociously nationalistic; many speakers emphasized the "sacredness" of Cambodia's territory; and quarrels arose with Vietnam about the ownership of offshore islands as early as July 1975. In 1976–1977, conflict between the two countries intensified. Full-scale warfare broke out toward the end of 1977. In December 1978 and January 1979, Vietnamese forces invaded Cambodia in strength; within two weeks they were in control of almost all of the country. Pol Pot and perhaps fifty thousand supporters, including most of his army, escaped—in many cases by rail—to the northwestern corner of Cambodia. Meanwhile, in Phnom Penh, the Vietnamese installed a government sympathetic to them made up of defectors from Pol Pot's Communist party, survivors from earlier regimes, and Cambodians trained in Hanoi in the 1950s and 1960s—a group that had been decimated by Pol Pot's faction when they were infiltrated into Cambodia by Vietnamese in the early 1970s.

As these lines are written (December 1982) most of Cambodia is occupied, quite peaceably, by Vietnamese troops and governed from Phnom Penh by a pro-Vietnamese group of radical Cambodians, styling themselves the People's Republic of Kampuchea. The systematic killings of certain opponents in Phnom Penh and the countryside have stopped. But guerrillas loyal to Pol Pot, or to the DK's form of revolution, and others loyal, perhaps, to Cambodia's precommunist past, as exemplified by Sihanouk and one of his former ministers, Son Sann, are poised along the Thai frontier, clashing occasionally with Vietnamese troops, occasionally with each other, while seeking foreign assistance and support. In the meantime, tens of thousands of Cambodia's bourgeoisie have taken up residence in the West. Others with less affluent connections are holed up in refugee camps in Thailand, fearful of going home and unable to find shelter somewhere else. Hundreds of thousands of Khmer of all social classes have had their families decimated over the last eleven years by warfare, starvation, assassination, purges, and disease. The PRK, in other words, is a society of survivors, like Germany or Japan in 1945–1946. With these two examples in mind, moreover, it is hazardous to talk about the "survival" or "extinction" of Cambodia.

It is less hazardous to point out some of the changes that have occurred. Over the past few years, the Cambodian people, removed for so long from the pages of their history, have burst upon the consciousness and conscience of other cultures as diplomatic playthings in a game of realpolitik, objects of pity, emblems of guilt, or exemplars of revolution. At enormous cost to themselves, only partly inflicted on them by outsiders, and without asking for the privilege, they have also come into their own history, perhaps only briefly, but probably for a longer time.

One result of this change is that Cambodians can no longer be treated merely as objects of study by "Orientalists" like myself. Instead, they have become subjects of history, capable of deciding on their future in ways that were not available to them and would have been difficult to predict in 1953. This is not to say that in the short run at least they will have much to contribute in an institutional way to determining the alliances that the PRK chooses to form or the priorities that it selects after consultation with Vietnam. But we should not conclude that the Cambodians are "puppets," as perhaps they once had been, or suggest that the forces at play in Cambodia today are merely another set of traditional *chaovay* "consuming" them. One side effect of the Pol Pot regime was that the governors came to be drawn from people with a wider range of social origins than at any point in Cambodian history. Similarly, many of the governed, or "new people," as they were called, were people who had assumed that they themselves constituted the Cambodian elite and thus were "born to rule." Because so many of these "new people" have left the country and hundreds of thousands of others have been killed, it seems unlikely that a foreseeable Cambodian government will be able or willing to fill its ranks with people who were "born to rule" before the revolution. Similarly, it is unlikely that any Cambodian government will be able to leave the rural poor out of its calculations to the same extent, or for the same reasons, as did so many of the governments depicted in this book. This is because a postrevolutionary society is not usually a counterrevolutionary one, not only because of government oppression but also because of a transformed consensus.

In the past what made Cambodians different from Vietnamese was in part their tendency to see hierarchy, injustice, and foreign hegemony as inevitable aspects of their lives. Cambodians (except those at the top) felt aggrieved, but they did not see themselves as belonging to classes or to a nation. Politics happened to them, arriving from outside. In the 1970s, this fatalistic perception of the world broke down. Much of Cambodia's material culture was destroyed in the process. Perhaps a million people died of hardship, warfare, and executions. In the 1970s, like Humpty Dumpty, Cambodia "had a great fall," far greater, I think, than what had happened in the fifteenth century or even in the 1840s, when members of the elite remained behind, when the Vietnamese had gone, to rebuild Cambodian life. When the 1970s were over, on the other hand, Cambodia's entrepreneurial minorities (Cham, Chinese, Sino-Cambodians, Europeans, Vietnamese) had left the country or been killed. So had Cambodia's "natural leaders" from the *sangha,* the royal family, the bureaucracy, and the army. If the society was to be rebuilt as before, where were the "builders" to come from?

Will survivors of the 1970s, and especially those born after 1979, be able to put their country "together again"? Even if they could do so, they may not be willing to reconstruct everything that the 1970s tore apart. The horrors of those years, ironically, liberated them more thoroughly from their history than ever before. This transformation has been carried out in most cases against their will and at enormous cost: The choices Cambodians have made, among death, subjugation, exile, and subsistence, are not ones to be faced by many readers of this book.

The society that lingered on in Phnom Penh until April 1975 cannot come back to life inside Cambodia, partly because it served the material interests of so few, partly because it has been so thoroughly dismantled, and partly because, for the people who have remained behind, the process of liberating themselves from their most recent indigenous tyranny—Pol

Pot's—has meant ushering in a new, open-ended period of foreign domination.

Looking back at what DK spokesmen referred to as "two thousand years of Cambodian history," we can perceive an alternation over the years among tyrannies, disorder, and foreign intervention, between local leaders who allowed themselves to be compared to gods and outsiders who have felt compelled, for various reasons, to redeem Cambodians from other foreigners or from themselves. For the Cambodian people, the price of allowing this process to repeat itself so often has been to postpone their independence and to force them back repeatedly onto reliance on a personal scheme of values. In the 1970s, I would suggest, these values came under sustained attack from a tyranny more systematic than any that preceded it. In the 1970s, Cambodians behaved like a nation, or like several nations, and suffered the destruction of nearly everything they had ever taken for granted. In coming back to life under what has so far been comparatively cautious guidance from Hanoi, they have been forced by what has happened to them (which is to say, to a large extent, what they have done to one another) to act for the first time as if their future were more important, and more easily perceived, than anything that has happened in their past.

For these reasons, the 1980s should not be seen as an interval between two periods of recognizably Cambodian history, following a period of disorder, but as the beginning of a wide-ranging transformation, whose characteristics, duration, and consequences are impossible to predict.

Notes

ABBREVIATIONS

AA	*Artibus Asiae*
AOM	France. *Archives d'outremer*
AP	*Asian Perspectives*
BEFEO	*Bulletin de l'Ecole Française d'Extrême Orient*
BSEI	*Bulletin de la Société des Etudes Indochinoises*
BSOAS	*Bulletin of the School of Oriental and African Studies*
CMH	*Chotmai Het* (Thai archival documents)
CSSH	*Comparative Studies in Society and History*
DNTL	*Dai Nam Thuc Luc Chinh Bien*
FA	*France Asie*
FBIS	United States. *Foreign Broadcast Information Service*
FEQ	*Far Eastern Quarterly*
IC	*Inscriptions du Cambodge*
JA	*Journal Asiatique*
JAS	*Journal of Asian Studies*
JESHO	*Journal of Economic and Social History of the Orient*
JMBRAS	*Journal of the Malay Branch of the Royal Asiatic Society*
JRAS	*Journal of the Royal Asiatic Society*
JSEAH	*Journal of Southeast Asian History*
JSEAS	*Journal of Southeast Asian Studies*
JSS	*Journal of the Siam Society*
MAS	*Modern Asian Studies*
PA	*Pacific Affairs*
RI	*Revue Indochinoise*

CHAPTER 1. INTRODUCTION

1. Adhémard Leclère, *Histoire du Cambodge* (Paris, 1914). See George Coedes's critical review in *Bulletin de l'Ecole Francaise d'Extrême Orient* (*BEFEO*), Vol. 14 (1914):47–54.

2. These subsequent surveys include Martin Herz, *A Short History of Cambodia* (New York, 1958); and A. Dauphin Meunier, *Histoire du Cambodge* (Paris, 1968). David P. Chandler, *The Land and People of Cambodia* (Philadelphia, 1972), is an even briefer account, geared to secondary schools.

3. See particularly Milton Osborne, *Politics and Power in Cambodia: The Sihanouk Years* (Melbourne, 1973). Prince Norodom Sihanouk has written several volumes of memoirs, including *Indochine vue de Pékin* (Paris, 1972), *My Wars with the CIA* (New York, 1973), *Chroniques de guerre . . . et de l'espoir* (Paris, 1979), and *Souvenirs doux et amers* (Paris, 1981). Other valuable studies of this period include Roger M. Smith, *Cambodia's Foreign Policy* (Ithaca, N.Y., 1966); and Charles Meyer, *Derrière le sourire khmer* (Paris, 1971).

4. Lon Nol's archives from the period have presumably been destroyed; those relating to U.S. involvement are heavily censored; and most of the major participants in the government of the Khmer Republic have disappeared. For a persuasive indictment of the U.S. role during the early 1970s, see William Shawcross, *Sideshow* (New York, 1979).

5. See Serge Thion and Ben Kiernan (eds.), *Khmer Rouge!* (Paris, 1981); Ben Kiernan and Chanthou Boua (eds.), *Peasants and Politics in Kampuchea, 1942–1981* (London, 1982); and David P. Chandler and Ben Kiernan (eds.), *Revolution and Its Aftermath in Kampuchea: Eight Essays* (New Haven, 1982). Ben Kiernan's work and the work of other scholars, including Anthony Barnett, Timothy Carney, Stephen Heder, and Michael Vickery, now in process, will do much to illuminate the period.

6. See Lucien Hanks, "Merit and Power in the Thai Social Order," *American Anthropologist,* Vol. 64 (1962):1247–1261; and David P. Chandler, "The Tragedy of Cambodian History," *Pacific Affairs (PA),* Vol. 52, No. 3 (Fall 1979):410–419.

7. See Centre d'Études et de Recherches Marxistes (comp.), *Sur le "mode de production asiatique,"* (Paris, 1969). Michael Vickery is now examining Angkorean society, especially in the eleventh century, in the light of this concept; see Chapters 3 and 4 below.

8. See David Joel Steinberg et al., (eds.), *In Search of Southeast Asia* (New York, 1971), pp. 169–238, for a discussion of the notion of "frameworks for nations."

9. On Cambodian demography, see J. Migozzi, *Cambodge: Faits et problèmes de population* (Paris, 1973).

10. For a discussion of this problem see David P. Chandler, "Seeing Red: Perceptions of Cambodian History in Democratic Kampuchea," in Chandler and Kiernan, *Revolution and its Aftermath.*

CHAPTER 2. THE BEGINNINGS OF CAMBODIAN HISTORY

1. C. Mourer, "The Prehistoric Industry of Laang Spean," *Archaeology and Physical Anthropology of Oceanea,* Vol. 5, No. 2 (1970):128–146. See also J. P. Carbonnel, "Recent Data on the Cambodian Neolithic," in R. B. Smith and W. Watson (eds.), *Early Southeast Asia* (Oxford, 1979), pp. 223–226; and Donn Bayard, "The Roots of Indo-Chinese Civilization: Recent Developments

in the Pre-history of Southeast Asia," *PA*, Vol. 53, No. 1 (Spring 1980):89–114.

2. See I. W. Mabbett, "The Indianization of Southeast Asia," *Journal of Southeast Asian Studies (JSEAS)*, Vol. 8, No. 1 (March 1977):1–14, and Vol. 8, No. 2 (September 1977):143–161; and Paul Mus, *India Seen from the East*, trans. by I. W. Mabbett and D. P. Chandler (Clayton, Australia, 1975). For linguistic evidence, see Judith M. Jacob, "Sanskrit Loanwords in Pre-Angkor Khmer," *Mon-Khmer Studies VI* (Honolulu, 1977), pp. 151–168.

3. G. Coedes, *The Making of Southeast Asia* (London, 1966), pp. 54–55.

4. See Paul Mus, *L'angle de l'Asie*, ed. S. Thion (Paris, 1977), especially, pp. 109–121.

5. I. W. Mabbett, "*Varnas* in Angkor and the Indian Caste System," *Journal of Asian Studies (JAS)*, Vol. 36, No. 3 (May 1977):429–442.

6. L. Finot, "Sur quelques traditions indochinoises,"*Bulletin de la Commission Archéologique de l'Indochine* (1911), pp. 20–37. See also Evéline Porée-Maspero, "Nouvelle étude sur le nagi Soma," *Journal Asiatique (JA)*, Vol. 238 (1955): 257–267.

7. K. Bhattacharya, *Les religions brahmaniques dans l'ancien Cambodge* (Paris, 1961), p. 11n.

8. Louis Malleret, *L'archéologie du delta du Mekong,* 4 vols. (Paris, 1959–1963), especially Vols. 1 and 2. See also G. Coedes, "Fouilles en Cochinchine," *Artibus Asiae (AA)*, Vol. 10 (1947):190–199.

9. See O. W. Wolters, *Early Indonesian Commerce: A Study of the Origins of Srivijaya* (Ithaca, N.Y., 1967); and Wang Gungwu, "The Nanhai Trade: A Study of the Early History of Chinese Trade in the South China Sea," *Journal of the Malay Branch of the Royal Asiatic Society (JMBRAS)*, Vol. 31, No. 2 (June 1958):31–45.

10. Cited by G. Coedes, *The Indianization of Southeast Asia* (Honolulu, 1968), p. 61.

11. Paul Wheatley, "The Mount of the Immortals: A Note on Tamil Cultural Influence in Fifth Century Indo-China," *Oriens Extremus*, Vol. 21, No. 1 (June 1974):97–109.

12. C. Jacques, " 'Funan,' 'Zhenla': The Reality Concealed by These Chinese Views of Indo-China," in Smith and Watson, *Early Southeast Asia*, pp. 371–379. See also O. W. Wolters, "Northwestern Cambodia in the 7th Century," *Bulletin of the School of Oriental and African Studies (BSOAS)*, Vol. 37, No. 2 (1974):355–384.

13. Cited by L. P. Briggs, *The Ancient Khmer Empire* (Philadelphia, 1951), p. 29.

14. Ibid., p. 28.

15. See P. Paris, "Anciens canaux reconnus sur photographes aeriennes dans les provinces de Takeo et Chaudoc," *BEFEO*, Vol. 31 (1931):221–224; and Paris, "Anciens canaux reconnus sur photographes aeriennes dans les provinces de Takeo, Chaudoc et Rach Gia" *BEFEO*, Vol. 41 (1941):365–370.

16. J.D.M. Derret, "Rajadharma," *JAS* Vol. 35, No. 4 (August 1976):605. The full quotation reads: "The agricultural population is fascinated with power, which is essential to its very life. The soil cannot be tilled without *protection* and *rain*."

17. K. Bhattacharya, "La secte des Pacupata dans l'ancien Cambodge." *JA*, Vol. 243 (1955):479–487.

18. O. W. Wolters, "Khmer 'Hinduism' in the Seventh Century," in Smith and Watson, *Early Southeast Asia,* pp. 427–442.

19. See David P. Chandler, "Royally Sponsored Human Sacrifices in Nineteenth Century Cambodia: The Cult of *Me Sa* (Uma Mahisasuramardini) at Ba Phnom," *Journal of the Siam Society, (JSS)*, Vol. 62, No. 2 (1974):207–221.

20. See Evéline Porée-Maspero, *Etude sur les rites agraires des cambodgiens,* 3 vols. (Paris, 1962–1969).

21. See Institut Bouddhique (comp.), *Prachum ruong preng phak ti 8* [Collected folktales, volume 8] (Phnom Penh, 1971), which is concerned with *nak ta;* and my review in *JSS,* Vol. 61, No. 2 (July 1973):219–221.

22. W. Solheim, "Regional Reports: Cambodia, Laos and Vietnam," *Asian Perspectives, (AP)*, Vol. 3 (1960):25.

23. Mus, *India Seen from the East,* pp. 13ff.

24. C. Jacques, "Etudes d'épigraphie cambodgienne IX: La stèle du Baphuon," *BEFEO,* Vol. 63 (1976):351–368; and K. 441, Sambor Prei Kuk inscription, *Inscriptions du Cambodge (IC),* Vol. 4, p. 14 ("K." preceding a number places the inscription in the inventory of the Ecole Française d'Extrême Orient).

25. See P. N. Jenner, *A Chronological Inventory of the Inscriptions of Cambodia* (Honolulu, 1980).

26. J. Jacob, "Pre-Angkor Cambodia," in Smith and Watson, *Early Southeast Asia,* pp. 406–426. For a stimulating discussion of state formation in early Southeast Asia from a Marxist perspective, see Jonathan Friedman, *System, Structure and Contradiction in the Evolution of "Asiatic" Social Formations.* (Ann Arbor, Mich., 1975), especially pp. 373ff.

27. See Briggs, *Ancient Khmer Empire,* pp. 38–57, for a summary of the evidence.

28. C. Jacques, " 'Funan', 'Zhenla'," p. 376. But cf., in the same volume, Ronald C. Ng, "The Geographical Habitat of Historical Settlement in Mainland Southeast Asia," p. 271, which mentions "the rise and fall of . . . important civilizations and centers of power, such as Funan, Chenla, Champa and finally Angkor."

29. Friedman, *System, Structure,* pp. 341–344. This discussion also draws on Michael Vickery, "Angkor and the Asiatic Mode of Production," unpublished seminar paper, Monash University, November 27, 1981.

CHAPTER 3. KINGSHIP AND SOCIETY AT ANGKOR

1. See B. P. Groslier, *Angkor et le Cambodge au XVIe siècle* (Paris, 1958).

2. G. Coedes, *The Indianized States of Southeast Asia* (Honolulu, 1968), and L. P. Briggs, *The Ancient Khmer Empire* (Philadelphia, 1952).

3. G. Coedes, "L'avenir des études khmères," *Bulletin de la Société des Etudes Indochinoises (BSEI),* Vol. 40 (1965):205–213. The rest of this chapter, like all scholarship on Cambodia, owes a great deal to Coedes's work and that of his colleagues and pupils at the Ecole Française d'Extrême Orient.

4. J. Boisselier, *Le Cambodge* (Paris, 1966), synthesizes the work of previous scholars.

5. G. Coedes and P. Dupont, "L'inscription de Sdok Kak Thom," *BEFEO*, Vol. 43 (1942–1943):57–134. See also I. W. Mabbett, "Devaraja," *JSEAH*, Vol. 10, No. 2 (1969):202–223; and Nidhi Aeusrivognse, "The *Devaraja* Cult and Khmer Kingship at Angkor," in K. R. Hall and J. K. Whitmore (eds.), *Explorations in Early Southeast Asian History* (Ann Arbor, Mich., 1976), pp. 107–148.

6. K. 956, from Wat Samrong, *IC*, Vol. 7, pp. 128–129.

7. C. Jacques, "La carrière de Jayavarman II," *BEFEO*, Vol. 59 (1972):194–220.

8. O. W. Wolters, "Jayavarman II's Military Power: The Territorial Foundation of the Angkor Empire," *Journal of the Royal Asiatic Society (JRAS)*, (1973):21–30.

9. K. 989, stele from Prasat Ben, *IC*, Vol. 7, pp. 21–30.

10. Hermann Kulke, *The Devaraja Cult*, trans. I. W. Mabbett (Ithaca, N.Y., 1978).

11. G. Coedes, "Les Capitales de Jayavarman II," *BEFEO*, Vol. 28 (1928):116.

12. P. Stern, "Diversité et rhythme des fondations royales khmères," *BEFEO*, Vol. 44, No. 2 (1951):649–685.

13. A. Bergaigne, *Les inscriptions sanscrites du Cambodge* (Paris, 1882), p. 127.

14. For a discussion of this style, see G. de Coral Remusat, "Influences javanaises dans l'art de Roluoh," *JA*, Vol. 223 (1933):190–192.

15. K. 713, stele from Preah Ko, *IC*, Vol. 1, pp. 18–31.

16. K. 809, from Prasat Kandol Dom, *IC*, Vol. 1, p. 43.

17. Cited in S. Sahai, *Institutions politiques et organisation administrative du Cambodge* (Paris, 1970), p. 42n.

18. R. Stencel and Eleanor Moron, "Astronomy and Cosmology at Angkor Wat," *Science*, Vol. 193 (July 23, 1978):281–287.

19. See G. Coedes, "A la recherche du Yasodharasrama," *BEFEO*, Vol. 32 (1932):84–112; and Bergaigne, *Inscriptions sanscrites*, pp. 166–211.

20. On the importance of the Northeast, see P. Paris, "L'importance rituelle du nord-est et ses applications en Indochine," *BEFEO*, Vol. 41, (1941):301–333.

21. See B. P. Groslier, *Inscriptions du Bayon* (Paris, 1973), p. 156; and David P. Chandler, "Maps for the Ancestors: Sacralized Topography and Echoes of Angkor in Two Cambodian Texts," *JSS*, Vol. 64, No. 2 (July 1976):170–187, especially note 28.

22. See V. Goloubew, "Le Phnom Bakheng et la ville de Yasovarman," *BEFEO*, Vol. 33 (1933):319–344; and V. Goloubew, "Nouvelles recherches autour de Phnom Bakheng," *BEFEO*, Vol. 34 (1934):576–600.

23. J.Filliozat, "Le symbolisme du monument du Phnom Bakheng," *BEFEO*, Vol. 44, No. 2 (1954):527–554.

24. See John Black, *The Lofty Sanctuary of Khao Prah Vihar* (Bangkok, 1976).

25. Bergaigne, *Inscriptions Sanscrites*, p. 322. For similar passages, see pp. 227, 376.

26. See G. Coedes, "Le véritable fondateur du culte de la royauté divine au Cambodge," in H. B. Sarkar (ed.), *R. C. Majumdar Felicitation Volume* (Calcutta, 1970), pp. 56–66. See also Sahai, *Institutions*, p. 46n.

27. Kulke, *Devaraja Cult*, 33ff.

28. G. Coedes, "Les inscriptions de Bat Chum," *JA*, Vol. 10, No. 8 (1908):213–254.

29. K. 806, Pre Rup stele, *IC*, Vol. 1, pp. 73–142.

30. See L. Finot and V. Goloubew, *Le Temple d'Içvarapura* (Paris, 1926).

31. K. 111, stele from Wat Sithor, *IC*, Vol. 6, pp. 195–211 at 196.

32. "L'Inscription de Toul Komnap Ta Kin (K. 125)," *BEFEO*, Vol.28, (1928):140–144.

33. Michael Vickery, "The Reign of Suryavarman I and the Dynamics of Angkorean Development," unpublished paper. I am grateful to Dr. Vickery for allowing me to consult this paper. On the notion of the Asiatic mode of production as related to Angkor, which Vickery discussed in detail, see L. Sedov, "La société angkorienne et le problème du mode de production asiatique," in Centre d'Études et de Recherches Marxistes (comp.), *Sur le "mode de production asiatique"* (Paris, 1969), pp. 327–344.

34. M. De Coral Remusat, "La date de Takev," *BEFEO*, Vol. 34, (1934):401–434 at 425.

35. G. Coedes, "Le serment des fonctionnaires de Suryavarman I," *BEFEO*, Vol. 13, No. 6 (1913):11–17. For a similar oath sworn by Cambodian officials in the nineteenth and twentieth centuries, see Chandler, "Maps for the Ancestors," passim.

36. H. de Mestrier du Bourg, "La première moitié du XIe siècle au Cambodge," *JA*, Vol. 258 (1970):281–314.

37. Kenneth Hall, "Eleventh Century Commercial Development in Angkor and Champa," *JSEAS*, Vol. X, No. 2 (September 1979):420–434; and K. Hall, "Khmer Commercial Development and Foreign Contacts Under Suryavarman," *Journal of Economic and Social History of the Orient* (*JESHO*), Vol. 18, No. 3 (1975):318–336. On the question of trade in early Southeast Asia, see Karl L. Hutterer (ed.), *Economic Exchange and Social Interaction in Southeast Asia: Perspectives from Prehistory, History and Ethnography* (Ann Arbor, Mich., 1977), especially the chapter by Brian Foster, "Trade, Social Conflict, and Social Integration: Rethinking Some Old Ideas on Exchange," pp. 3–22.

38. A. Barth, *Inscriptions sanscrites du Cambodge* (Paris, 1885), p. 139.

39. I. W. Mabbett, "Kingship at Angkor," *JSS*, Vol. 66, No. 2 (July 1978):1–58.

40. I. W. Mabbett, "Some Remarks on the Present State of Knowledge About Slavery at Angkor," in Anthony Reid (ed.), *Slavery in Southeast Asia* (forthcoming). I am grateful to Dr. Mabbett for allowing me to consult this manuscript. See also C. Jacques, "A propos de l'esclavage dans l'ancien Cambodge," in B. P. Lafont (ed.), *L'Asie du sud-est continentale* (Paris, 1976), Vol. 1, pp. 71–76.

41. Institut Bouddhique, Phnom Penh, Commission des Moeurs et Coutumes Cambodgiennes (CMCC), Archive number 94.004.

42. L. Finot, "L'inscription de Ban Theat (K. 364)," *BEFEO*, Vol. 12 (1912):1–27 at stanzas 33–34.

43. R. Stencel and Eleanor Moron, "Astronomy and Cosmology at Angkor Wat," *Science*, Vol. 193 (July 23, 1978):281–287.

44. For a summary of the debate, see G. Coedes, *Pour mieux comprendre Angkor* (Paris, 1947), pp. 68–84.

45. Eleanor Moron, "Configuration of Time and Space at Angkor Wat," *Studies in Indo-Asian Art and Culture,* Vol. 5 (1977):217–267.

46. Stencel et al., "Astronomy and Cosmology," pp. 281–287.

47. Groslier, *Inscriptions du Bayon,* p. 141.

48. Briggs, *Ancient Khmer Empire,* p. 206.

49. For a review of the literature, see B. P. Groslier, "La cité hydraulique angkorienne. Exploitation ou surexploitation du sol?" *BEFEO,* Vol. 66 (1979):161–202. See also B. P. Groslier, "Agriculture et religion dans L'empire angkorien," *Etudes rurales,* Nos. 53–56 (January–December, 1974):95–117. For a contrary argument advanced by a hydraulic engineer, see W. J. Van Liere, "Traditional Water Management in the Lower Mekong Basin," *World Archaeology,* Vol. 11, No. 3 (Fall 1980):265–280. Van Liere suggested that the artificial lakes at Angkor had no distributive function but served merely as adjuncts to the metaphysical world view of Angkorean kings. The farming of the shores of the Tonle Sap when the lake receded, however, was quite advanced and may have been able to support the sizable populations needed to build the temples and serve in them.

50. See also Rhoads Murphey, "The Ruin of Ancient Ceylon," *JAS,* Vol. 16, No. 1 (February 1957):181–200.

51. Michael Coe, "The Khmer Settlement Pattern: A Possible Analogy with That of the Maya," *American Antiquity,* Vol. 22 (1957):409–410; and M. Coe, "Social Typology and Tropical Forest Civilizations," *Comparative Studies in Society and History (CSSH),* Vol. 4 (1961–1962):65–85.

CHAPTER 4. JAYAVARMAN VII AND THE CRISIS OF THE THIRTEENTH CENTURY

1. G. Coedes, *Pour mieux comprendre Angkor,* (Paris, 1947), pp. 176–210.

2. B. P. Groslier, *Inscriptions du Bayon,* (Paris, 1973), p. 141.

3. This statue was discovered in 1958. See G. Coedes, "Le portrait dans l'art khmer," *AA,* Vol. 7, No. 3 (1960):179–188.

4. See J. Boisselier, "Reflexions sur l'art du Jayavarman VII," *BSEI,* Vol. 27, No. 3 (1952):261–273; Paul Mus, "Angkor at the Time of Jayavarman VII," *Indian Arts and Letters,* Vol. 11 (1937):65–75; and P. Mus, "Angkor vu du Japon," *France Asie, (FA),* Nos. 175–176 (1962):521–538. Groslier, *Inscriptions du Bayon,* p. 118, makes the valuable point that Jayavarman VII, unlike some of his predecessors, restored no temples dedicated by earlier kings.

5. G. Maspero, *Le royaume de Champa* (Paris, 1928), p. 164.

6. Ibid.

7. K. 485, stele from Phimeanakas, *IC,* Vol. 2, p. 171.

8. Ibid., p. 175.

9. Coedes, "Le portrait." Groslier, *Inscriptions du Bayon,* p. 194, however, claims that Coedes's inventory of portrait statues is incomplete.

10. L. Finot, "L'inscription sanscrite de Say-Fong," *BEFEO,* Vol. 3, No.2 (1903):18–33. See also G. Coedes, "Les hôpitaux de Jayavarman VII," *BEFEO,* Vol. 40 (1940):344–347.

11. Boisselier,"Réflexions," p. 263.

12. P. Stern, *Les monuments khmers du style de Bayon et Jayavarman VII* (Paris, 1965), passim. See also J. Auboyer, "Aspects de l'art bouddhique au pays khmer au temps de Jayavarman VII," in W. Watson (ed.), *Mahayanist Art After AD 900* (London, 1977), pp. 66–74; and H. W. Woodward, Jr., *Studies in the Art of Central Siam, 950–1350 AD* (Ann Arbor, Mich., 1975).

13. K.273, Ta Prohm inscription, *BEFEO*, Vol. 6, No. 2 (1906):44-81.

14. G. Coedes, "Les gites d'étape à la fin du XIIIe siècle," *BEFEO*, Vol. 40, (1940):347–349.

15. See G. Coedes, "Le stèle de Preah Khan," *BEFEO*, Vol. 41 (1941): 256–301. The passage quoted appears on p. 287.

16. Groslier, *Inscriptions du Bayon*, p. 167.

17. This passage derives in large part from arguments advanced by Hiram W. Woodward, Jr., in private communications.

18. See Ta Prohm inscription.

19. See L. Finot and V. Goloubew, "Le symbolisme de Nak Pean," *BEFEO*, Vol. 23 (1923):401-405; and V. Goloubew, "Le cheval Balaha," *BEFEO*, Vol. 27 (1927):223-238.

20. J. Boisselier, "Pouvoir royal et symbolisme architectural: Neak Pean et son importance pour la royauté angkorienne," *AA*, Vol. 21 (1970):91-107.

21. See Chapter 3, note 20, above.

22. J. Boisselier, "Notes sur l'art du bronze dans l'ancien Cambodge," *AA*, Vol. 29 (1967):275-350.

23. See G. Groslier, *A l'ombre d'Angkor* (Paris, 1916), pp. 148–182; and G. Groslier, "Etude sur le temps passé à la construction d'un grand temple khmer (Banteay Chhmar)" *BEFEO*, Vol. 35 (1935):159-176.

24. See Jacques Dumarcay, *Le Bayon, Histoire architecturale du temple* (Paris, 1973), especially pp. 57–64. For an interesting explanation of changes in the iconography of the Bayon, see Hiram W. Woodward, Jr., "Tantric Buddhism at Angkor Thom," *Ars Orientalis*, Vol. 12 (1981):57–68.

25. K.287, stele from Prasat Chrung, *IC*, Vol. 4, pp. 207–253 at p. 250.

26. See Jean Boisselier and David Snellgrove (eds.), *The Image of the Buddha* (Paris, 1978), p. 410.

27. For a detailed discussion of this conversion, see G. Coedes, "Documents sur l'histoire politique et religieuse du Laos occidental," *BEFEO*, Vol. 25, (1925):1–202. See also N. A. Jayawickrama (trans.), *The Sheaf of Garlands of the Epochs of the Conqueror* (London, 1968); and A. Leclère, *Le bouddhisme au Cambodge* (Paris, 1899), pp. 1–34.

28. L.P. Briggs, *The Ancient Khmer Empire* (Philadelphia, 1952), pp. 242 and 259.

29. P. Pelliot (ed.), *Mémoires sur les coutumes du Cambodge de Tcheou Ta Kuan* (Paris, 1951).

30. K.287, stele from Prasat Chrung, *IC*, Vol. 4, p. 208.

31. Jan Myrdal and Gun Kessle, *Angkor: An Essay on Art and Imperialism* (New York, 1970), p. 140.

32. For a summary of the evidence, see David P. Chandler, "Folk Memories of Angkor in Nineteenth Century Cambodia: The Legend of the Leper King," *JSS*, Vol. 67, No. 1 (January 1979):54–62.

33. G. Coedes, "Une période critique dans l'Asie du Sud Est: Le XIIIe siècle," *BSEI*, Vol. 33 (1958):387–400.

34. Pelliot, *Mémoires*, pp. 411–420.

35. Interestingly, although Cambodian classical literature makes almost no mention of slaves, one of the most popular folktale cycles is concerned with the triumphs of an unscrupulous slave who outwits everyone he meets, including the emperor of China. See Pierre Bitard (trans.), *La merveilleuse histoire de Thmenh Chey l'astucieux* (Saigon, 1956).

36. M. C. Ricklefs, "Land and Law in the Epigraphy of Tenth Century Cambodia," *JAS*, Vol. 26, No. 3 (May 1967).

37. Finot et al., *Le temple d'Içvarapura*, p. 83.

38. L. Finot, "Temple de Mangalatha a Angkor Thom," *BEFEO*, Vol. 25 (1925):393–406.

CHAPTER 5. CAMBODIA'S DARK AGES

1. O. W. Wolters, "The Khmer King at Basan," *Asia Major*, Vol. 12, No. 1 (1966):86.

2. Michael Vickery, "The 2/k 125 fragment: A Lost Chronicle of Ayuthaya," *JSS*, Vol. 65, No. 1 (January 1977):1–80.

3. G. Coedes, "La fondation du Phnom Penh," *BEFEO*, Vol. 13, No. 3 (1913):6–11.

4. See J. M. Gullick, *Indigenous Political Systems of Western Malaya* (London, 1958), especially pp. 125–143.

5. Vickery, "The 2/k 125 fragment," pp. 60–62.

6. See B. P. Groslier, *Le Cambodge au XVIe siècle* (Paris, 1958), pp. 142–144.

7. This and the quotation in the preceding paragraph are taken from C. R. Boxer (ed.), *South China in the Sixteenth Century* (London, 1953), p. 63.

8. Groslier, *Le Cambodge au XVIe siècle*, p. 69. See also J. Dumarcay, "Le prasat prei près d'Angkor Wat," *BEFEO*, Vol. 59 (1970):189–192; and G. Coedes, "La date d'exécution des deux bas-reliefs tardifs d'Angkor Wat," *JA*, Vol. 250 (1962):235–243.

9. Khin Sok, "Deux inscriptions tardives du Phnom Bakheng," *BEFEO*, Vol. 65, No. 1 (1978):271–280.

10. Khin Sok, "L'inscription de Vatta Romlock," *BEFEO*, Vol. 67 (1980): 125–131; and Saveros Pou, "Inscription du Vat Romlok," *BEFEO*, Vol. 70 (1981): 126–130.

11. See G. Janneau, *Manuel pratique pour le cambodgien* (Saigon, 1876), pp. 87–88. See also E. Porée-Maspero, *Étude*, p. 11. A seven-volume version of the legend, in verse, was published in Phnom Penh in 1952.

12. See A. Cabaton (ed. and trans.), *Brève et véridique relation des évènements du Cambodge par Gabriel Quiroga de San Antonio* (Paris, 1941). See also L.

P. Briggs, "Spanish Intervention in Cambodia," *T'oung Pao* (1949), pp. 132–160.

13. See W.J.M. Buch, "La compagnie des Indes et l'Indochine," *BEFEO,* Vol. 36 (1936):97–196, and Vol. 37 (1937):121–237; H.P.N. Muller, *De Oost-Indische compagnie in Camboja en Laos* (The Hague, 1917); and also D. K. Basset, "The Trade of the English East India Company in Cambodia, 1651–1656," *JRAS* (1962), pp. 35–62.

14. Cabaton, *Brève et véridique relation,* p. 100.

15. Jean Delvert, *Le paysan cambodgien.* (The Hague, 1961), especially pp. 371ff.

16. Cabaton, *Brève et véridique relation,* p. 208.

17. See the nineteenth-century prose chronicle numbered P-6 in the Fonds Phnom Penh collection of the Ecole Française d'Extrême Orient in Paris.

18. S. Pou, *Etudes sur le Ramakerti* (Paris, 1977), pp. 48–49.

19. See *BEFEO,* Vol. 62 (1975):369–384; *BEFEO,* Vol. 63 (1976):313–350; and Saveros Pou, "*Subhasit* and *Cpap* in Khmer Literature," in *Ludwik Sternbach Felicitation Volume* (Lucknow, 1979), pp. 331–348. See also Saveros Pou and K. Haksrea, "Liste d'ouvrages de *Cpap,*" *JA,* Vol. 269 (1981):467–483.

20. Clifford Geertz, *The Religion of Java* (New York, 1960), pp. 248–260.

21. Saveros Pou's three-volume edition and critique of the *Ramakerti* was published by *BEFEO* in Paris in 1977–1979. The volumes include a Cambodian text, a French translation, and a volume of commentary, *Etudes sur le Ramakerti.* See also Saveros Pou, "Etudes ramakertiennes," and Saveros Pou, Lan Sunnary, and K. Haksrea, "Inventaire des oeuvres sur le Ramayana khmer (Ramakerti)," *Seksa Khmer,* Vol. 3, Nos. 3-4 (December 1981):87–126.

22. See E. Porée-Maspero, *Etude sur les rites agraires des cambodgiens,* 3 vols. (Paris and the Hague, 1962–1969), p. 528; and Saveros Pou, "Etudes ramakertiennes," p. 93, note 15.

23. F. Bizot (ed.), *Histoire de Reamker* (Phnom Penh, 1973). According to Thong Thel (personal communication), this Khmer text resembles Thai-language versions more closely than it does the seventeenth-century Cambodian text.

24. See David P. Chandler, "Songs at the Edge of the Forest: Perceptions of Order in Three Cambodian Texts," in Alexander Woodside and David K. Wyatt (eds.), *Moral Order and the Question of Change: Essays on Southeast Asian Thought* (New Haven, 1982), pp. 53–77; and Peter Carey, *The Cultural Ecology of Early Nineteenth Century Java* (Singapore, 1974), p. 4.

25. See F. Martini, "Quelques notes sur le Reamker" *AA,* Vol. 24, Nos. 3–4 (1961):351–362; and F. Martini, *La gloire de Rama* (Paris, 1978), pp. 19–30.

26. I am grateful to Barbara Hatley for this insight into *wayang.*

27. A. Leclère, *Les codes cambodgiens,* 2 vols. (Paris, 1898), pp. 123–175.

28. Mak Phoeun, "Les chroniques royales du Cambodge," Doctoral thesis, University of Paris IV, 1974, p. 176.

29. On Vietnam's "march south" and early relations with Cambodia, see Michael Cotter, "Toward a Social History of the Vietnamese Southward Movement," *JSEAH,* Vol. 9, No. 1 (March 1968):12–24; Thai Van Kiem, "La plaine aux cerfs et la princesse de jade," *BSEI,* Vol. 34 (1959):378–393; and Pham Dinh Khiem, "Une grande page d'histoire oubliée: De l'alliance des cours de Hué et d'Oudong

à la première ambassade à demeure du Vietnam au Cambodge au début du XVIIe siècle," *Etudes interdisciplinaires sur le Vietnam,* Vol. 1 (1974):145–164.

30. E. Gaspardone, "Un chinois des mers du sud," *JA,* Vol. 240, No. 3 (1952):361–385.

31. See Saveros Pou, "Les inscriptions modernes d'Angkor," *JA,* Vol. 260, No. 242 (1972):107–129; and David P. Chandler, "An Eighteenth Century Inscription from Angkor Wat," *JSS,* Vol. 59, No. 2 (July 1971):151–159.

32. On Taksin's reign, see C. J. Reynolds, "Religious Historical Writing and the Legitimation of the First Bangkok Reign," in Anthony Reid and David Marr (eds.), *Perceptions of the Past in Southeast Asia* (Singapore, 1979), pp. 90–107; and Lorraine Gesick, "The Rise and Fall of King Taksin: A Drama of Buddhist Kingship," draft paper prepared for Classical State in Southeast Asia Workshop, Santa Cruz, Calif., 1978.

33. Frank Huffman, "Thai and Cambodian: A Case of Syntactic Borrowing?" *JAS,* Vol. 93, No. 4 (1973):488–589; and idem, "Khmer Loan-Words in Thai," unpublished paper prepared for a seminar at the Center of South and Southeast Asian Studies, University of Michigan, 1980. I am grateful to Professor Huffman for allowing me to read this paper.

34. See Clifford Geertz, *Negara: The Theater State in Nineteenth Century Bali* (Princeton, N. J., 1980), especially, pp. 110–127. I am grateful to Professor Geertz for inviting me to attend two successive seminars on "The Classical State in Southeast Asia," sponsored by the Social Science Research Council in 1977 and 1978. My ideas about Cambodian kingship benefited greatly from discussions with the other guests at these occasions.

CHAPTER 6. STATE, SOCIETY, AND FOREIGN RELATIONS, 1794–1848

1. For a discussion of Asian "maps," see David P. Chandler, "Maps for the Ancestors: Sacralized Topography and Echoes of Angkor in Two Cambodian Texts," *JSS,* Vol. 64, No. 2 (July 1976): passim.; and E. R. Leach, "The Frontiers of 'Burma'," *CSSH,* Vol. 3 (1960–1961):49–68. According to Adhémard Leclère, *Recherches sur le droit publique des cambodgiens* (Paris, 1894), p. 221, the boundaries of a *sruk* in traditional Cambodia were "those of the rice fields belonging to it." These varied from year to year.

2. National Library, Bangkok, *Chotmai Het (CMH)* 1203/1 *kho* 41, mentions a Thai map of Cambodia; and Democratic Republic of Vietnam, Bureau of Historical Research (comp.), *Dai nam thuc luc chinh bien* [Primary compilation of the veritable records of imperial Vietnam] *(DNTL),* Vol. 19, p. 240, mentions a Vietnamese one; these have not survived.

3. Eng Sut, *Akkasar mahaboros khmaer,* [Documents about Khmer heroes] (Phnom Penh, 1969), p. 1148.

4. *DNTL,* Vol. 15, p. 115; and *DNTL,* Vol. 22, p. 157.

5. E. Aymonier, *Géographie du Cambodge* (Paris, 1876), pp. 31–59.

6. Ibid., p. 49.

7. *CMH* 3/1192/4/1; and *CMH* 3/1204/1 *ko*/2.

8. See W. E. Willmott, "History and Sociology of the Chinese in Cambodia Prior to the French Protectorate," *JSEAH*, Vol. 7, No. 1 (March 1966): 15–38.

9. C. E. Bouillevaux, *Voyage en Indochine* (Paris, 1858), p. 168. See also Alexander Hamilton, *A New Account of the East Indies* (London, 1727, reprinted 1930), p. 106: "There are about two hundred *Topasses,* or *Indian Portugeze* settled and married in *Cambodia,* and some of them have pretty good posts in the Government, and live great after the Fashion of that Country."

10. On the ethnography of nineteenth-century Cambodia, see Wolfgang Vollman, "Notes sur les relations inter-ethniques au Cambodge du XIXe siècle," *Asie du Sud-Est et Monde Insulindien,* Vol. 4, No. 2 (1973):172–207, drawn entirely from Western-language sources.

11. *DNTL,* Vol. 15, p. 171.

12. *DNTL,* Vol. 3, p. 385. See also C. Flood (trans.), *The Dynastic Chronicles, Bangkok Era, the Fourth Reign,* 3 vols. (Tokyo, 1965–1967), p. 171, which quotes King Duang of Cambodia as writing the French in 1858: "Cambodia wanted to build ships, put masts on them and sail them in order to trade with other countries, but Vietnam would not permit Cambodia to sail in and out."

13. William Milburn, *Oriental Commerce* (London, 1813), pp. 449–450.

14. See Chapter 4.

15. Saveros Lewitz, "La toponymie khmère," *BEFEO,* Vol. 53, No. 2 (1967).

16. For a description of rice-growing villages, see Jean Delvert, *Le paysan cambodgien* (Paris, 1962), pp. 322–370.

17. See Institut Bouddhique, *Brajum roung preng bhak ti 4* [Collected folk stories, vol. 4] (Phnom Penh, 1966), pp. 1–10. Both texts are analyzed in Chandler, "Songs at the Edge of the Forest."

18. France, Archives outremer, Aix-en-Provence (AOM), Fonds Indochinois A-30 (22), "Rapport confidentiel sur le Cambodge," August 1874.

19. Truong Buu Lam, "L'autorité dans les villages vietnamiens du XIXe siècle," in G. Wijawardene (ed.), *Leadership and Authority* (Singapore 1968), pp. 65–74.

20. G. Janneau, "Le Cambodge d'autrefois," *Revue Indochinoise (RI),* Vol. 17, No. 3 (March 1914):266.

21. See H. D. Evers (ed.), *Loosely Structured Social Systems: Thailand in Comparative Perspective* (New Haven, 1969); and Robert Textor, "The 'Loose Structure' of Thai Society: A Paradigm Under Pressure," *PA,* Vol. 50, No. 3 (Fall 1977):467–473.

22. See Eric Wolf, "Kinship, Friendship, and Patron-Client Relations," in M. Banton (ed.), *The Social Anthropology of Complex Societies* (London, 1966), pp. 1–22.

23. Louis Finot, "Proverbes cambodgiens," *RI,* Vol. 7, No. 2 (January 1904):74.

24. Tiounn, "Cérémonial cambodgien concernant la prise des fonctions des mandarins nouveaux promus," *RI,* Vol. 10, No. 1 (January 1907):75. See also P. Bitard, "Les songes et leurs interprétations chez les cambodgiens," in *Sources orientales II: Les songes et leur interprétations* (Paris, 1959), p. 258, which reports that to dream of eating human flesh or a freshly severed head means that one will become a provincial governor.

25. See Chapter 7.

26. J. Gonda, *Ancient Indian Kingship from a Religious Point of View* (Leiden: 1966), p. 91.

27. The Thai system is discussed in A. Rabibhadana, *Organization of Thai Society in the Early Bangkok Period* (Ithaca, N. Y., 1969), pp. 98–104.

28. See Chapter 3.

29. See manuscript chronicle P-6, Fonds Phnom Penh collection, Ecole Française d'Extrême Orient, pp. 11–12.

30. Rabibhadana, *Organization of Thai Society,* p. 44.

31. See A. Leclère, "Sdach tranh," *RI,* Vol. 7 (1905):1378–1384.

32. Gonda, *Ancient Indian Kingship, p. 36.*

33. A. Leclère, *Les codes cambodgiens,* (Paris, 1898), Vol. 1, p. 216.

34. For an analysis of the Chinese system, see John K. Fairbank (ed.), *The Chinese World Order* (Cambridge, Mass., 1968), especially pp. 1–19 and 63–89.

35. See P. Boudet and A. Masson (eds.), *Iconographie historique de l'Indochine française* (Paris, 1931), plates 128–129.

36. See D. G. Deveria, *Histoire des relations de la Chine avec Annam du XVIe au XIXe siècles* (Paris, 1880), pp. 52–54.

37. See W. Vella, *Siam under Rama III* (Locust Valley, N. Y., 1957), p. 60.

38. John Crawfurd, *Journal of an Embassy to the Courts of Siam and Cochin-China* (London, 1828), p. 146: "The Cochin-Chinese Ambassadors were yesterday presented to the King. They were received, I am told, without much ceremony, the intercourse being considered of so friendly and familiar a nature as not to call for extraordinary formalities."

39. AOM, Fonds Indochinois A-30 (6), Carton 10.

40. Institut Bouddhique, manuscript chronicle from *wat* Srolauv, p. 23.

41. Rama III, *Collected Writings* (in Thai) (Bangkok, 1967), p. 140.

CHAPTER 7. THE CRISIS OF THE NINETEENTH CENTURY

1. Eng Sut, *Akkasar mahaboros khmaer* [Documents about Khmer heroes] (Phnom Penh, 1969), p. 1013.

2. AOM A-30 (12) Carton 11. Letter from Doudart de Lagrée to Governor of Cochinchina, January 8, 1866.

3. Quoted in C. Wilson, *State and Society in the Reign of Mongkut, 1851–1867* (Ann Arbor, Mich., 1971), p. 983.

4. For a summary of Thai evidence, see David P. Chandler, *Cambodia Before the French: Politics in a Tributary Kingdom 1794–1847* (Ann Arbor, Mich., 1974), pp. 83–84.

5. *CMH* 2/1173/19ko. See also *DNTL,* Vol. 3, pp. 146–147.

6. For a discussion of the rebellion, see David P. Chandler, "An Anti-Vietnamese Rebellion in Early Nineteenth Century Cambodia," *JSEAS,* Vol. 6, No. 1 (March 1975):16–24. See also *DNTL,* Vol. 5, pp. 85ff.; *DNTL,* Vol. 6, p. 107; and L. Malleret, *Archéologie du delta de Mekong,* 4 vols. (Paris, 1959–1963), Vol. 1, pp. 27–33.

7. Institut Bouddhique, manuscript chronicle from Wat Prek Kuy (1874), p. 27.

8. See David P. Chandler, "Royally Sponsored Human Sacrifices in Nineteenth Century Cambodia: The Cult of *Me Sa* (Uma Mahisasuramardini) at Ba Phnom," *JSS,* Vol. 62, No. 2 (1974):207–221.

9. See Chapter 9.

10. Manuscript chronicle from Wat Prek Kuy, p. 58.

11. A. Leclère, *Recherches sur le droit publique des cambodgiens* (Paris, 1894), p. 151.

12. *DNTL,* Vol. 7, p. 79.

13. *DNTL,* Vol. 14, p. 123.

14. Rama III, *Collected Writings,* (Bangkok, 1967), p. 142.

15. The campaign is discussed in Chandler, *Cambodia Before the French,* pp. 113–118.

16. Chronicle from Wat Prek Kuy, p. 61.

17. *DNTL,* Vol. 14, pp. 53–54.

18. *DNTL,* Vol. 15, p. 113.

19. Ibid., p. 232.

20. *DNTL,* Vol. 16, pp. 21–22, 106.

21. *DNTL,* Vol. 18, pp. 249–250. See also *DNTL,* Vol. 19, p. 55, which discusses some shortcomings of the system. Most convicts and military colonists were expected to spend at least three years in Cambodia.

22. *DNTL,* Vol. 17, p. 30.

23. Ibid., p. 230.

24. *DNTL,* Vol. 19, p. 238.

25. Ibid., p. 329.

26. G. Aubaret (trans.), *Gia Dinh Thung Chi* [History and description of lower Cochin China] (Paris, 1867), p. 131.

27. See Milton Osborne, *Aggression and Annexation: Kampuchea's Condemnation of Vietnam* (Canberra: Australian National University, Research School of Pacific Studies, Working Paper No. 15, 1979).

28. *DNTL,* Vol. 19, p. 310.

29. *DNTL,* Vol. 18, p. 225. In 1839, Minh Mang ordered a survey of Cambodia's raw materials: *DNTL,* Vol. 21, pp. 239–240.

30. *DNTL,* Vol. 21, pp. 173, 235.

31. *DNTL,* Vol. 19, pp. 88–89; see also *DNTL,* Vol. 16, p. 109.

32. Thipakarawong, *Phraratchapongsawadan Chaophraya* [Royal chronicle] (Bangkok, repr. 1961), Vol. 2, p. 9. In 1838, one of Minh Mang's advisers suggested that "indigenous people be allowed to rule themselves and collect taxes" so as to save the Vietnamese money. He was told by the emperor to desist from making suggestions of this sort.

33. See, for example, Nguyen Khac Vien and Françoise Corrèze, *Kampuchea 1981: Témoignages* (Hanoi, 1981). A detailed comparison of the Vietnamese tutelage of the 1830s and that of the 1980s would make an interesting study.

34. *DNTL,* Vol. 21, pp. 269–272.

35. Chandler, *Cambodia Before the French,* pp. 140–141.

36. *DNTL,* Vol. 20, p. 263.

37. *DNTL,* Vol. 22, p. 157.

38. *DNTL*, Vol. 20, p. 7.

39. See Chandler, *Cambodia Before the French*, p. 25, note 37.

40. For an eyewitness report, see CMH, ratchakan thi 3 [Official correspondence from the third reign of the Bangkok period] 3/1202/43 ko 10.

41. Thailand, Royal Institute, *Chotmaihet ruang thap yuan khrang ratchakan thi 3* [Correspondence about the Vietnamese army in the third reign] (Bangkok, 1933), p. 17.

42. *DNTL*, Vol. 23, p. 112.

43. *DNTL*, Vol. 22, p. 228.

44. *DNTL*, Vol. 23, p. 155.

45. Ibid., p. 114.

46. Thailand, Royal Institute, *Chotmaihet*, p. 38.

47. Thailand, Royal Institute, *Chotmaihet*, p. 33, and *CMH*, 3/1202/40.

48. Chandler, *Cambodia Before the French*, pp. 156–158.

49. K.S.R. Kulap (pseud.), *Sayam Anam yut* [Siam's wars with Vietnam] (Bangkok, 1906, repr. 1971), p. 916.

50. *DNTL*, Vol. 23, p. 351.

51. Chandler, *Cambodia Before the French*, p. 155.

52. *CMH*, 3/1206/6.

53. Chandler, *Cambodia Before the French*, pp. 179–181.

54. David P. Chandler, "Going Through the Motions: Ritual and Restorative Aspects of the Reign of King Duang of Cambodia," paper prepared for Classical State in Southeast Asia Workshop, Santa Cruz, Calif., 1978.

55. Eng Sut, *Akkasar mahaboros*, p. 1027.

56. Inscription K. 142, from Wat Baray, translated in E. Aymonier, *Le Cambodge* (Paris, 1904), pp. 349–351.

57. For a discussion of these, see Chandler, "Going Through the Motions," passim. See also A. Leclère, *Histoire du Cambodge* (Paris, 1914), p. 441. For a political history of Duang's reign, see Bun Srun Theam, "Cambodia in the Mid-Nineteenth Century: A Quest for Survival, 1840–1863," M.A. thesis, Asian Studies, Australian National University, 1981, especially pp. 104–168.

58. Many of these are contained in Thailand, Office of the Prime Minister (comp.), *Thai sathapana kasat khamen* [The Thai establish the Khmer kingdom], (Bangkok, 1971), especially pp. 49–65.

59. Charles Meyniard, *Le second empire en Indochine* (Paris, 1891), p. 461. Minh Mang had noted in 1822 that "Cambodia is in the midst of powerful neighbors, and the fear of being invaded is great." Bun Srun Theam, "Cambodia in the Mid-Nineteenth Century," pp. 138–167, discusses the mission in some detail.

CHAPTER 8. THE EARLY STAGES OF THE FRENCH PROTECTORATE

1. Jean Delvert, *Le paysan cambodgien* (The Hague, 1961), pp. 425–428.

2. Charles Meyniard, *Le second empire en Indochine* (Paris, 1891), pp. 403–408.

3. Henri Mouhot, *Voyage dans les royaumes de Siam, du Cambodge, et de Laos* (Paris, 1972), pp. 174–176.

4. See G. Taboulet (ed.), *La geste française en Indochine,* 2 vols. (Paris, 1955), p. 334; and Milton Osborne, *The French Presence in Cochinchina and Cambodia: Rule and Response (1859–1905)* (Ithaca, N. Y., 1969), p. 27.

5. F. Julien, *Lettres d'un précurseur* (Paris, 1885), p. 46.

6. See Taboulet, *La geste,* pp. 621–629; and R. S. Thomson, "Establishment of the French Protectorate over Cambodia," *Far Eastern Quarterly (FEQ),* Vol. 4 (1945):313–340.

7. Taboulet, *Le geste,* pp. 630–635. See also Eng Sut, *Akkasar mahaboros khmaer* [Documents about Khmer heroes] (Phnom Penh, 1969), p. 1113.

8. For a stirring discussion of this expedition, see Milton Osborne, *River Road to China* (London, 1975).

9. Osborne, *French Presence,* pp. 211–214; and Eng Sut, *Akkasar mahaboras,* p. 1172.

10. For the full text of the treaty, see Taboulet, *La geste,* pp. 67–72. See also Khing Hoc Dy, "Santhor MOK, poète et chroniqueur du XIXe siècle," *Seksa Khmer,* Vol. 3, Nos. 3-4 (December 1981):137–160 at p. 142. Mok, a courtier, tried to keep Thomson from entering Norodom's quarters. Thomson kicked him out of the way, and Mok later composed a poem about the incident, beginning, "Oh Frenchman, you miserable robber, you dared to lift your foot and kick the secretary to the king."

11. For a discussion of the rebellion, see Osborne, *French Presence,* pp. 206–228. See also Ke Khi You, "L'insurrection générale de 1885–1886 au Cambodge," *Mémoire de maîtrise,* University of Paris VII, 1971.

12. Luc Durtain, *Dieux blancs, hommes jaunes* (Paris, 1930), p. 261.

13. L. Henry, *Promenade au Cambodge et au Laos* (Paris, 1894), p. 64n.

14. Osborne, *French Presence,* p. 237.

15. AOM, 3E 3(i), report from Kandal, May 1898.

16. Jean Hess, *L'affaire Yukanthor* (Paris, 1900), p. 77. For discussions of this crisis, see P. Doumer, *l'Indochine française* (Paris, 1905), pp. 230–231; Osborne, *French Presence,* pp. 243–246; and Alain Forest, *Le Cambodge et la colonisation française: Histoire d'une colonisation sans heurts* (Paris, 1980), pp. 59–78.

17. AOM, 3 E-10 (2), second trimester report from Stung Treng, 1923.

18. Manuscript chronicle of Sisowath's reign, formerly in library of royal palace, microfilmed by Centre for East Asian Studies, Tokyo (hereafter Sisowath chronicle), p. 1025.

19. Ibid,. p. 1034.

20. See Harry Franck, *East of Siam* (New York, 1926), pp. 24–25. A Pannetier, *Notes cambodgiennes* (Paris, 1921), p. 140, asserted that opium addiction was widespread among the Cambodian militia. See also R. Meyer, *Saramani* (Paris, 1922), pp. 122–123. P. Collard, *Cambodge et cambodgiens* (Paris, 1926), p. 277, mentioned Sisowath's addiction to opium but added that the drug is "not harmful to Asiatics."

21. A. Leclère, *Cambodge: Fêtes civiles* (Paris, 1916), pp. 30–31. See also Sisowath chronicle, pp. 1068–1074.

22. See Meyer, *Saramani,* pp. 132–151; Jean Ajalbert, *Ces phénomènes, artisans de l' Empire* (Paris, 1941), pp. 189–192; and Forest, *Le Cambodge,* pp. v–vii.

23. Sisowath chronicle, pp. 1077–1086.

24. Cambodian dancers participated in the colonial exhibition of 1930 and also performed at the New York World's Fair in 1939–1940.

25. For a discussion of the retrocession, see L. P. Briggs, "The Treaty of March 23, 1907, Between France and Siam, *FEQ,* Vol. 5 (1946):439–454.

26. Sisowath chronicle, pp. 1107–1110.

27. See C. Wilson, "The *Nai Kong* of Battambang, 1824–1868," in C. Wilson et al. (eds.), *Royalty and Commoners,* Contributions to Asian Studies, Vol. 15 (1980): pp. 66–72; and *Phongsawadan muang phratabong* [Chronicle of the region of Battambang]; No. 16 of series, *Prachum Phongsawadan* [Collected chronicles] (Bangkok, 1969), pp. 94–106.

28. The unusual frequency of landlordism, sharecropping, and outsiders in these two regions was extrapolated by radical theorists in the 1970s to characterize rural society throughout the country. According to Pol Pot, landlordism, which was in fact rare on a national scale, was the "major problem" facing pre-revolutionary Cambodia. Communist party favoritism toward poor peasants flowed from this analysis. See William Willmott, "Analytical Errors of the Kampuchean Communist Party," *PA,* Vol. 54, No. 2. (Summer, 1981):209–227.

CHAPTER 9. CAMBODIA'S RESPONSE
TO FRANCE, 1916–1945

1. Manuscript chronicle of Sisowath's reign, microfilmed by Centre for East Asian Studies, Tokyo (hereafter Sisowath chronicle), pp. 1166–1167.

2. AOM 3 E12 (2), report from Svay Rieng, 1915.

3. For a discussion of developments in Cambodia in the 1920s, see F. Baudouin, *Le Cambodge pendant et après la grande guerre* (Paris, 1927); and A. Silverstein, *Le Cambodge administratif* (Phnom Penh, 1924). See also Réné Morizon, *Monographie sur le Cambodge* (Paris, 1930).

4. See A. Souyris-Rolland, "Les pirates au Cambodge," *BSEI,* Vo. 25, No. 4 (1950):307–313. The rubric *piraterie* follows immediately after *situation politique* in the format of monthly French reports from the various *résidences,* but banditry is seen in the reports in terms of security rather than ideological dissidence. AOM 3 E12(2), a report from Svay Rieng in 1921, dismissively asserts that "a life of raiding others, full of the unexpected, composed of tricks, pursuits and ambushes, all without great physical danger, is one of the sports to which Cambodians are addicted." See also Alain Forest, *Le Cambodge et la colonisation française : Histoire d'une colonisation sans heurts* (Paris, 1980), pp. 373–412. For a Thai perspective, see David Johnston, "Bandit, *Nakleng* and Peasant in Rural Thai Society," in C. Wilson et al. (eds.), *Royalty and Commoners, Contributions to Asian Studies,* Vol. 15 (1980): 90–101; and more generally, E. Hobsbawm, *Bandits* (London, 1969).

5. A. Pannetier, *Notes cambodgiennes* (Paris, 1921), p. 75.

6. The sculpture was carved by Louis Bottinelly. For a study of the influence of Indochina on French imaginative writers, see L. Malleret, *L'exotisme indochinois dans la litterature française depuis 1860* (Paris, 1934), especially pp. 183–192, 216–244. Novels set in Cambodia dating from this period include Charles Bellan, *Fleur de lotus* (Paris, 1924); Pierre Benoit, *Le roi lépreux* (Paris, 1927); Jean Dorsenne, *Sous le soleil des bonzes* (Paris, 1934); and André Malraux, *Le voie royale* (Paris, 1930). See also "Neang," *Echo du Cambodge*, July 30, 1927.

7. AOM 3E 8(3), Report from Prey Veng, 1924. Félix Louis Bardez, born in Paris in 1882, had served in Indochina, largely in Cambodia, since 1908.

8. For a detailed account of the incidents see David P. Chandler, "The Assassination of *Résident* Bardez (1925)," *JSS* (forthcoming). See also *L'Echo du Cambodge*, especially the issues of December 1925; Walter Langlois, *André Malraux: The Indo-China Adventure* (New York, 1966), pp. 185–188; and Luc Durtain, *Dieux blancs, hommes jaunes* (Paris, 1930), pp. 264–265.

9. For the French text of this ordinance, see Dik Keam, *Phum Direchan* [Bestiality village] (Phnom Penh, 1971), pp. 154–159.

10. I am grateful to Ben Kiernan for lending me his recorded interview with one of the assailants, Sok Bith, which took place in September 1980. Bith served a fifteen-year sentence for the assault.

11. AOM 3E 7 (6); Annual report from Kratie, 1925–1926.

12. This newspaper has not yet received the scholarly attention it deserves. See Buncchan Muul, *Kuk Niyobay* [Political prison] (Phnom Penh, 1971), pp. 8–14.

13. Like *Nagara Vatta*, the colonial issues of *Kambuja Surya*, which effectively *publish* Cambodian-language literature for the first time, deserve detailed attention.

14. For a discussion of these two texts, see David P. Chandler, "Cambodian Royal Chronicles (*Rajabangsavatar*), 1927–1949: Kingship and Historiography in the Colonial Era," in Anthony Reid and David Marr (eds.), *Perceptions of the Past in Southeast Asia* (Singapore, 1979), pp. 207–217; and David P. Chandler, "Instructions for the Corps of Royal Scribes: An Undated Cambodian Manuscript from the Colonial Era," *JSS*, Vol. 63, No. 2 (July 1975):343–348.

15. William E. Willmott, *The Chinese in Cambodia* (Vancouver, 1967); and W. E. Willmott, "History and Sociology of the Chinese in Cambodia Before the French Protectorate," *JSEAH*, Vol. 7, No. 1 (March 1966): 15–38. See also *L'Echo du Cambodge*, September 7, 1938, which reports on the continuing influx of Chinese immigrants.

16. On education, see Forest, *Le Cambodge*, pp. 143–165; and Jacques Nepote, "Education et développement; dans le Cambodge moderne," *Mondes et développement*, No. 28 (1974):767–792. See also Jean Delvert, "L'oeuvre française d'enseignement au Cambodge," *FA*, Nos. 125–127 (October–December 1956), p. 309–322.

17. For reports on the effects of the depression on Cambodia, see, for example, AOM 3E 15 (8), Annual reports from Kampot; AOM 3 (5), from Kandal; and AOM 3E 10 (4), from Srung Treng.

Alert to positive developments, one French administrator reported in 1933 that the crash had led to the collapse of private fortunes throughout Takeo, adding that "a powerful form of solidarity was born in shared poverty, making a *table rase* of ancient antagonisms of class and even of race." AOM 3E 7 (6), report from Takeo.

18. Norodom Sihanouk, *L'Indochine vue de Pékin* (Paris, 1972), pp. 27–28.

19. See H. de Grauclade, *Le réveil du peuple khmer* (Hanoi, 1935). For a less optimistic view, see G. de Pourtales, *Nous, à qui rien n'appartient* (Paris, 1931), pp. 115ff.

20. See, for example, Ben Kiernan, "Origins of Khmer Communism," in *Southeast Asian Affairs 1981* (Singapore, 1980), pp. 161–180.

21. See Chapter 9 for a description of Thanh's activities during and after World War II.

22. See, for example, AOM 3E 8 (12), 1923 annual report of the governor of Prey Veng.

23. *Écho du Cambodge,* July 19, 1933.

24. The most recent study of this period, although it says very little about Cambodia, is A. W. McCoy (ed.), *Southeast Asia Under Japanese Occupation* (New Haven: Yale University Southeast Asian Studies, Monograph series No. 22, 1980).

25. Decoux has discussed this period in his memoirs, *A la barre de l'Indochine* (Paris, 1949). See also N. Sihanouk, *Souvenirs doux et amers* (Paris, 1981), pp. 59–114.

26. Charles Robequain, *The Economic Development of French Indo-China* (Oxford, England, 1944), p. 366.

27. See Milton Osborne, "King-making in Cambodia: From Sisowath to Sihanouk," *JSEAS,* Vol. 4, No. 3 (September 1973):169–185.

28. Sihanouk, *L'Indochine vue de Pékin,* pp. 19–30; and Sihanouk, *Souvenirs doux et amers,* pp. 35–50.

29. Manuscript chronicle of Sihanouk's reign, covering the years 1941–1949, microfilmed by Centre for East Asian Studies, Tokyo (hereafter Sihanouk chronicle), pp. 136–140.

30. See V. M. Reddi, *A History of the Cambodian Independence Movement 1863–1955* (Tirupati, 1971), pp. 82–84; Bunchhan Muul, *Kuk niyobay,* [Political prison] (Phnom Penh, 1971); and Kong Somkar, *Achar Hem Chieu* [Venerable Hem Chieu] (Phnom Penh, 1971).

31. This information is drawn from unpublished correspondence between Son Ngoc Thanh, in exile in 1943, and his nationalist colleagues in Cambodia.

32. Interestingly, Sok Bith, the illiterate farmer implicated in Bardez's assassination (see note 10 above) knew about Hem Chieu, but about few other nationalist figures.

33. G. Gautier, *Jeune Cambodge* (Phnom Penh, 1943). See also *Indochine,* No. 153 (August 5, 1943), and No. 210 (August 10, 1944). AOM E 11 (7), note from Pursat, 1944, states that romanized Khmer was being taught at that time in all Cambodian schools with mixed, not necessarily unhappy, results (Eveline Porée-Maspero, letter of August 27, 1982).

34. Robert Ollivier, "Le protectorat français au Cambodge," (Ph. D. dissertation, University of Paris, 1969), p. 213.

35. Ibid., p. 198. The French name for the kingdom became "Cambodge" again in 1946.

36. Lt. Tadakame, attached as a political adviser to the palace, remained in Cambodia after the war, later even joining an Issarak band.

37. Sihanouk chronicle, p. 493.

38. See Charles Meyer, *Derrière le sourire khmer* (Paris, 1971), pp. 115–116; Ollivier, "Le protectorat français," p. 242; Reddi, *History of the Cambodian Independence Movement,* pp. 105–109 and *Realités cambodgiennes,* July 9 and 16, 1967.

CHAPTER 10. ROADS TO INDEPENDENCE AND REVOLUTION

1. Ollivier, "Le protectorat français," p. 267.

2. V. M. Reddi, *History of the Cambodian Independence Movement 1863–1955* (Tirupati, 1971), p. 124.

3. The material in this paragraph is drawn from Ben Kiernan, "Origins of Khmer Communism," in *Southeast Asian Affairs 1981* (Singapore, 1980), pp. 161–180; Bunchhan Muul, *Charet Khmer* [Khmer mores] (Phnom Penh, 1974); and Wilfred Burchett, *Mekong Upstream* (Hanoi, 1957).

4. Ollivier, "Le protectorat français," pp. 282–290; P. Preschez, *Essai sur la democratie au Cambodge* (Paris, 1961), pp. 17–19; Reddi, *History of the Cambodian Independence Movement,* pp. 124–126; and AOM, Cambodge, 7 F 29 (4), "Etude sur l'évolution de la politique intérieure et les partis politiques khmers" (1951), passim.

5. AOM, Cambodge 7F 29 (7) "Etude sur les mouvements rebelles au Cambodge, 1942–1952," (hereafter "Etude sur les mouvements") pp. 9–10. According to Ben Kiernan (personal communication), material in this report crosschecks nicely with interview material obtained in 1980–1981 by Kiernan and Chanthou Boua.

6. Reddi, *History of the Cambodian Independence Movement,* p. 129.

7. "Etude sur les mouvements." See also Kiernan, "Origins of Khmer Communism," pp. 163–167; and Reddi, *A History of the Cambodian Independence Movement,* pp. 151–154.

8. See Norodom Sihanouk, *Souvenirs doux et amers* (Paris, 1981), pp. 134–142. Yuthevong, a fascinating figure, has not been studied in detail. When he died while undergoing treatment for tuberculosis in a French hospital in Phnom Penh in 1947, rumors spread that he had been assassinated by the French; see Reddi, *History of the Cambodian Independence Movement,* p. 137n.; and Burchett, *Mekong Upstream,* p. 112.

9. Sihanouk, *Souvenirs,* pp. 158–168; Ollivier, "Le protectorat français," pp. 314–320; Reddi, *History of the Cambodian Independence Movement,* pp. 165–173.

10. Ollivier, "Le protectorat français," pp. 323–325. See also Martin Herz, *A Short History of Cambodia* (New York and London, 1958), p. 83.

11. Sihanouk, *Souvenirs,* pp. 170–173, reprinted from an article in *Réalités cambodgiennes* (October 1958). Ollivier "Le protectorat français" p. 326, quoted from a Poitiers newspaper, *Libre Poitou,* of October 20, 1951, in which Son Ngoc Thanh in an interview claimed to have been prime minister of Cambodia in 1939 and to be of aristocratic descent.

12. United States, Foreign Broadcast Information Service (FBIS), *Broadcasts from the Far East,* November 7, 1951.

13. Ollivier, "Le protectorat français," p. 330.

14. Reddi, *History of the Cambodian Independence Movement,* p. 183.

15. Interview with Channa Samudvijana, Bangkok, August 27, 1981.

16. See Donald Lancaster, *The Emancipation of French Indo-China* (Oxford, 1961), p. 272; and Herz, *Short History of Cambodia,* pp. 84–85. See also M. Laurent, *L'armée au Cambodge et dans les pays en voie de développement en Sud Est Asiatique* (Paris, 1968), especially pp. 283–291.

17. "Étude sur les mouvements," p. 64ff. Ollivier, "Le protectorat français," pp. 320–322. The constitution prepared at this time drew in large part on its earlier Vietnamese counterpart and even included quotations from the U.S. Declaration of Independence.

18. Kiernan, "Origins of Khmer Communism," p. 168.

19. See "Étude sur les mouvements," pp. 84, 87. The second citation notes that some "autarchic collective farms, like *kholkozes* have been noted . . . in Kompong Cham" in 1952. Interestingly, this region was a stronghold of radical activity in the 1950s and the 1960s, and a seedbed in the 1970s for cadres in Democratic Kampuchea.

20. FBIS, November 28, 1951.

21. FBIS, April 4, 1979.

22. Ollivier, "Le protectorat français," pp. 333–334.

23. "Lettre de l'Association des Étudiants Khmers en France à sa Majesté Norodom Sihanouk," Paris, July 6, 1952. According to Ben Kiernan, this document was the work of Hou Youn, a Cambodian radical assassinated at Pol Pot's behest in 1975. The manifesto appeared in Khmer in *Khmer Nisut* [Khmer student] No. 14 (August 1952). In the same issue, writing as "Khmer Daom" [Original Khmer], Saloth Sar, later known as Pol Pot, contributed two essays, both strongly critical of the Cambodian monarchy. One of these ("Monarchy or Democracy?") has been translated as an appendix to Ben Kiernan and Serge Thion, *Khmers Rouges!* (Paris, 1981), pp. 357–360. The other, entitled "The Royal Trip to European Countries," closes with a short poem, claiming that "royal edicts are dishonest" and seek to destroy the "solidarity of students." Interestingly, none of the articles in the periodical takes an internationalist view of the Indochina war; the antimonarchic, pro-Assembly position they all assume suggests instead that Pol Pot and his colleagues, at this stage in their careers, supported Son Ngoc Thanh's form of dissidence rather than the Vietnamese-sponsored KPRP.

24. Reddi, *History of the Cambodian Independence Movement,* p. 205. For this period, see also Norodom Sihanouk, *La monarchie cambodgienne et la croisade royale pour l'indépendence* (Phnom Penh, n.d., c. 1957), passim.

25. Norodom Sihanouk and Wilfred Burchett, *My War with the CIA* (Harmondsworth, 1973), p. 153; Reddi, *History of the Cambodian Independence Movement,* p. 20.

26. Ollivier, "Le protectorat français," pp. 344–346.

27. Ibid., pp. 358ff., conveys the impression of approaching anarchy in Phnom Penh; such an atmosphere may well have accelerated French willingness to negotiate with the king.

28. Sihanouk, *Souvenirs,* pp. 209–212.

29. Kiernan, "Origins of Khmer Communism," p. 179.

30. In 1981, Nhek Tioulong stated that, in the mid-1950s, when he served in Sihanouk's cabinet, it soon became almost impossible for the newly independent Cambodian regime to collect taxes levied on land and harvests. To Cambodian peasants, it seems, "independence" meant being relieved of these particular levies (interview with Nhek Tioulong, Bangkok, August 29, 1981).

31. Some of the ideas that follow can be traced to David P. Chandler, "The Tragedy of Cambodian History," *PA,* Vol. 52, No. 3 (Fall 1979):410–419; and to my conversations over the last four years or so with Ben Kiernan, Michael Vickery, and Milton Osborne. See also William E. Willmott, "Analytical Errors of the Kampuchean Communist Party," *PA,* Vol. 54, No. 2 (Summer 1981):209–227; and Kiernan and Thion, *Khmers Rouges!* passim.

Bibliographic Essay

Readers competent to read Thai, Cambodian, and Vietnamese sources are directed to the appropriate footnote references in the text. This brief essay will try to select and evaluate a few major primary and secondary sources for Cambodian history available in French and English. A reading knowledge of French is essential for students interested in Cambodian history before 1953.

GENERAL WORKS

The most recent bibliographic introduction to Cambodia is Charles F. Keyes, *Southeast Asian Research Tools: Cambodia* (Honolulu, 1979).

An early attempt to synthesize Cambodian history, relying heavily on chronicle histories, is Adhémard Leclère's *Histoire du Cambodge* (Paris, 1914; reprinted 1975). Unfortunately, Leclère is cavalier in his use of sources and is difficult to verify. Martin Herz wrote *A Short History of Cambodia* (New York and London, 1958) shortly after completing a tour of duty in Phnom Penh as a U.S. Foreign Service officer. The chapters on the 1940s and 1950s are better than those dealing with earlier times. A. Dauphin Meunier's brief *Histoire du Cambodge* (Paris, 1968) is more judicious. David P. Chandler, *The Land and People of Cambodia* (Philadelphia, 1972), aimed at high-school students, is largely historical in its approach. Perhaps the best brief synthesis of Cambodian culture is Solange Thierry's *Les Khmers* (Paris, 1964).

There are no serious studies of Cambodian urban life. Those that examine rural conditions are also rare and are dominated by Jean Delvert's magisterial *Le paysan cambodgien* (Paris and the Hague, 1961). The most thorough examination of folk beliefs and rituals in Cambodia is E. Porée-Maspero's three-volume study, *Etude sur les rites agraires des cambodgiens* (Paris and the Hague, 1962–1969).Two good monographic studies of village life are May Ebihara, *Svay* (Ann Arbor: University Microfilms, 1971) and G. Martel, *Lovea* (Paris, 1975). On Cambodian Buddhism, see François Bizot, *Le figuier a cinq branches: Recherche sur le bouddhisme khmer* (Paris, 1976). The postcolonial economy is ably discussed in Rémy Prud'homme, *L'économie du Cambodge* (Paris, 1969); and A. Migozzi approaches demographic issues in his monograph, *Cambodge: Faits et problèmes de population* (Paris, 1973).

FROM PREHISTORY TO THE DECLINE OF ANGKOR

Work on prehistory is not as advanced in Cambodia as in neighboring Vietnam and Thailand. The best introduction to the subject is Donn Bayard, "The Roots of Indo-Chinese Civilization," *Pacific Affairs,* Vol. 53, No. 1 (Spring 1980):89–114. See also C. Mourer and R. Mourer, "Prehistoric Research in Cambodia During the Last Ten Years," *Asian Perspectives,* Vol. 14 (1971):35–42.

Fortunately for English-speaking readers, L. P. Briggs, *The Ancient Khmer Empire* (Philadelphia, 1951), and Christopher Pym's stylistically more accessible *The Ancient Civilization of Angkor* (New York, 1968) are both excellent. So is the English version of G. Coedes, *Angkor* (London, 1962).

A magisterial overview of this early period is G. Coedes, *The Indianized States of Southeast Asia* (Honolulu, 1975). Students wishing to examine Cambodian inscriptions may consult A. Barth and A. Bergaigne, *Inscriptions sanscrites du Cambodge* 2 vols. (Paris 1885, 1893); and G. Coedes, *Les inscriptions du Cambodge,* 8 vols. (Hanoi and Paris, 1937–1966). The eighth volume of Coedes's compilation is an index of the entire corpus. See also P. N. Jenner, *A Chronological Inventory of the Inscriptions of Cambodia* (Honolulu, 1980); and P. N. Jenner, *A Chrestomathy of Pre-Angkorean Khmer,* 3 vols. (Honolulu, 1980). Many inscriptions have been translated into French over the years in the *Bulletin de l'Ecole Française d'Extrême Orient* (1900–). The *Bulletin* also contains important studies of classical Cambodia: Many of these have been cited in the footnotes to Chapters 2 and 3. Monographic studies of Cambodian culture and institutions in this period include S. Sahai, *Les institutions politiques et l'organisation administrative du Cambodge ancien* (Paris, 1970); Jean Boisselier, *Le Cambodge* (Paris, 1966), an archaeological handbook; and B. P. Groslier and Jacques Arthaud, *Angkor: Art and Civilization* (New York, 1966), a well-illustrated introduction.

Two important studies of kingship and its relation to religion at Angkor have recently appeared. These are H. Kulke, *The Devaraja Cult* (Ithaca, N. Y., 1978); and Ian Mabbett, "Kingship in Angkor," *Journal of the Siam Society,* Vol. 66, No. 2 (July 1978):1–58. Mabbett's perceptive article has a helpful bibliography. Another stimulating study is Eleanor Moron, "Configuration of Time and Space at Angkor Wat." *Studies in Indo-Asian Art and Culture,* No. 5 (1977):217–267.

The most detailed study of the reign of Jayavarman VII is B. P. Groslier, *Les inscriptions du Bayon* (Paris, 1973), which has a good bibliography. Students should also consult Phillipe Stern, *Les monuments khmers du style du Bayon et Jayavarman VII* (Paris, 1965).

The best introduction to everyday life at Angkor is P. Pelliot (ed.), *Mémoires sur les coutumes du Cambodge de Tcheou Takouan* (Paris, 1951), which is quoted frequently in Chapter 4.

CAMBODIA'S DARK AGES: C. 1400–1863

This crucial period of Cambodian history has not yet been studied in much detail. One reason for this is that the Cambodian chronicle texts are so unreliable, as Michael Vickery has shown in his *Cambodia After Angkor: The Chronicular Evidence for the Fourteenth to Sixteenth Centuries* (Ann Arbor, Mich., 1977). Vickery's last chapter is a valiant attempt to make sense of the period as a whole. For the sixteenth century, B. P. Groslier, *Angkor et le Cambodge au XVIe siècle d'après les sources portugaises et espagnoles* (Paris, 1958), is a helpful compilation and contains useful data about the economy of Angkor. Inscriptions from Angkor from the sixteenth century to the eighteenth have been ably edited by Saveros Pou *Bulletin de l'Ecole Française d'Extrême Orient,* Vol. 59 [1972], and Vol. 62 [1975]; see also S. Pou, "Les inscriptions modernes d'Angkor," *Journal Asiatique,* Vol. 260 (1972). In addition, Pou has edited and translated the *chef d'oeuvre* of classical Cambodian literature, the *Reamker,* 3 vols. (Paris, 1977–1979). See also François Martini (trans.), *La gloire de Rama: Ramakerti* (Paris, 1978). For an analysis of post-Angkorean artistic styles, see M. Giteau, *L'iconographie du Cambodge post-angkoréen* (Paris, 1975).

The eighteenth century is a period of Cambodian history that has not yet been seriously studied, but it should be, as chronicle histories for this period appear to be factually reliable and can be checked against the comparatively voluminous Thai and Vietnamese sources.

For the first half of the nineteenth century, see David P. Chandler, *Cambodia Before the French: Politics in a Tributary Kingdom, 1794–1847* (Ann Arbor, Mich., 1974).

CAMBODIAN HISTORY SINCE 1863

For the early colonial period, G. Taboulet (ed.), *La geste française en Indochine,* 2 vols. (Paris, 1955) is useful, and so is Milton Osborne's pioneering study, *The French Presence in Cochinchina and Cambodia: Rule and Response (1859–1905)* (Ithaca, N. Y., 1969). The early twentieth century is intelligently treated in Alain Forest, *Le Cambodge et la colonisation française: Histoire d'une colonisation sans heurts (1897–1920)* (Paris, 1980), but the 1920s and the 1930s have not yet been studied systematically. Robert Ollivier, "Le protectorat français au Cambodge," (Ph.D. dissertation, University of Paris, 1969) is useful for the period 1940–1953; so is Philippe Preschez's monograph, *Essai sur la démocratie au Cambodge* (Paris, 1961), which is especially good on the proliferation of political parties in Cambodia after World War II. See also V. M. Reddi, *A History of the Cambodian Independence Movement 1863–1955* (Tirupati, 1971). Milton Osborne's *Politics and Power in Cambodia* (Camberwell, Australia, 1973) also contains a good summary of politics in this period. For analyses of postwar Cambodian radicalism, see Wilfred Burchett, *Mekong Upstream* (Berlin, 1959); Charles Meyer, *Derrière le sourire khmer* (Paris, 1971); and J. C. Pomonti and Serge Thion, *Des courtesans aux partisans: La crise cambodgienne* (Paris, 1971). Ben Kiernan and Chanthou Boua (eds.), *Peasants and Politics in Kampuchea, 1942–1981* (London, 1982) contains much valuable primary material, some of it translated for the first time from Khmer. For a discussion of decolonization in Cambodia, see Donald Lancaster, *The Emancipation of French Indo-China* (New York, 1961). Norodom Sihanouk's memoirs, *L'Indochine vue de Pékin* (Paris, 1972) and *Souvenirs doux et amers* (Paris, 1981), may be used with caution by historians of the period.

Developments in Cambodia in the 1970s are discussed in David P. Chandler and Ben Kiernan (eds.), *Revolution and Its Aftermath in Kampuchea: Eight Essays* (New Haven, Conn., 1983), and in Ben Kiernan, "How Pol Pot Came to Power: The History of Radicalism in Kampuchea," Ph.D. dissertation in progress, Monash University. See also Francois Ponchaud, *Cambodia Year Zero* (New York, 1977); Pin Yathay, *L'Utopie meurtrière* (Paris, 1980); and Serge Thion and Ben Kiernan, *Khmers Rouges!* (Paris, 1981). Relations between Cambodia and the United States in this period are discussed from different perspectives in William Shawcross, *Sideshow* (New York, 1980), and Noam Chomsky and Edward S. Herman, *After the Cataclysm: Postwar Indo-China and the Reconstruction of Imperial Ideology* (Boston, 1979), pp. 135–300. See also Timothy Carney, *Communist Party Power in Kampuchea (Cambodia): Documents and Discussion* (Ithaca, N. Y., 1977). Finally, students may consult Ines Rodrigues, "Selected, Annotated, English-Language Bibliography of the Kampuchean Revolution, 1970–1979, *Southeast Asian Research Materials Group Newsletter* (Australian National University Library), No. 18 (May, 1981):1–28.

Index

This book was set in Korinna
by the typesetting division
of Westview Press